The Jesuit Mission to the Lakota Sioux

The Jesuit Mission to the Lakota Sioux

Pastoral Theology and Ministry, 1886-1945

Ross Alexander Enochs

Sheed & Ward
Kansas City

Sheed & Ward™ is a service of The National Catholic Reporter Publishing Company.

————————————————◆————————————————

Library of Congress Cataloguing-in-Publication Data

Enochs, Ross Alexander, 1963-
    The Jesuit mission to the Lakota Sioux : pastoral theology and ministry, 1886-1945 / Ross Alexander Enochs.
       p.   cm.
    Includes bibliographical references and index.
    ISBN: 1-55612-813-4 (alk. paper)
    1. Teton Indians—Missions. 2. Teton Indians—Religion. 3. Teton Indians—History—Sources. 4. Jesuits—Missions—South Dakota—Rosebud Indian Reservation—History—Sources. 5. Jesuits—Missions—South Dakota—Pine Ridge Indian Reservation—History—Sources. 6. Rosebud Indian Reservation (S.D.)—History—Sources. 7. Pine Ridge Indian Reservation (S.D.)—History—Sources. I. Title
E99.T34E56   1995
266'.2783 089975—dc20   95-9250
                                                          CIP

————————————————◆————————————————

Published by: Sheed & Ward
               115 E. Armour Blvd.
               P.O. Box 419492
               Kansas City, MO 64141-6492

To order, call: (800) 333-7373

Contents

Dedicated to my mother and father with love.
Thank you for everything.

Preface

THIS STUDY TRACES THE DEVELOPMENT OF PASTORAL THEOLOGY AND ministry at the St. Francis and Holy Rosary missions in South Dakota primarily by examining the Jesuits' diaries, published articles, sermons, retreat notes, and other personal papers. All these sources illustrate the techniques that they used to convert the Lakota and their views on Lakota culture and religion. To understand the perspective of the Lakota Catholics, this study analyzes their organizations and their writings. Moreover, since the memories of several people on Rosebud and Pine Ridge reach back to the 1920's and 30's, the author interviewed about 30 Lakota elders and a few Jesuits, who provided valuable information. Finally, the method of this study is to look for patterns in missiology. Rather than examining a single Jesuit or a few anecdotes, this study examines the patterns in the writings of the Jesuits on Pine Ridge and Rosebud through sixty years of mission history.

I owe a great deal of thanks to Fr. Gerald Fogarty, S.J., Mark Thiel, Fr. Michael Steltenkamp, S.J., and Chris Vecsey for all their help. I would also like to thank Chuck Elston, Fr. William Mugen, John LeDoux, Susan Stawicki-Vrobel, Leah Halepeska, Carrie Ronnander, Diane Duffey, Phil Runkel, Joe Horn Cloud, Viola Packard, Bernard Flood, Harry Bluethunder, Jessie Crow, Fr. Richard Jones, Fr. C.P. Jordan, Maggie Brown, Daisy Whirlwind-Horse, Fr. Bernard Fagan, Francis Hairy Chin, Fr. Ted Zuern, Francis Apple, Mildred Apple, Juanita Conners, Jessie Eagleheart, Olivia Pourier, Hobert Pourier, Phylis Clifford, Fr. John Scott, Fr. Lawrence Helmueller, Lawrence Whiting, Martha Whiting, Sarah Brave, Joe Whiting, Myrtle Crow Eagle, Sister Pat Mylott, Fr. Eugene Zimmerman, Kate Omaha Boy, Fr. Raymond Burger, Sister Helen, Sister Pat, Rosie Red Hair, Leo Chasing-in-Timber, Fr. Paul Manhart, and Fr. John Hatcher, S.J.

Key to Abbreviations

HRM = Holy Rosary Mission collection at the Marquette University
         Archives.
SFM = St. Francis Mission collection at the Marquette University
         Archives.
BCIM = Bureau of Catholic Indian Missions collection at the Marquette
         University Archives.

Numbers after abbreviation refer to the number of the series-box-folder.

Example: "HRM 4-1-2" cites the Holy Rosary Mission collection, series
4, box 1, folder 2.

These collections are all housed at the Marquette University Archives,
Milwaukee, Wisconsin.

Introduction

AT ONE TIME IN 1673, THE MENOMINEES WERE UNSUCCESSFUL IN CATCHING sturgeon. To remedy the situation, they prayed to the sun, and put a painted image of the sun on a pole in the water to seek divine intervention for their problem. Louis Andre, a Jesuit missionary who stayed with them, described the situation:

> [The Menominees] believed that the sun was the master of life and of fishing, the dispenser of all things. . . . After disabusing them of the idea which they had of the sun, and explaining to them in a few words the principal points of our Faith, I asked them whether they would consent to my removing the picture of the sun, and replacing it by the image of Jesus crucified. . . . They consented. . . . I put my crucifix in the place of the picture of the sun. On the following morning, sturgeon entered the river, in such great abundance that these poor people were delighted.[1]

Andre retained a practice that was familiar to the Menominees but replaced the Menominee symbol for God with the crucifix. He retained the form but changed the content of the ritual. In many ways the Jesuits at the Holy Rosary and St. Francis missions did the same in their mission to the Lakota Sioux two hundred years later.

Since the beginning of the Church, Catholic missionaries have tried to convince peoples with different customs, religions, languages, and moral systems that the Catholic faith was universally valid. But though Catholics in different countries share a common faith, they never had a common culture. Rather they all had unique ethnic and national customs that they retained after becoming Catholic.

According to Catholic tradition, the Church began as a missionary enterprise at Pentecost when Jesus sent the disciples out to preach and the

---

1. James T. Moore, *Indian and Jesuit: A Seventeenth Century Encounter* (Chicago: Loyola University Press, 1982), 146. *Jesuit Relations and Allied Documents,* Travels and Explorations of the Jesuit Missionaries in New France, 1610-1791, ed. Reuben Gold Thwaites, 73 vols. (Pagent Book Company: New York, 1959), 58:273-275

Holy Spirit gave them a miraculous ability to communicate with people who did not speak their language. Derived from the Latin word *missa*, meaning "sent," a missionary was one whom the Church sent to preach. Moreover, the Gospels passed down several injunctions to spread the faith: "As the Father has sent me, so I send you" (Jn. 20:21), and "Go make disciples of all nations" (Mt. 28:19). Thus Christians always believed that spreading the Gospel was an essential aspect and a demand of their faith.

In the 1960's and 1970's, however, mission history became an ideological battleground. On one side were those who argued that missionaries were arrogant people who attempted to destroy the religion and culture of indigenous people and resorted to coercion to do this. In regard to the Native American missions, some claimed that the Catholic missionaries attempted to eradicate Native American culture and sought to replace it with American culture; some argued that the Jesuits regarded Native American religion as "Devil-dominated heathenism."[2]

Although Catholic missionaries at times attempted to eliminate certain specific Native American beliefs and rites, this book provides evidence that the Jesuit missionaries accepted many aspects of Lakota culture and participated in several Lakota rituals and customs throughout their time among the Lakotas. Furthermore, it shows that the Jesuits sought to preserve those aspects of Lakota culture and religion that they believed were good, and attempted to abolish only those practices or beliefs that they thought were in conflict with either the Catholic faith or the Lakotas' well-being.

This study focuses on the mission method and pastoral ministry of the Jesuits at the St. Francis and Holy Rosary missions in South Dakota from 1886 to 1945. The years 1886 and 1945 marked points of significant change in the history of these missions. In 1886, John Jutz, S.J., founded St. Francis Mission, which marked the beginning of the permanent presence of the Jesuits on the Rosebud Reservation. One year later, Jutz founded Holy Rosary Mission on the Pine Ridge Reservation. As

---

2. In his influential book *Custer Died for Your Sins* (New York: Avon, 1969) Vine Deloria, Jr. accused missionaries of destroying Native American culture, condemning Native American religion as demonic, using a patronizing mission method, excluding Native Americans from positions of authority in the Church, causing inter-tribal rivalry, and coercing them to accept Christianity. In Harvey Markowitz's article, "The Catholic Mission and the Sioux: a Crisis in the Early Paradigm," *Sioux Indian Religion* (Norman: University of Oklahoma, 1987) Markowitz asserted that the Jesuits viewed Lakota religion as "Devil-dominated heathenism." Speaking of the Jesuits on Pine Ridge, Markowitz wrote: "The idea that 'Devil-dominated heathenism' and Christianity might be phases of a single process of religious growth – parallel to sociocultural development – was totally unacceptable to Catholic missionaries. Instead, they viewed these two forms as antithetical. To replace Sioux heathenism with the sacraments represented a religious revolution, not evolution. Given such a perspective, missionaries rejected the notion that a Lakota could participate in traditional Indian ceremonies and simultaneously be a Catholic" (p. 124).

this study shows, from 1886 to 1945 the Jesuits' approach to pastoral ministry and the Catholic traditions on these reservations changed only gradually. Before 1945, the reservations were remote enough to be insulated from much of the secularism and skepticism of modern America. But the Second World War brought to the reservations profound cultural change which had a significant impact on the religious character of these missions. The increased secularization that occurred on the reservations after the War, and the resulting decrease in religious zeal among the Lakota Catholics, also influenced the Jesuits in the Dakotas to alter their methods of pastoral ministry significantly.

Located just eighty miles apart on reservations that bordered on each other, the St. Francis and Holy Rosary missions were similar in many ways. Jesuits and Franciscan sisters ran both these missions and taught in the schools. The Jesuits at these missions also always kept in close contact with each other. Quite frequently the Jesuit superiors, school superintendents, and other priests worked in one of these missions for a few years and then transferred to the other for the next few years.[3] Since these two missions tended to share personnel, the Jesuits employed the same methods of pastoral ministry at both missions.

As an additional point of comparison, both of these missions served two closely related bands of the Teton Sioux: the Oglala and the Brule. The Sioux Nation was really a confederation of seven "council fires" or divisions: the Teton, Yankton, Yanktonnais, Mdewakanton, Wahpeton, Sisseton, and Wahpekute. Grouping the latter four divisions together, scholars referred to the Mdewakanton, Wahpeton, Sisseton, and Wahpekute as the Santee Sioux. The Teton Sioux division contained seven sub-divisions or seven bands: the Oglala, Brule, Hunkpapa, Minneconjous, Blackfeet, Two Kettle, and Sans Arcs. On Pine Ridge Reservation, most of the Sioux were Oglalas, and on Rosebud most were Brules.[4]

To complicate the terminology further, the term "Sioux" actually came from *Nadouesioux*, a French corruption of the Ojibwa word for the Sioux which meant "little snakes." Since the Ojibwas and the Sioux traditionally were enemies, this name was not meant as a compliment. The Sioux referred to themselves as the Lakotas, Dakotas, or Nakotas, depending on the dialect they spoke, and this meant "friends" or "allies." The names of the three Sioux dialects, Lakota, Dakota and Nakota, also served as the names for the Sioux bands which spoke these dialects. Therefore, since the Oglalas and Brules spoke Lakota, they referred to themselves as the Lakotas. In this study, the term "Sioux" refers to the Sioux Nation as a whole, and "Lakotas" refers to the Sioux on Pine Ridge and Rosebud, most of whom were Lakotas.[5]

---

3. See appendix.

4. William Powers, *Oglala Religion* (Lincoln: University of Nebraska, 1975), 5-13.

5. *Ibid.*, 5-13.

This study principally concerns mission method and pastoral ministry and shows that the Jesuits' methods were not simply the sum total of the techniques and ideas that they brought with them to convert the Lakotas. Rather, their pastoral ministry involved a continual exchange of thoughts between them and the Lakotas. On Pine Ridge and Rosebud, the Jesuits did not only use Western techniques to convert the Lakotas, but also learned from the Lakotas how best to transmit Catholic doctrine to them. Rather than passively receiving the new teachings, the Lakotas themselves actively engaged in reconciling their culture with Catholic doctrine. Furthermore, this study shows that the Jesuits at Holy Rosary and St. Francis respected some aspects of the Lakota religion, and taught that some continuity existed between the traditional Lakota religion and the Catholic faith. Contrary to the beliefs of some scholars,[6] the Jesuits recognized virtue in the Lakota religion, participated in Lakota rituals, and sought to preserve aspects of the Lakota culture throughout their time at the St. Francis and Holy Rosary missions.

---

6. Harvey Markowitz, "The Catholic Mission and the Sioux: a Crisis in the Early Paradigm," in *Sioux Indian Religion*, ed. Raymond DeMaille and Douglas Parks (Norman: University of Oklahoma, 1987), 136-137.

CHAPTER ONE

The Beginnings
of the Sioux Mission

THE JESUITS AND FRANCISCANS OF NEW FRANCE BEGAN THE CATHOLIC mission to the Sioux. From 1666 to 1702, four of these missionaries, Claude Jean Allouez, S.J., Jacques Marquette, S.J., Joseph Marest, S.J., and Louis Hennepin, O.F.M., contacted the Sioux. In 1666, Allouez had a brief and peaceful meeting with the Sioux, during which he baptized one of their dying children.[1] Four years later, through the use of a messenger, Marquette negotiated with the Sioux and secured from them a promise of safe passage for Catholic priests in their lands.[2] Between 1688 and 1702, Marest made two expeditions of unknown duration into their lands. Though his contemporary Jesuit brothers recorded little about his expeditions, they referred to him as the "missionary to the Sioux."[3]

The Belgian Franciscan, Louis Hennepin, was the first missionary on record to live with the Sioux and study the Dakota dialect.[4] In 1680 the Santee Sioux captured Hennepin on the Mississippi River and forced him to travel and live with them for four months.[5] During this time, however, they befriended Hennepin and, as Hennepin later described, their Chief, Aquipaguetin, adopted him into his family:

> One of the leading Issati [Santee] chiefs gave us his peace calu-
> met [pipe] to smoke and accepted the one we had brought. He
> gave us a bark platter of wild rice which the Indian women had
> seasoned with blue-berries. . . . At the close of this feast, the best

---

1. Thwaites, *Jesuit Relations*, 51:53-54.

2. *Ibid.*, 54:193, 56:115-117.

3. *Ibid.*, 66:107, 338.

4. Louis Hennepin, *A New Discovery of a Vast Country in America* (Chicago: A.C. McClurg, 1903), 1:188, 217.

5. Louis Hennepin, *A Description of Louisiana* (University of Minnesota Press, 1938), 94-114.

meal we had for seven or eight days, each of the chiefs who had
adopted us in place of their sons killed in the war took one of us
to his village. . . . The five wives of [Aquipaguetin] who called
me *Mitchinchi*, or his son, met us with three bark canoes and
took us a short league farther to an island where their wigwams
were. . . . The day after our arrival, Aquipaguetin, who is chief of
a large family, covered me with a robe made of ten large dressed
beaver skins trimmed with porcupine quills. He showed me five
or six of his wives and told them, as I afterward learned, that they
were to treat me as one of their sons.[6]

Adoption into a Sioux family was a religious rite and certainly a great
honor. After this ritual, the members of the chief's family referred to
Hennepin as "son," "nephew," "brother," or "grandson."[7]

Hennepin participated in several Sioux rituals during this time. On
several occasions, he took a sweat bath with Aquipaguetin, and said that it
improved his health.[8] He also said that he smoked the calumet, which was
a long pipe that the Native Americans considered sacred. Among the Natives of North America, smoking the sacred pipe was a universal symbol
of good will and a sacred rite. If a Native American consented to smoke
the pipe with someone, it was a sign that all that he said in the context of
that meeting was in good faith. But if he refused to smoke, this signified
that he had unfriendly intentions. When they first met the Santee, Hennepin's group had a sacred pipe with them which they offered to the Santee as a sign of their good will. At that time, however, the Santee refused
it. Later Hennepin smoked the sacred pipe with the Santee several times
and also with other Native Americans whom he encountered. Hennepin
himself carried a sacred pipe, which a French commander gave him, to
help him gain acceptance among the Native Americans.[9] Likewise, Marquette carried a pipe which the Illinois gave him and which he used to
show his friendly intentions to any Native Americans that he might encounter.[10] On one occasion when a Native American band attacked Marquette, he displayed the pipe and this had the effect of pacifying them.[11]
By smoking with the Native Americans, both Hennepin and Marquette
participated in a significant indigenous ritual for the purpose of communicating with and befriending the Native Americans.

Although Hennepin made several attempts to instruct the Sioux in
Christianity, he admitted, however, that his efforts were mostly unsuccess-

---

6. *Ibid.*, 106-108.

7. *Ibid.*, 107-111.

8. *Ibid.*, 108.

9. *Ibid.*, 44, 84, 103, 106.

10. Thwaites, 59:131.

11. Paul Steinmetz, S.J., "The Sacred Pipe in American Indian Religions," in *American
Indian Culture and Research Journal* 8 (1984) 61. Thwaites, 59:151.

ful.[12] Nevertheless, he did establish friendly relations with them. When Hennepin was about to leave them, they offered him a pile of beaver pelts to induce him to stay with them and to repay him for the items they stole from him when they captured him.[13] They also apologized for the harsh treatment that they gave him at first. After leaving them for a few months, he returned to them later that year. At that time, he stayed with them for a month, feasted with them, and left them on good terms.[14]

The major factor in the success of the missions of New France was the missionaries' ability to learn the Native American languages. They also traveled with the Native Americans, paddled their canoes, lived in their tepees, ate their food, and smoked their pipes. The willingness of Hennepin and the other Catholic missionaries of New France to participate in Native American rituals and to live in much the same way as did the Native Americans showed that they adapted, at least in some respects, to the Native American lifestyle. But their early meetings with the Sioux were brief, and the Jesuits were not able to establish a permanent mission to the Sioux in the Eighteenth century. Before they could establish a permanent mission, the French government in 1763 banished the Jesuits from Louisiana,[15] and in 1773 Pope Clement XIV suppressed the entire Society of Jesus.

In 1814 Pius VII restored the Society of Jesus, and twenty-five years later the Jesuits resumed their mission to the Sioux. In 1839, the Belgian Jesuit, Pierre De Smet, met with the Sioux, and two years later the French missionary Father Augustine Ravoux began to live and travel with several Sioux bands. When Ravoux was undergoing his seminary training in Le Puy, France in 1838, Bishop Jean Mathias Loras of Dubuque, Iowa, paid him a visit. Loras was in France to recruit missionaries for his territory. After hearing the bishop address his seminary class, Ravoux offered his services and accompanied him back to Iowa.[16] In 1841, Loras sent him to establish a mission among the Dakota Sioux, and he immediately began to study the Dakota dialect.

Visiting the Dakota Sioux primarily in Wisconsin and Minnesota, Ravoux reported that they were kind to him and aided him in learning their language.[17] The French traders who were friendly with the Sioux also helped him learn Dakota, and encouraged him in his efforts to evangelize the Dakotas.[18] By 1843, he knew the Sioux language well enough

12. Hennepin, *A New Discovery of a Vast Country in America,* 1:217.

13. Hennepin, *Description of Louisiana,* 110-111.

14. *Ibid.,* 93-125.

15. Thwaites, 70:213-219.

16. Augustine Ravoux, *Reminiscences, Memoirs and Lectures of Monsignor A. Ravoux* (St. Paul: Brown, Treacy, and Co., 1890), 1.

17. Augustine Ravoux, *The Labors of Mgr. A. Ravoux Among the Sioux or Dakota Indians* (Pioneer Press Co.: St. Paul, 1897), 1-10.

to write in Dakota the first Catholic Sioux catechism, *Wakantanka Tiki Chanku*, meaning "The Path to the House of God."[19] The book contained a Bible history, catechism, prayers, and hymns translated from French into Dakota. In this catechism were twenty songs that he took great pains to translate from the French into Dakota, and he commented that he had a small choir of Dakotas who were part French, and who sang in French as well as Dakota.[20] Since he was French, Ravoux quickly became close to several Native Americans, most of whom were half-French, and also many French traders. In Minnesota, he even lived for a time at a trading post which did business with the Dakotas, since he found that it was a good environment in which to evangelize them.[21] He also reported that the Dakotas listened respectfully to his teachings and came to hear him preach at Ft. Pierre.[22]

Like the missionaries before him, Ravoux conformed his ways, to some extent, to those of the Sioux. He participated in many traditional Sioux feasts, and used these opportunities to attempt to teach them the principal Catholic doctrines. On at least one occasion, the Sioux showed their esteem for him by serving him a Sioux delicacy, roast dog, which he consented to eat.[23] In addition to participating in traditional Sioux feasts, he also conformed to the Native American culture by wearing some of their clothing. Since the Sioux called the Catholic missionaries "Blackrobes" or "Blackgowns," the Sioux band with whom he lived gave him a gift to match his name. In a book he wrote over fifty years after his first contact with the Sioux, he described their gift:

> Black Gown! This word brings to my recollection a fine black cassock that I wore over fifty years ago. It was really a production of the industry of the land. The material was deerskin, dyed by Indian women, and the cassock was made by them. Clad in my new cassock, which I wore two or three years, I thought was as fine and rich a cassock as I had ever seen before. After about twelve months it was no more a black cassock. Its color had become purple. A year or two later it shrunk so much that I could wear it no longer. Then by Indian industry, it was turned into several pairs of moccasins which were very useful to me.[24]

For four years, he traveled widely in Wisconsin, Minnesota and the Dakota Territory visiting, baptizing, and living with the Santee, Brule,

---

18. *Ibid.*, 2-3.
19. *Ibid.*, 4.
20. Ravoux, *Labors*, 5.
21. *Ibid.*, 6.
22. Ravoux, *Reminiscences*, 25.
23. *Ibid.*, 17.
24. Ravoux, *Labors*, 6-7.

Hunkpapa, Blackfeet, and other bands of the Sioux who he reported always welcomed him.[25] But after this time, his bishop assigned him to St. Paul and Mendota, Minnesota to minister to the needs of French and English Catholics there. But he still continued to visit the Sioux throughout the next thirty years.

At that time, priests were scarce in Minnesota and few were available to stay with all the scattered Sioux bands. Though he spent years laboring to convert the Sioux, he had to travel over a vast territory. He encountered many different Sioux bands, and sometimes stayed only a few months among them. Though he no doubt had difficulties communicating a deep knowledge of the Catholic faith to the Sioux under these conditions, he established friendly relations with several Sioux bands and advanced the Blackrobes' reputation among them.

Two years before Ravoux contacted the Sioux, the Belgian Jesuit, Pierre De Smet, met with them in 1839, and established a friendship that he maintained until his death in 1873. De Smet actually became interested in the Native American missions in much the same way as did Ravoux. When De Smet attended seminary in Belgium, an American priest came to his school seeking missionaries. Along with several of his classmates, he decided to make the journey to America in 1821. After beginning his Jesuit training in Maryland, he traveled to Missouri in 1823 where he completed his studies at the newly established Jesuit seminary at Florissant.[26] That year the Bishop of New Orleans, Louis Dubourg, S.S., a former president of Georgetown College, decided to give the Jesuits the land and all the buildings at Florissant to establish a seminary. Making an agreement with the Jesuit Superior in Maryland, Charles Neale, he entrusted the Jesuits with the care of all the missions to the Native Americans and whites on the Missouri River and its tributaries. Dubourg and Neale also agreed that the Jesuits at Florissant would train priests for the missions, and establish a mission among the Potawatomis.[27]

In 1838 De Smet began his missionary work among the Native Americans, and carried out Dubourg's plan of founding a mission to the Potawatomis at Council Bluffs near Omaha. After establishing good relations with the Potawatomis, in 1839 he sought to negotiate a peace between the warring Potawatomis and the Yankton Sioux. At De Smet's first meeting with the Yankton Sioux in 1839, they welcomed him, and he successfully convinced the Yanktons that peace with the Potawatomis was in their best interest. At the peace talks, De Smet encouraged them to make peace in the traditional Native American fashion:

25. Ravoux, *Reminiscences*, 17, 25, 82. Ravoux, *Labors*, 1-10.

26. H.M. Chittenden and A.T. Richardson, *Life, Letters, and Travels of Pierre-Jean DeSmet* (New York: Francis P. Harper, 1905), 1:6.

27. Gilbert Garraghan, S.J., *The Jesuits of the Middle United States* (New York: America Press, 1938), 1:55, 61-64.

> I persuaded the Sioux to make some presents to the children of
> such of our Potawatomis as they had killed, which is called *cover-*
> *ing the dead* and to come and smoke with them the calumet of
> peace.[28]

Offering presents to the afflicted and smoking the pipe together were Native American customs which served to reconcile the two parties. In the
evening after the successful negotiations, De Smet recounted that they
showed their appreciation for his actions by honoring him with the calumet dance.[29] By attending their dances, taking part in their feasts, and
encouraging other Native American customs, he adapted, to some extent,
to the Native American culture and by doing so, won their trust.

De Smet met with many different Native American nations and most
received him enthusiastically. In 1840, he described the reception the
Cheyennes gave him:

> The head chiefs of the villages invited me to a feast and put me
> through all the ceremonies of the calumet, as follows: first they
> give the Great Spirit to smoke, holding the pipe towards the heav-
> ens, then towards the sun, the earth and the water; then the calu-
> met goes the rounds of the lodge three times; it passes from hand
> to hand, and everyone takes half a dozen puffs. Then the chief
> embraced me and greeted me saying, "Black-robe, my heart was
> very glad when I learned who you were. Never has my lodge
> seen a greater day. As soon as I received the news of your com-
> ing, I had my kettle filled to give you a feast in the midst of my
> warriors. Be welcome. I have had my three best dogs killed in
> your honor." Do not wonder when I tell you that this is their
> great feast, and that the flesh of wild dog is very delicate and
> extremely good.[30]

Like Ravoux, De Smet participated in their traditional feasts even though
the food differed from his accustomed fare. By taking part in "all the
ceremonies of the calumet," he also showed his willingness to participate
in Native American rituals. He smoked the sacred pipe with many of the
Native Americans he met including the Sioux. When he met with the
Yanktonnais and Santee Sioux in 1840, he smoked the sacred pipe with
them.[31] At one of his meetings with the Sioux, the Sioux chiefs gave
him a sacred pipe, pipe bag, and tobacco pouch.[32] On another occasion,

---

28. H.M. Chittenden and A.T. Richardson, *Life, Letters and Travels of Pierre-Jean
DeSmet: 1801-1873*, 1:190.

29. *Ibid.*, 1:190.

30. *Ibid.*, 1:211-212.

31. *Ibid.*, 1:251.

32. *Ibid.*, 3:1008.

the Yankton Sioux Chief Ite-ech-tshe, Cut Face, gave him another sacred pipe.[33]

During his travels, De Smet smoked with many Native American bands knowing that the sacred pipe was an important piece of religious paraphernalia. He understood that the Sioux and other Native Americans offered the smoke of the pipe to the Great Spirit before they smoked.[34] Thus he was well aware that by smoking the pipe, he took part in a religious ritual that was common to most Natives of North America. He also had a good knowledge of the significance of smoking the pipe in various contexts. Describing the pipe, he said the

> calumet is the object which the American Indian prizes most highly, he who does not own one is in their eyes a very poor wretch. It is often tastefully and ingeniously decorated and carved. . . . The calumet presides at all their gatherings, in all their councils with their neighbors, at the ratification of all treaties, their religious festivals and friendly toasts. Anyone who refuses to smoke the calumet is excluded from taking part and is obliged to withdraw. To refuse to accept the calumet, as between two different tribes, is equivalent to a declaration of war, and on the other hand to accept it is always, among the savages, a sign of good harmony, fraternity and mutual charity, ready to aid one another in case of need.[35]

When De Smet visited the different Sioux bands, he came to them unarmed, usually accompanied only by a native translator, so they knew that he did not come with hostile intentions. He also spoke about religion often, and they took religious matters seriously. In 1840, he met with the Blackfeet Sioux, who received him with enthusiasm and smoked the pipe with him. As was shown by De Smet's description of his first encounter with the Blackfeet Sioux, the Blackrobes' reputation apparently was spreading among the Sioux at that time:

> My long black robe and the missionary's cross that I bore upon my breast excited [the Sioux chief's] curiosity. The Canadian [De Smet's translator] answered him . . . "It is the man who talks to the Great Spirit. It is a chief or Black-gown of the Frenchmen." His fierce look at once changed; he ordered his warriors to put away their weapons and they all shook hands with me. I made them a present of a big twist of tobacco, and everybody sat down in a circle and smoked the pipe of peace and friendship.[36]

---

33. *Ibid.*, 3:1008.
34. *Ibid.*, 1:211-212, 3:914.
35. *Ibid.*, 3:1008-1011.
36. *Ibid.*, 1:252.

The Blackfeet Sioux Chief then invited him back to his village for a feast in De Smet's honor. When they arrived at the camp, they asked De Smet to sit on a buffalo robe. Upon doing this, much to his surprise, they grabbed the robe by the corners, lifted him up, and carried him to the feast.[37]

De Smet had a particular fondness for the Flatheads whom he began to meet with in 1840. Though he was the first priest to visit their nation, he was not the first Catholic to contact them. In the early 1800's, a group of Catholic Iroquois made contact with the Flatheads and convinced them of the virtue of the Blackrobes' religion. Not wanting to wait for a missionary to visit them, the Flatheads sent a delegation to Bishop Joseph Rosati in St. Louis in 1839 to request Catholic priests for their band. On this journey, they met De Smet and he promised to visit them.[38] When he finally arrived at the Flathead camp in 1840, he received a hero's welcome. He had remarkable success in converting them and they accepted the Catholic faith almost immediately.[39]

De Smet's work among the Flatheads illustrated his plan for the ideal mission. In just a few years he persuaded the Flatheads to change from a nomadic to an agrarian society. He also encouraged them to spread the Catholic faith through their own example. Before he left them, he assigned a Flathead Chief[40] to be their catechist in his absence since the chief was zealous in learning the Catholic prayers.[41]

In his effort to found a mission among the Flatheads, De Smet had several difficulties to overcome. Since the Flatheads allowed men to have many wives and allowed divorce (which was common), he endeavored to discourage these practices.[42] He also believed that instilling a work ethic was essential for any people, and he found them willing to comply with the requests that he made of them.[43] The first project that he gave to them was the construction of a church, a school, and several houses. With their own labor, the Flatheads built these buildings,[44] which served as the basis of a settled lifestyle and helped De Smet organize the community's public worship. Following the pattern established by the Jesuits in Paraguay,[45] he called the entire Flathead community together in the morning and evening for prayer. He also provided catechism at a certain hour of

---

37. *Ibid.*, 1:251-253.
38. *Ibid.*, 1:19-30.
39. *Ibid.*, 1:339.
40. De Smet does not provide the name of this chief.
41. Chittenden, 1:226.
42. *Ibid.*, 2:572.
43. *Ibid.*, 1:329.
44. *Ibid.*, 1:331.
45. *Ibid.*, 1:315-317.

the day, and with the assistance of translators, he developed a catechism in the Flathead language.[46]

De Smet praised the Flatheads for their temperament and described them as generous, honest, and hospitable. Noting that they had no thieves among them, he wrote: "I have often asked myself: 'Is it these people whom the civilized nations dare to call by the name of savages?'"[47] His writings indicated that he recognized that the Native Americans had many good qualities, and that they often, in his words, learned vices from "whites who, guided by the insatiable thirst for sordid gain, endeavor to corrupt [the Native Americans] and encourage them by their example."[48] Moreover, he condemned the liquor trade of the whites with the Native Americans, and frequently complained to the government about the liquor trafficking.[49] Though he persuaded the Flatheads to abandon their nomadic lifestyle, he did not want them to become like the other whites of the frontier. Rather, he wanted to insulate them from what he saw as the corruption of the age and the white frontiersmen who he thought were prone to so many vices.[50]

De Smet believed that because of their willingness to accept the Catholic faith, the Flatheads were, in his words, "a chosen people, the elect of God."[51] For instance, when the Flatheads battled the Crows, they had remarkable success that he attributed to the special protection of God: "I look upon the miraculous escape of our Christian warriors, in this fierce contest, as further evidence of the peculiar protection of heaven."[52] The zeal with which the Flatheads practiced devotions, he believed, was also a sign of God's grace. Describing the services, he wrote:

> I rang the bell for prayer, and from the first day to the last, they continued to show the same avidity to hear God's word. Their eagerness was so great that they would run to get a good place; even the sick got themselves carried thither. What a lesson for the cowardly and pusillanimous Christians of the old Catholic countries, who have always plenty of time for coming to the divine services, and think they do enough if they are in time for the first gospel.[53]

---

46. *Ibid.*, 1:336-338.
47. *Ibid.*, 1:227.
48. *Ibid.*, 1:228.
49. *Ibid.*, 1:184-185.
50. *Ibid.*, 1:329.
51. *Ibid.*, 1:327.
52. *Ibid.*, 2:577.
53. *Ibid.*, 1:225-227.

De Smet's remarkable success with the Flathead mission drew the attention of Edward Geary, the government agent on the Flatheads' land. In his report to the Commissioner of Indian Affairs in 1860, he said that

> the Flatheads and the cognate tribes are a noble race, magnanimous and brave. They have been for twenty-five years under the spiritual direction of the Catholic missionaries, and all profess Christianity.[54]

By 1849, De Smet also helped to establish missions to the Coeur d'Alene, Pend d'Oreilles, Osages, Potawatomis, and Miamis. At this time, Catholic priests and nuns ran schools at the Osage, Potawatomi, and Miami missions and received federal aid from the education fund for the Indians.[55]

De Smet met for the first time with the Oglala Sioux in 1849. When he arrived at the meeting, the Oglala Chief Red Fish had just suffered a defeat in battle when he attacked the Crows. During the battle, the Crows captured the Chief's daughter. Red Fish told De Smet of his loss:

> I have lost my beloved daughter. Pity me, for I have learned that the medicine of the Black-gown (prayer) is powerful before the Great Spirit. Speak to the Master of Life in my favor, and I will still preserve hope of seeing my child.[56]

After berating the Chief for attacking the Crows, De Smet consented to pray for his cause. Shortly afterwards, Red Fish learned that his daughter had just escaped from the Crows unharmed. De Smet reported that the Oglalas all attributed her escape to the efficacy his prayers, and word of this event traveled through the Sioux villages.[57]

In 1851 De Smet met with the Arapahos, Cheyennes and Sioux, including the Oglalas and Brules, at the Great Council at Ft. Laramie, a gathering of over 10,000 Native Americans. At this council, he acted as a mediator between the Native Americans and the government, and all the chiefs present signed the treaty. During the eighteen-day assembly, he visited with the different bands, participated in their feasts and attended their dances, which he described as "perfectly innocent."[58] He also reported that the Oglalas invited him to stay with them. During this time, he instructed the Sioux and baptized 239 Oglalas, 280 Brules and Osages, and 61 Native Americans of mixed ancestry.[59]

---

54. Edward Geary, Oct 1, 1860, Portland, Oregon, *Report of the Commissioner of Indian Affairs Accompanying the Annual Report of the Secretary of the Interior for the year 1860* (Washington: George W. Bowman, 1860), 181.

55. Chittenden, 4:1307.

56. *Ibid.*, 2:630.

57. *Ibid.*, 2:631.

58. *Ibid.*, 2:680.

59. *Ibid.*, 2:678-679. The phrase "mixed ancestry" refers to those Native Americans who had a parent or ancestor who came from Europe.

At this council, De Smet spoke of the many French Catholics living in the "Indian territory" who sought priests.[60] The presence of Sioux of mixed ancestry and French at this council and in the Dakota Territory indicated that even in the 1850's a mixing of cultures had taken place.[61] Since he was Belgian, he had an ethnic and linguistic background similar to that of the French. His background actually helped him gain the trust of many Native Americans who were quite close to French people. The Sioux knew the French since many French men married Sioux women, lived with the Sioux, and spoke Sioux dialects. During his travels, De Smet encountered many natives of mixed ancestry and French men who were interpreters, traders and trappers. Many of these men were Catholic, and they frequently aided and accompanied him.[62] At times he even held Mass for the French, natives of mixed ancestry, and Native Americans gathered together, at which they sang hymns in French, Latin and the Native American languages.[63] He also encountered a great many natives of mixed ancestry, most often part French, who helped him to make contacts with other Native Americans. On several occasions when he met with natives of mixed ancestry, he reported that he was able to baptize them.[64]

Christian Hoecken, S.J., a missionary who accompanied De Smet to a Santee Sioux camp in 1850, also noted the presence of many Sioux of mixed ancestry, and he hoped that the Church could spare missionaries for them:

> Do not imagine that the number of these poor children [the Santee], all baptized by Father De Smet and others is insignificant. The halfbreeds exist in great numbers everywhere, with thousands of Indians.[65]

Thus, even in the mid-nineteenth century, Jesuit missionaries evangelized natives of mixed ancestry whose religious heritage came both from Europe and America. Since the seventeenth century, many of the French travelers and trappers in the Dakotas married Sioux women, and brought the Catholic faith to the Sioux through marriage.[66] Unlike the English, the French did not bring many women with them when they colonized America and they often married Native Americans.

---

60. *Ibid.*, 2:677-679.

61. *Ibid.*, 2:684.

62. *Ibid.*, 1:264.

63. *Ibid.*, 1:262.

64. *Ibid.*, 2:677.

65. *Ibid.*, 4:1256. Christian Hoeken, S.J., to Father Provincial John A. Elet, Territory of the Platte, Dec. 28, 1850.

66. Sister M. Claudia Duratschek, O.S.B., *The Beginnings of Catholicism in South Dakota,* 8-10.

In the 1850's, several Native American bands requested that Catholic priests live with them. Oddly enough, they often made these requests to the government agents. In September 1857, the Superintendent of Indian Affairs, W.J. Cullen, met with the Sisseton and Wahpeton bands of the Santee Sioux at Yellow Medicine, Minnesota, and published the minutes of the meeting in *The Annual Report of the Commissioner of Indian Affairs*. The minutes stated that these Sioux bands

> desire to have a Catholic priest sent among them; he will do them good; their present missionaries are not of any benefit to them, and [the Sioux] are unwilling that they shall be paid from their education fund, but are willing that when a Catholic priest is sent he shall be paid out of it. . . . [Sioux Chief Cloudman said] "The school fund comes off of us, and we want Catholic priests. We do not blame the Great Father, he wishes to do right, but he sends us lazy people who do nothing for us."[67]

Similarly and in that same year, Colonel Alfred Vaughan, a Protestant government agent to the Blackfeet (not the Blackfeet Sioux), wrote a letter to De Smet encouraging him to establish a Catholic mission among the Blackfeet:

> I take great pleasure in testifying that the Catholic Church, to which you belong, has everywhere obtained the most pre-eminent success. The Catholic missionaries have always succeeded in gaining the Indians' hearts, in controlling their brutal outbreaks and ameliorating their condition in every respect. Being fully convinced of this, the object of this letter is to obtain your intercession with your superiors for the formation of a mission among the Blackfeet. Such a mission would advance the interests of the government and those of the Indians at the same time.[68]

At this time and for the next twelve years, the government encouraged the Catholic missionaries' work, as pacifying the Native Americans was in their interest.

The government also asked De Smet several times to serve as a mediator between them and the Native Americans. In 1858 John Floyd, the Secretary of War, wrote De Smet a letter which said that "the President is desirous to engage you to attend the Army for Utah to officiate as chap-

---

67. "Minutes of a council held with the chiefs and head men of the Sisseton and Wahpeton bands of upper Sioux, held at Yellow Medicine, at the conclusion of the payment of their annuities, on Monday, the 21st of September, 1857," *Report of the Commissioner of Indian Affairs Accompanying the Annual Report of the Secretary of the Interior for the year 1857*, 113-114. The Sioux chiefs at this council were *Mazomani, Mahpiya-wicasa, Akicita-majin,* and *Oksida Waste.* Thomas Williamson (Presbyterian minister) and Stephan R. Riggs (Congregational minister) were missionaries among the Sisseton and Wahpeton at this time.

68. Chittenden, 4:1317. Colonel Vaughan to De Smet, May 20, 1857. De Smet quoted this letter in his letter dated June, 1857.

lain."[69] At this time the Flatheads, Pend d'Oreilles, Coeur d'Alenes and others engaged the Army in several battles. Since De Smet had friendly relations with all these Native American nations, the Army chose him to mediate the peace negotiations. Accepting this assignment,[70] he had a conference in April, 1859 with the chiefs of these nations at which he persuaded them to renew the peace treaty with the government.[71] Captain A. Pleasonton, Assistant Adjutant-General, wrote a note saying that De Smet "accomplished in a highly satisfactory manner the important duties confided to his charge in Special Orders No. 4 of October 28, 1858 [the pacification of the Coeur d'Alene]."[72]

In 1864, the government again sought De Smet's services, and he complied. Commissioner of Indian Affairs William Dole wrote him saying,

> I have now to state that I am desirous of availing of your experience upon the subject of our relations with the Indians generally, and your knowledge of their character and habits, as also your influence over the particular bands of the Sioux who have given us so much trouble in Dakota, and solicit you to accompany the expedition, with a hope that they may be induced to lay down their arms and establish peaceful relations with the government.[73]

De Smet traveled to Fort Berthold that year and met with a small group of Yanktonnais and other bands of the Sioux. After having a council with them, he sent them to the main Sioux camp with a present of tobacco and an invitation to the principle chiefs to meet with him. Responding to his appeal for a council, about two hundred Sioux returned to Fort Berthold. The chiefs smoked the pipe with him, and as always, he counseled them to maintain friendly relations with the government.[74] After his meetings with the Sioux, he sent several letters to Commissioner Dole telling him of the results of his meetings.[75]

From 1864 to 1868, De Smet visited the Yanktonnais, Santee, Yankton, Brule, Two Kettle, Hunkpapa, and Oglala Sioux bands, all of whom

---

69. *Ibid.*, 4:1569. John Floyd, Secretary of War to De Smet, War Department, Washington, May 13, 1858.

70. *Ibid.*, 2:716-717. De Smet to John P. Floyd, St. Louis University, May 18, 1858.

71. *Ibid.*, 2:766.

72. *Ibid*, 4:1581. A. Pleasonton, Captain Second Dragoons, Assistant Adjutant-General by order of General Harney, Fort Vancouver, Washington Territory, June 1, 1859. For Special Orders No. 4 see Chittenden, 4:1573.

73. William P. Dole to De Smet, March 21, 1864, *Report of the Commissioner of Indian Affairs for the year 1864*, 275.

74. De Smet to William Dole, July 15, 1864, *Report of the Commissioner of Indian Affairs in the year 1864*, 280.

75. De Smet to William Dole, Fort Berthold, June 24, 1864, *Report of the Commissioner of Indian Affairs for the year 1864*, 277.

received him well. He counseled peace at these meetings and also took the opportunity to provide Catholic instruction to the Sioux.[76] He wrote that at one of the meetings the Yankton Chief Pananniapapi, Struck by the Ree, whom he baptized in 1864,[77] told him that he desired a Catholic mission among his people.[78] Furthermore, in 1866 five chiefs of the Yankton Sioux – Struck by the Ree, Little Swan, Feather in the Ear, Medicine Cow and Jumping Thunder – sent a joint letter to De Smet requesting a school and teachers:

> There is another religious [teacher] that wants to come and remain with us. He wants to teach us the Santee language, but we do not want them. We want no other but you and your religion. The other wants to learn us how to read and sing in the Indian language and which we know how to do in our own way. What we want is to learn the American language and their ways. We know enough of the Indian ways. I am now very old and before I die I want to see a school and the children learn how to read and write in the American language, and if you try and get with us, I will be very happy.[79]

The Sioux also communicated their desire to have Catholic priests to the generals whom they met at the councils. In a letter to De Smet in 1866, Brigadier General and Special Indian Commissioner Alfred Sully commented that the Sioux asked for Catholic priests:

> Knowing the great interest you take in the welfare of the Indians, I write you in their behalf that you may interest yourself and such as may so be disposed to assist in the establishment of religious missions in the Indian Country. I would suggest as a commencement such institutions be established, one at the [?] village, Fort Berthold, another at the Yankton Agency, Dakota Territory. I would recommend the establishment of others as soon as the means could be procured. In making this request I am only asking what the Indians at these two above mentioned places have repeatedly requested me to do. Their predilections are decidedly in favor of the Catholic religion to the exclusion of any other. As I do not profess myself to be a Catholic, I can speak of the great good they have done towards civilizing the savage without fear of being accused of prejudice. In fact, I can say that the priests are the only missionaries I have ever seen who have been successful

---

76. Chittenden, 3:874.

77. *Ibid.*, 4:1526. De Smet to General Meagher, St. Louis University, Nov, 6, 1886. Sister M. Claudia Duratschek, O.S.B., *Builders of God's Kingdom: the History of Catholicism in South Dakota* (Yankton: Diocese of Sioux Falls, 1979), 10.

78. Chittenden, 3:884. Chittenden translates "Struck by the Ree" as "Man who Strikes the Ree."

79. *Ibid.*, 4:1287. Yankton Chiefs to De Smet, Greenwood, Dakota Territory, July 26, 1866, letter dictated to J.B. Chardon, and signed by Struck by the Ree, Little Swan, Feather in the Ear, Medicine Cow, and Jumping Thunder.

in improving the condition of the Indians to any great extent. . . . The Fathers should be, if possible, French, the Sisters also, on account of the half-breeds who live with the Indians being French.[80]

Encouraging De Smet in his labors to establish missions among the Sioux, Sully also recognized that the intermarriage of the French and Sioux built up friendships and family ties upon which the missionaries could build.

In 1867, however, several bands of the Sioux, including the Brules and Hunkpapas, were at war with the Army, and the Secretary of the Interior, O.H. Browning, asked De Smet to serve as an envoy and pacify them.[81] In May and June of that year, at Fort Thompson and Fort Sully, De Smet held several councils with the chiefs of the several Sioux bands: the Brules, Two Kettles, Yanktonnais, Yanktons, San Arcs, Minneconjous, Oglalas and Blackfeet Sioux. C.T. Campell, the government agent at Fort Sully at that time, commented on De Smet's stature at these meetings:

> The appearance among them again of Father De Smet has an astonishing influence. They adopt his religion, made plain to them by his peculiar zeal and manner of instruction; they adhere to it and revere with pride the medal of the Holy Cross, as a charm that may lead them to good acts, knowledge, and happiness.[82]

Assuring the Sioux that the government desired only peace with them, De Smet counseled them of the "absolute necessity of keeping aloof of the hostile bands."[83] The councils at Forts Thompson and Sully went smoothly, and he left with promises from most that they would refrain from initiating any aggressive actions against the Army. At this time, however, the government failed to follow through on its promises to provide them with the means to farm the land without which they were vulnerable to famine. Several bands also bitterly complained of the presence of soldiers on their land.[84]

Still acting as an envoy of the government, De Smet met with the Hunkpapa Sioux and several other bands who were at war with the Army. Sitting Bull, the Hunkpapa Sioux Chief and shaman, no longer desired to negotiate with any white people. Nevertheless, in 1868, De Smet sent a

---

80. Sully to De Smet, Feb. 28, 1866, in *The Jesuits of the Middle United States,* by Gilbert Garraghan, S.J., 2:481.

81. Chittenden, 3:859.

82. C.T. Campell to N.G. Taylor, Commissioner of Indian Affairs, Yankton, D.T., June 13, 1867, *Report on Indian Affairs by the Acting Commissioner for the year 1867,* 238.

83. De Smet to N.G. Taylor, Commissioner of Indian Affairs, Old Fort Sully, June 1, 1867, *Report on Indian Affairs by the Acting Commissioner for the year 1867,* 241-242.

84. Brig. General Alfred Sully to N.G. Taylor, Commissioner of Indian Affairs, Fort Sully, June 9, 1867, *Report on Indian Affairs by the Acting Commissioner for the year 1867,* 244.

scout to Sitting Bull's camp with a present of tobacco, a token expressing his desire to negotiate. Sitting Bull accepted his tobacco and allowed De Smet to enter his camp. The scouts told De Smet that Sitting Bull's band would have killed any other white man who tried to enter their camp at that time.[85]

Carrying a banner of the Blessed Virgin, De Smet rode into Sitting Bull's camp escorted by Red Cloud, the Head Chief of the Oglalas, and several other Sioux chiefs.[86] The camp welcomed him, and the Sioux there were so impressed by the banner that he gave it to them. After the chiefs offered the sacred pipe to the Great Spirit and smoked with him, the Chiefs Black Moon, Sitting Bull, Two Bears and others made speeches in which they complained of the unprovoked assaults upon them by the Army. Arguing for peace with the Army, De Smet convinced most of the chiefs to attend a council at Fort Rice.

As a result of De Smet's intervention, several of these Sioux chiefs went to Fort Rice, located on the Missouri River in North Dakota, and signed a peace treaty in 1868.[87] Major General William Harney, Commissioner John Sanborn, and Major General Alfred Terry wrote a joint letter to De Smet thanking him for his work at this council:

> We the undersigned members of the Indian Peace Commission who have been present at the council just terminated at this post, desire to express to you our high appreciation of the great value of the services which you rendered to us and to the country by your devoted and happily successful efforts to induce the hostile bands to meet us and enter into treaty relations to the government. We are satisfied that but for your long and painful journey into the heart of the hostile country, and but for the influence over even the most hostile of the tribes which your years of labor among them have given to you, the results of which we have reached here could not have been accomplished.[88]

Though he acted as a government envoy on many occasions, De Smet actually believed that the whites were mostly to blame for the violence on the plains:

> The grievances of the [Sioux] Indians against the whites are very numerous, and the vengeances which they on their side provoke are often most cruel and frightful. Nevertheless, one is compelled to admit that they are less guilty than the whites. Nine times out of ten, the provocations come from the latter – that is to say, from

---

85. Chittenden, 3:909.

86. *Ibid.*, 3:904-908.

87. *Ibid.*, 3:921. Harney, Sanborn, and Terry to De Smet, Fort Rice, Dakota Territory, July 3, 1868.

88. *Ibid.*

the scum of civilization, who bring to them the lowest and gross-
est vices, and none of the virtues, of civilized men.[89]

He recognized, however, that the Native American culture and ethics had
both positive and negative aspects. For example, he sharply criticized
the Sioux, Pawnees, and Snakes for their "barbarous custom of abandon-
ing the old and the sick pitilessly to the ferocious beasts of the desert."[90]
In several of his letters, he described the brutal tortures that Native
Americans inflicted upon rival bands. He was also astonished that the
band as a whole performed these acts of cruelty and not just the men.
For example, after visiting a Snake camp and leaving without incident,
he said that they often took prisoners whom they tortured. On one occasion that he learned of, he said that after killing the men of the neighbor-
ing band, the Snakes took the women captives back to their camp. They
then handed the captive women "to their wives, mothers and sisters.
These women immediately butcher[ed the captive women] with their
hatchets and knives."[91]   The Native Americans, De Smet commented,
saw revenge as a virtue.[92]   In Native American society, wars between
different bands were often based on a never ending cycle of revenge for
killings, and they encouraged each other to take revenge on their enemies.

The Sioux were among those whom De Smet condemned for their
violent actions. One time when he visited the Sioux, he described the
scene following a Sioux war party's return from a "battle" with the Oma-
has. In this battle he said that the Sioux waited until the Omaha men
were away hunting. In their absence, the Sioux entered the Omaha village
and slaughtered the old men, women, and children. They returned with
the scalps of their enemies to perform the scalp dance.[93]   Throughout his
extensive writings, he provided several examples of the hostility of Native
American nations toward each other; however, he also provided many examples of their kindness and of the order that existed in the Native American communities.

De Smet's long account of the virtues of Louise Sighouin, daughter
of a Coeur d'Alene chief, was an example of his recognition of the piety
and zeal of many Native Americans. When he was among the Coeur
d'Alenes, he received a great deal of help from Sighouin in converting
this nation. He described her as having all the virtues of a saint. Soon
after he baptized her, she made known that she was willing to devote herself wholly to the Church. He wrote a long tribute lauding her piety:

---

89. *Ibid.*, 3:856. De Smet, letter, Fort Benton, Montana, June 10, 1866.
90. *Ibid.*, 1:219.
91. *Ibid.*, 1:220.
92. *Ibid.*, 1:285.
93. *Ibid.*, 2:628-629.

The zeal and fervor in the service of God, which she manifested immediately after her baptism were the unfailing tokens of a pre-destined soul, filled with extraordinary gifts from heaven. These privileged favors were manifested in all their light by her admirable gentleness, which the greatest opposition could not disturb, by her patience under every trial, by her truly angelic modesty, by her fervent and sustained piety. She seemed, as it were, absorbed in prayer, and nothing apparently could then distract her thoughts. . . . In the different missions, many neophytes are distinguished by a zeal and piety truly worthy of the primitive Christians, by a rare assiduity at all religious exercises, by a faithful accomplishment of all the duties of a good Christian, in a word, by all the virtues which we have just seen in their highest form in Louise Sighouin.[94]

De Smet also indicated that even before the Native Americans converted to Christianity, their culture and religion had some virtue:

By most persons the capacity of the Indians has been greatly underrated. They are generally considered as low in intellect, wild men thirsting after blood, hunting for game or plunder, debased in their habits and groveling in their ideas. Quite the contrary is the case. They show order in their national government, order and dignity in the management of their domestic affairs, zeal in what they believe to be their religious duties, sagacity and shrewdness in their dealings and often a display of reasoning powers far above the medium of uneducated white men or Europeans. Their religion, as a system, is far superior to that of the inhabitants of Hindostan or Japan. . . . All these Indians believe in the existence of a Great Spirit, the creator of all things, and this appears to be an inherent inborn idea.[95]

Here he demonstrated his belief that the Native Americans had some, however obscure, knowledge of God. He believed that their religion was relatively advanced since they believed in the Creator, the Great Spirit. Since he said that the Native American religions were more advanced than Hinduism, he clearly recognized some truth in the Native American religions.

Moreover, De Smet frequently used the term "Great Spirit" as a translation for "God." At a meeting with the Sioux Chiefs including Red Cloud in 1868, he prayed with them to the Great Spirit:

We were all assembled; a large circle was formed, in which several officers for the fort and some of the soldiers joined, besides a

---

94. *Ibid.*, 3:1146-1175.

95. *Ibid.*, 3:1063-1064. De Smet to the Provincial of the Missouri Province Thomas O'Neil, St. Louis University, Sept, 1866.

great number of Indians from all these different tribes [primarily different Sioux bands]. I then offered a solemn prayer to the Great Spirit to put us in his keeping, and made a short address to the numerous friends who surrounded us. . . . [later that night when the Sioux were telling stories] I took occasion to give them various lectures, instructing them in the good custom of offering their prayers of devotion to the Great Spirit, every morning on arising and before going to bed.[96]

By using the term "Great Spirit," he indicated to the Sioux that continuity existed between the Sioux religion and his religion. Rather than discouraging prayer to the Great Spirit, he gave them new prayers to offer to the Great Spirit.

In addition to participating in several Sioux ceremonies, De Smet became a member of the Yanktonnais Sioux when Two Bears, the Head Chief of that band, adopted him as a brother.[97] In De Smet's later letters, he referred to Two Bears as his "brother" or "adopted brother,"[98] and the tone of his letters suggested that he was proud of this distinction. Because of his contact with De Smet, Two Bears favored the idea of having Catholic priests among his people, and General David Stanley, writing in 1868, recorded one of Two Bears's requests for Catholic priests:

When we are settled down sowing grain, raising cattle and living in houses, we want Father De Smet to come and live with us, and to bring us other Black-robes to live among us also.[99]

Before De Smet contacted them, the Sioux and other Native Americans were profoundly religious people, and their community life revolved around their religious beliefs. When De Smet arrived, they were naturally interested in his religion. Either through coincidence or some other factors, he and his religion acquired the reputation of having great power, and some called him the "Big Medicine Man."[100] Moreover, his intervention between Native Americans who fought each other indicated to them that he had their interests at heart.

De Smet acquired a reputation of trustworthiness among the Sioux, even though they never quite trusted the Army or the government. Speaking of the Sioux, General Stanley wrote that De Smet was "the only man for whom I have ever seen Indians evince a real affection. They say in

---

96. *Ibid.*, 3:904-905.

97. *Ibid.*, 3:903-904.

98. *Ibid.*, 4:1291, 1537.

99. *Ibid.*, 4:1588. Major General David S. Stanley to Archbishop Purcell, Fort Sully, Dakota Territory, July 12, 1868. In Chittenden, this letter is incorrectly dated July 12, 1864. It should be July 12, 1868 since the Fort Rice council he described took place in 1868.

100. *Ibid.*, 4:1585.

their simple and open language, that he is the only white man who has not a forked tongue."[101]   In 1870 J.A. Hearn, the government agent at the Grand River Agency in South Dakota, made a similar comment about De Smet's reputation.   In his report to the Commissioner of Indian Affairs, Hearn wrote:

> Rev. Father De Smet visited the [Sioux] in July, they were all very well pleased to see him, he intends starting a mission school below this point next Spring, as the Indians are desirous of having their children educated; any assistance rendered him would be of great benefit to the Indians, as he has a great deal of influence, and the Indians think he is one white man that does not lie to them.[102]

The Sioux trusted him because they viewed the Blackrobes as belonging to a different class of people than the Army. The Native Americans did not look at the world simply in terms of whites and Native Americans, but rather distinguished between different "tribes" or groups of white people. The Native Americans referred to the different groups as "Black-robes," "Shortcoats" (Presbyterians), "Whiterobes" (Episcopalians), and "Longknives" (U.S. military). The Catholic priests' celibacy was one of the characteristics that distinguished the Blackrobes from other whites. Since they were unmarried, Catholic priests had the ability to travel far and fast without having to worry about the safety or prosperity of their families. Thus, celibacy was an ideal state for a missionary who had to travel with nomads.

Though De Smet was on friendly terms with the government and worked closely with them to pacify the Native Americans when they were nomadic, the fortunes of the Catholic missions suffered a sharp change of fate when President Grant enacted his "Peace Policy" in 1870. During the 1860's, several of the Sioux bands, including the Yankton and Santee, began to settle down to farm, and the government provided them with farming equipment, log houses, and rations.[103] Supporting this movement toward an agrarian lifestyle, Grant established a policy to "civilize" and Christianize the Native Americans. He and the Department of the Interior thought that Christianizing them was an integral step to "civilizing" and also pacifying them.[104] To carry out his plan, he decided to assign one

---

101. *Ibid.*, 4:1585.

102. J.A. Hearn, report, Grand River Agency, Dakota Territory, Sept. 14, 1870, *Annual Report of the Commissioner of Indian Affairs to the Secretary of the Interior for the year 1870,* 222. Grand River Agency is presently on Standing Rock Reservation.

103. Ben Thompson, report, Lake Traverse, D.T., Oct.12, 1869, *Report of the Commissioner of Indian Affairs,* 323-326. P.H. Conger, report, Yankton Agency, D.T. June 9, 1869, *Report of the Commissioner of Indian Affairs,* 306-308.

104. E.S. Parker, "Report of the Commissioner of Indian Affairs," Oct. 31, 1870 in *Annual Report of the Commissioner of Indian Affairs,* 10. Parker explained the reasoning behind

Christian denomination to each reservation. Once a denomination received an assignment, it had the exclusive right to evangelize the Native Americans on that reservation. Under this plan, a denomination could not evangelize any Native American nation or band to which the government did not assign it. By prohibiting interdenominational competition, Grant attempted to insulate the Native Americans from the bitter tension that existed between many religious denominations, since he knew that this competition would hinder their acceptance of Christianity. Under the Peace Policy, the federal government also provided funding to run the schools that the Protestant and Catholic missionaries established in their assigned areas.

Grant's plan, however, outraged De Smet, who wrote that "in the whole of this affair the Indians have not been consulted as to the religion they desired to belong to."[105] Also disturbed by these developments, the Catholic hierarchy appointed De Smet to lobby against the policy, but despite his pleas, the Grant administration ignored him. Though Grant promised to assign denominations to Native American nations and bands on the basis of the success which a denomination had in evangelizing a particular nation or band, Catholics believed that they received far fewer assignments than they deserved.[106] Consequently, Catholics condemned the Grant administration, particularly the Department of the Interior, for harboring an anti-Catholic bias.

Though the Catholic missionaries gained exclusive rights to evangelize the Sioux of Standing Rock Reservation (located on the border of present day North and South Dakota) and Devil's Lake Reservation (North Dakota),[107] the government assigned the Brules and Oglalas to the Episco-

---

the Grant administration's policy saying "it has seemed to the humanitarian, that the more the Indian was brought into contact with modern civilization the more degraded he became learning only its vices and adopting none of its virtues. Not, therefore, as a dernier resort to save a dying race, but from the highest moral conviction of Christian humanity, the President wisely determined to invoke the cooperation of the entire religious element of the country, to help, by their labors and counsels, to bring about and produce the greatest amount of good from the expenditure of the munificent annual appropriation of money by Congress, for the civilization and Christianization of the Indian race."

105. Chittenden, 4:1336, De Smet to Father D'Aste, St. Louis University, Feb. 11, 1871.

106. Peter Rahill, *The Catholic Indian Missions and Grant's Peace Policy: 1870-1884*, (Washington: Catholic University, 1953), 60. The government assigned Catholics to these agencies: Umatilla in Oregon, Tulalip in Washington, Flathead in Montana, Grande Ronde in Oregon, Standing Rock in North and South Dakota, Devil's Lake in North Dakota, Colville in Washington, and Papago in Arizona. BCIM 4/3-2-7, "Management of the Catholic Indian Bureau at Washington," Feb. 25, 1878, p. 2.

107. Sister M. Claudia Duratschek, O.S.B., *Builders of God's Kingdom.* (Yankton: Sacred Heart Convent, 1985), 27. Sister M. Claudia Duratschek, O.S.B., *Crusading Along Sioux Trails.* (Yankton: Grail, 1947), 28. The Hunkpapas, Yanktonnais, and Blackfeet Sioux settled at Standing Rock Reservation. The Two Kettle, Minneconjous, and Sans Arc and

palians. After the government created the Pine Ridge and Rosebud reservations in 1876, the Episcopalians gained the exclusive right to evangelize the Lakotas on these two reservations.

Most of the Oglalas and Brules, however, did not want the Episcopalians. In 1875 Red Cloud, Head Chief of the Oglala Sioux, met in South Dakota with a commission from the Office of Indian Affairs, and requested Catholic priests for the Oglala people.[108] After traveling to Washington, D.C, to attend a series of meetings with President Hayes beginning on September 26, 1877, Chief Red Cloud, Oglala Chief Little Wound, and Brule Head Chief Spotted Tail, all specifically requested Blackrobes for their bands. At these meetings, Red Cloud said:

> I would like to have stock of all kinds to work with, and live like white people; I also desire to have farming implements of all kinds. I also want schools to enable my children to read and write, so they will be as wise as the white man's children. . . [On the second day of meetings he said] I want you to give me school teachers, so that we will have a good school house, and learn my children how to write and read. Catholic priests are good, and I want you to give me one of them also. . . . [On the third day he continued] We would like to have Catholic priests and nuns, so that they could teach our people how to read and write.[109]

Little Wound stated:

> I wish to have all the provisions that a white man has – the animals that he has, so I can learn and bring my children up in the same way the whites do theirs. We want farming implements of all kinds to cultivate the soil. I also want a Catholic Priest.[110]

Similarly, Spotted Tail said:

> My Great Father, I would like to say something about a teacher. My children, all of them, would like to learn how to talk English. They would like to learn how to read and write. We have teachers there, but all they teach us is to talk Sioux, and to write Sioux, and that is not necessary. I would like to get Catholic

---

Blackfeet Sioux settled at the Cheyenne River Reservation. The Santee made their home at Devil's Lake, N.D. and at the Santee Reservation in Nebraska. The Yanktonnais and Two Kettle Sioux moved to the Crow Creek reservation. Part of the Brule Sioux band went to the Lower Brule Reservation.

108. James Olson, *Red Cloud and the Sioux Problem* (Lincoln: University of Nebraska, 1965), 209. "Report of the Commission Appointed to Treaty with the Sioux Indians," *Annual Report of the Commissioner of Indian Affairs*, (1875), 184-201.

109. Transcript of Meeting between Chiefs Red Cloud, Spotted Tail and other Chiefs and President Hayes, Executive Mansion, Sept. 26, 1877, Council Proceedings May 26, 1875 -April 19, 1894, RG 75, Box 779, National Archives, Kansas City Branch, 201, 216, 226.

110. *Ibid.*, 204-205.

priests. Those who wear black dresses. These men will teach us how to read and write English. We would like to get black-smiths, and men who will work on the farm, and men who will learn us, and instruct us how to do everything. I would like to have a saw mill. I would like to have plows, and seeds, and implements of the farm.[111]

Even though the Episcopalians had worked among the Oglalas and Brules since 1875,[112] the Sioux Chiefs still desired Catholic priests. Moreover, on July 15, 1878, the *New York Times* reported that at a council in South Dakota with E.A. Hayt, Commissioner of Indian Affairs, Red Cloud repeated his request for a Catholic priest.[113]

In the meantime, in 1874 the Catholic hierarchy established the Bureau of Catholic Indian Missions (BCIM) in Washington, D.C. as a response to Grant's Peace Policy. The purpose of the BCIM was to gain legal rights for Catholic missionaries to evangelize freely on all the reservations, and eventually to gain greater government funding for the mission schools they established. To aid the missions, the hierarchy promoted membership in a lay fund raising society called the Ladies' Catholic Indian Missionary Association, which was a group of Catholic women in Washington, D.C. founded in 1875. Working closely with the BCIM, the Missionary Association raised over $16,000 from 1875 to 1877 for the support of the missions.[114] The BCIM used these and other funds it collected to build schools on reservations that the government assigned to the Catholic Church. This initial investment in the schools was crucial since, once the missionaries built the schools, the BCIM acquired contracts from the government to fund them. The combined efforts of the BCIM and the Missionary Association helped the Catholic mission schools in the United States grow from two boarding and five day schools in 1873, to eleven boarding and seventeen day schools by 1877.[115]

In the Dakota Territory, the priest who did the most to further the BCIM's plan of establishing schools among the Native Americans was Martin Marty, O.S.B. Marty was a Swiss Benedictine who in 1860 came

---

111. *Ibid.*, 223-224.

112. E.A. Howard, report, Spotted Tail Agency, Nebraska, Sept. 20, 1875, *Annual Report of the Commissioner of Indian Affairs to the Secretary of the Interior for the year 1875,* 254-255. James J. Hastings, report, Red Cloud Agency, Aug. 10, 1876, *Annual Report of the Commissioner of Indian Affairs to the Secretary of the Interior for the year 1875,* 33. He noted that an Episcopal missionary, Rev. Cleveland, served both the Oglalas and Brules since the winter of 1875-76.

113. "Red Cloud in an Ugly Temper," *New York Times,* July 15, 1878, p.1.

114. BCIM 4/3-1-16, "Financial Statement," *Annals of the Catholic Indian Missions of America* 1 (Jan. 1877):28. BCIM 4/3-2-6, "Work of the Bureau," *Annals of the Catholic Indian Missions of America* 2 (Jan. 1878):30.

115. BCIM 4/3-2-6, "Work of the Bureau," *Annals of the Catholic Indian Missions of America* 2 (Jan. 1878):30-31.

to St. Meinrad's Abbey in Indiana where eventually he became the Abbot in 1871.[116] As Abbot, he encouraged the Benedictines to evangelize the Sioux. In 1876, he began to meet with the Sioux, and immediately started to study the Dakota dialect.[117] During this year, the government established the Standing Rock, Pine Ridge, and Rosebud reservations after forcing the Sioux to cede the Black Hills. In return, the government promised the Sioux schools, farming equipment and rations.[118] In that same year, Marty traveled to the Sioux Standing Rock Reservation and assigned three Benedictines to establish a mission there. Two years later he persuaded four Benedictine sisters to join this mission and teach the Sioux girls in the school that the Benedictine Fathers established.[119] Because of a lack of funding, in 1883 Marty had to transfer control of the mission school to the government, but the sisters and priests still taught in the classrooms.[120]

Like De Smet before him, Marty tried to make peace between the Sioux and the government. After the Sioux defeated the Seventh Cavalry at the Little Big Horn in 1876, Sitting Bull's band, which had participated in the battle, sought refuge in Canada. Marty then decided to travel to Canada to attempt to negotiate a peace between Sitting Bull and the Army. After receiving authorization from the War Department, Marty met Sitting Bull on May 26, 1887.[121] Though he stayed with Sitting Bull for eight days, Marty was unable to persuade him to trust the Army after it had so many times betrayed him.

Despite the government ban on interdenominational competition, Marty also visited both Chief Spotted Tail and Chief Red Cloud in 1877 and 1878, and he reported that both chiefs welcomed him.[122] In 1878, a Catholic priest, Father A.H. Frederick, also stayed with Spotted Tail's band for a short time. In a letter to the Bishop of Omaha, James O'Connor, Frederick described a meeting he attended with Spotted Tail:

> Spotted Tail again urged the question about having a Catholic priest amongst his people. His words are as follows: "I and my people are very glad to see that a Catho. priest has arrived amongst us, and I want government to erect two larger buildings, so that the Father can teach my children."[123]

116. Robert F. Karolevitz, *Bishop Martin Marty: The Black Robe Lean Chief* (Privately printed in South Dakota, 1980), 41-42.

117. *Ibid.*, 53, 69.

118. Sister M. Claudia Duratschek, *The Beginnings of Catholicism in South Dakota* (Washington, D.C.: Catholic University, 1943), 193.

119. Duratschek, *Crusading Along Sioux Trails,* 77-78.

120. *Ibid.,* 88.

121. Rahill, *The Catholic Indian Missions,* 238-243. BCIM 4/3-2-6, "Abbot Martin Visits Sitting Bull," *Annals of the Catholic Indian Missions of America* 2 (Jan. 1878):7-8.

122. Duratchek, *Builders of God's Kingdom,* 45.

In 1878, the government agents still did not force Catholic priests off the Rosebud Reservation,[124] but this was soon to change. By the next year, tensions mounted between the Catholic missionaries and the government.

Desiring to test the resolve of the government to keep Catholic priests off the Pine Ridge Reservation, Marty sent Meinrad McCarthy, O.S.B., of St. Meinrad Abbey to minister to the Lakotas in 1879. Marty, however, underestimated the government's determination, and the government agent on Pine Ridge, Valentine McGillicuddy, ordered McCarthy to leave the reservation.[125] McCarthy, however, moved to Nebraska just two miles away from the southern border of Pine Ridge, and the Sioux visited him there to receive the sacraments. Protesting McCarthy's removal, Red Cloud and other Oglala chiefs told McGillicuddy that they wanted McCarthy allowed on the reservation, and McGillicuddy had their requests forwarded to President Hayes.[126] In his letter to Bishop O'Connor in 1879, McCarthy also indicated that the Lakotas desired Catholic priests:

> I wish you could have seen Red Cloud when I asked him the question [if the Indians wanted Catholic priests and nuns] some three weeks ago as with uplifted hand he said: "Friend, I have seen on my way to Washington many people and many churches. They may be good, but for myself, for my people, and for my children, I want to worship God, who is but one, as the Black Gown worships Him, and we want Black Gowns and Sisters to teach us to do this. Rest assured friend that this is the sentiment of every chief, man, woman and child of the Oglala tribe. We hail your advent with gladness [and] hope the great father will assist you to build schools and churches."[127]

Ultimately the government's policy to prohibit interdenominational competition fell under attack from both Protestants and Catholics. Though the government ordered Catholic missionaries off reservations, Protestants also desired to evangelize on reservations assigned to Catholics. The controversy came to a head in 1880 when a government agent ordered a Congregational minister to leave the Devil's Lake Reservation, which the government assigned to the Catholics.[128] After this incident, the combined lobbying efforts of Catholics and Protestants forced the govern-

---

123. SFM 1/1-1-1, Fr. A. H. Frederick to O'Connor, New Spotted Tail Agency, March 15, 1878.

124. BCIM 1-4-3, A.H. Frederick to Rev. Brouillet, New Spotted Tail Agency, July 10, 1878.

125. Duratschek, *Builders of God's Kingdom,* 40. Rahill, 277-278.

126. Duratschek, *Builders of God's Kingdom,* 40.

127. Henry Casper, S.J., *History of the Catholic Church in Nebraska* (Milwaukee: Bruce Press, 1960), 256. Archives of the Archdiocese of Omaha, McCarthy to Bishop O'Connor, June, 4, 1879.

128. Rahill, 305.

ment to rescind the ban in 1881, and consequently all denominations gained the legal right of access to all reservations.[129]

Marty took advantage of this new freedom and began to establish Catholic missions on the Sioux reservations in the Dakota Territory. Recognizing Marty's interest in the Sioux, Pope Leo XIII appointed him Titular Bishop and Vicar Apostolic of the Dakota Territory in 1880.[130] This appointment was prudent since Marty was successful in recruiting both priests and sisters to serve in the Sioux missions. Using his ties to the Benedictines, he helped establish several Sioux missions in the Dakota Territory. He had Benedictine priests sent from St. Meinrad Abbey and Conception Abbey (Missouri) to Devil's Lake Reservation in 1878, Crow Creek Reservation in 1887, and Cheyenne River Reservation in 1891.[131] In 1885, he invited Jesuits and Franciscan sisters to establish missions on Rosebud and Pine Ridge.[132]

Marty was also quite successful in acquiring funding for the Sioux missions. In 1884, Marty attended the Third Plenary Council where he requested aid for the Sioux missions. The Council accepted Marty's petitions and issued a directive to initiate a national annual collection to fund the Native American missions.[133] To provide additional support for the missions, the Council established the BCIM as a permanent organization, and organized the Commission for Catholic Missions among the Colored People and the Indians as a fund raising association.[134] These actions had the effect of organizing the Catholic missionary effort on a national scale.

During this time, however, Marty had not forgotten about the Lakotas on Pine Ridge and Rosebud. In 1883, Marty sent three secular priests, Father Francis Craft, Father Joseph Bushman, and Father Casper Hospenthal, to minister to the Lakotas on Pine Ridge and Rosebud.[135] From 1883 to 1885, these priests baptized 800 Lakotas, and Bushman baptized Chief Red Cloud, Red Cloud's family and five other Lakota chiefs in 1884.[136] Red Cloud's conversion was especially significant since he was the Head Chief of the Lakotas and commanded a great deal of influence.

129. *Ibid.*, 305-307.

130. Robert F. Karolevitz, *Bishop Martin Marty: The Black Robe Lean Chief*, 79.

131. Duratschek, *Builders of God's Kingdom*, 71, 98, 111-114, 149. Duratschek, *Crusading along Sioux Trails*, 164, 228. Philip Bantin and Mark Thiel, *Guide to Catholic Indian Mission School Records*, (Milwaukee: Marquette, 1984), 308-309.

132. Duratschek, *Builders of God's Kingdom*, 99. Duratschek, *The Beginnings of Catholicism in South Dakota*, 96. Duratschek, *Crusading Along Sioux Trails,* chapters 6-10.

133. John Tracy Ellis, *The Life of James Cardinal Gibbons*, (Westminster: Christian Classics, 1987), 1:284-285. Rahill, 312.

134. *Catholic Almanac: 1988*, (Huntington: Our Sunday Visitor, 1988), 518.

135. Duratchek, *Builders of God's Kingdom*, 84.

136. Theo. Henry, S.J., "Holy Rosary Mission," *Indian Sentinel* 1 (April 1919): 15. Duratschek, *Builders of God's Kingdom*, 84. Duratschek, *Crusading Along Sioux Trails*, 125.

In 1884 Father Craft, who had once studied to become a Jesuit,[137] opened a school for the Lakotas on Rosebud that ran for only two months, and had about 80 students.[138] Craft also made many conversions, and was a charismatic and colorful character on the reservation. Since he was fluent in Lakota, he catechized the Lakotas in their own language.[139] Craft also had an ethnic bond with the Native Americans since he was part Mohawk. On account of his charisma and language abilities, he also gained a great deal of influence among them. Furthermore, according to Craft, when Spotted Tail was dying, this Chief declared that he wanted a Blackrobe to succeed him as chief. Since Craft was the first Blackrobe to arrive after Spotted Tail's death, the Lakotas appointed him Chief, and gave him the name "Hovering Eagle."[140]

Although Craft had to decline the chieftainship, he became a part of the Brule band when Chief Spotted Tail's family adopted him.[141] After 1885, Craft did not reside permanently with the Lakotas, but visited the Pine Ridge and Rosebud reservations through 1891. On one of his visits in 1890, Fr. Florentine Digmann, S.J., superior of St. Francis Mission from 1896 to 1916, spoke of Craft's relationship with his adopted family:

> Father Francis Craft came on a visit. He had worked on the Reserve for about three years, spoke the Sioux [language] perfectly, and was almost adored by our Indians. Many came to visit him. He preached on the two following Sundays, exhorting them to follow the missionaries and do what they would tell them, though they would not understand the reason at once. I visited with him the Spotted Tail family in which he had been adopted. He called Mrs. Spotted Tail *"ina"* mother, and her children brother and sister.[142]

Craft also wrote about his adoption in his March 21, 1888 journal entry:

> When the Sicangus [Brules] adopted me into their nation & into the family of their head chief, & made me their chief in his place, it seemed to be the will of God that I should be a savage among the savages to win the savages to Christ. . . . The Son of God made

---

137. Thomas W. Foley. *Hovering Eagle: the Lives, the Legends, the Letters, and the Journals of Rev. Francis M. Craft.* unpublished manuscript, Marquette University Archives, 12.

138. James G. Wright, report, Rosebud Agency, Aug. 25, 1884, *Annual Report of the Commissioner of Indian Affairs to the Secretary of the Interior for the year 1884,* 45.

139. "Catholic Indian Schools: St. Francis," *Indian Sentinel* (1907 annual edition):22. SFM 1/1-1-4, n.a. Report on Indian Missions, 1934, p.3.

140. HRM 8-4-3, "Father Craft's Good Work Among the Sioux," *Irish World,* Jan. 10, 1891. HRM 8-8-5, " 'Hovering Eagle' on the Indian Scare," *Freeman's Journal,* Nov. 29, 1890.

141. "Father Craft," *New York Freeman's Journal,* Jan 3, 1891.

142. HRM 7-14-8, Digmann, diary, March 15, 1890.

Himself man to save man, & bore the consequences to the death, & still does not desert them. I have become an Indian to save the Indians, & I should stand by the consequences of my act to the end.[143]

Thus Craft tried to adapt to the Sioux lifestyle, and as an indication that they accepted him, the Lakotas gave him an eagle feather, a symbol of the Sioux Nation, which he wore in his hat.[144] In an entry he made in his diary on March 24, 1888, Craft also made a clear statement of his opinion about the Sioux customs:

The time has surely come when they must decide between giving up Indian ways, & adopting civilized habits, or perishing miserably. The Church does not condemn what is either good or indifferent, & when at Rosebud I told them that, though their customs required for their integrity the freedom of the old life, & must necessarily deteriorate when brought into contact, with civilization, still I would not condemn them in toto, but would encourage what was good, as long as it remained so.[145]

Here, Craft noted that even though the Sioux would have to discontinue some of their customs, the Church allowed the "good or indifferent" indigenous customs to continue.

Though Craft maintained a friendly and even familial relationship with the Sioux, he never achieved even a cordial relationship with the government. For example, in 1884, the government attempted to recruit Brule students for an industrial school in Genoa, Nebraska, which was 100 miles west of Omaha. But when the Lakotas protested against the plan, the government agent at Rosebud, James Wright, accused Craft of inciting the Lakotas against the proposal. Wright even threatened to take away the Brule's rations if they did not comply.[146] In 1884 Wright complained about Craft to Hiram Price, the Commissioner of Indian Affairs, and described the priest's influence among the Brules:

The effect of these remarks of Rev. Mr. Craft was soon manifest by the Indians, informing me they would not send their children to Genoa, and unceremoniously leaving the room. These remarks of Priest Craft have been the subject of comment and conversation among the Indians, and all classes at the Agency since they were made, all concur in the opinion that he has set at defiance all law and authority; if allowed to pass unnoticed it must in effect undermine the Agent's control and authority, leading the Indians to look to the Priest as their law-giver, and leaving the Agent but an non-entity.[147]

---

143. Foley, *Hovering Eagle*, 2-5.

144. *Ibid.*, 39.

145. *Ibid.*, 21.

146. BCIM 1-4-3, James G. Wright to Hiram Price, Commissioner of Indian Affairs, Rosebud Agency, Jan. 16, 1884.

Though Craft denied the accusations that he turned the Lakotas against the government school, he clearly had significant authority among the Lakotas. Though the government, by this time, granted equal access to all denominations, the Commissioner of Indian Affairs ordered Craft removed from Rosebud.[148] This conflict between Craft and the Indian Office illustrated the growing adversarial relationship between the Catholic Church and the government on Native American issues.

In 1885 Craft moved to the Standing Rock Reservation where he ministered to the Dakota Sioux. Recognizing the interest that the Sioux women had for a Native American sisterhood, Craft founded an order of Sioux nuns in 1891 called the Congregation of American Sisters among the Dakota Sioux of Standing Rock. This order dedicated itself to teaching the Sioux, caring for them, and helping them adapt to modern society. At its peak it had twenty nuns, but it lasted only a decade. This effort, nevertheless, showed that Craft was committed to developing religious orders among the Sioux.

After Craft left for Standing Rock, Father John Jutz, S.J., and Brother Ursus Nunlist, S.J., arrived at Rosebud Reservation on December 31, 1885. On the first day of 1886, they founded the St. Francis Mission and assumed responsibility for the evangelization of the Brule Lakotas.[149] A year later, Jutz traveled to Pine Ridge Reservation and founded the Holy Rosary Mission. By 1890, St. Francis had three priests, Florentine Digmann, S.J., Aloysius Bosch, S.J., and Joseph Lindebner, S.J., and ten Jesuit Brothers. In that same year, Holy Rosary had two priests, John Jutz, S.J., and Emil Perrig, S.J., and six Jesuit brothers. From 1900 to 1940, each mission had a staff of 14 to 25 Jesuits in residence at all times.

The Jesuits who established the Holy Rosary and St. Francis missions were mostly Germans, Austrians, and Swiss who came to America after Bismark expelled them from Germany during the *Kulturkampf.* Going first to Canisius College in Buffalo, New York or Campion College in Prairie du Chien, Wisconsin where they continued their studies or taught, they then traveled to South Dakota. These Jesuits belonged to what they called the Buffalo Mission, so named because the Jesuits first established it in Buffalo, New York in 1869. The Buffalo Mission was part of the German Province of the Society of Jesus, which supplied a few priests and brothers to the Dakota missions even after 1907 when St. Francis and Holy Rosary became part of the California Province of the Society of Jesus. After 1907, however, American Jesuits also staffed these two mis-

147. *Ibid.*

148. BCIM 1-4-3, Craft to Lusk, Yankton, Dakota Territory, March 12, 1884; Copy of proceedings of Council with Father Craft and Brule Sioux. S. F. Tappan Superintendent Industrial School, Genoa, Nebraska. Rosebud Agency, Jan. 14, 1884.

149. HRM 7-14-8, Digmann, diary, 1885-1886 entry.

sions. In 1913, the Jesuits transferred Holy Rosary and St. Francis to the Missouri Province, and thereafter this province sent most of the additional priests and brothers to the Dakota missions.[150]

When the Jesuits[151] reached South Dakota, they were a bit out of their reckoning and were quite surprised to learn that the territory for which they were responsible covered more area than Connecticut and Rhode Island combined.[152] They also knew nothing of the Lakota language. At this time, however, several Benedictines on other Sioux reservations had already mastered the Sioux tongue at the urging of Bishop Marty. One of these language scholars was Jerome Hunt, O.S.B., whom Marty assigned to the Sioux mission at the Standing Rock Reservation in 1876, and who later moved to the mission at Devil's Lake Reservation. When the Jesuits arrived at St. Francis and Holy Rosary, Hunt taught them the Sioux language. Even though Hunt knew Dakota, the Lakota and Dakota dialects were quite similar, and the Lakotas understood the Dakota dialect.

Hunt also showed the Jesuits how to read and use Ravoux's catechism.[153] Eventually, Hunt published his own works in the Dakota dialect, *Katholik Wocekiye Wowapi: Prayers, Instructions, and Hymns in the Sioux Indian Language* (1899) and *Catechism, Prayers and Instructions in the Sioux Indian Language* (c. 1900), which the Jesuits also used.[154] By 1908, the Jesuits distributed about 2000 of Hunt's prayerbooks on the reservations.[155] Among the German, Austrian, and Swiss Jesuits at Holy Rosary and St. Francis, Eugene Buechel, Henry Grotegeers, Placidus Sialm, Emil Perrig, Henry Billings, Joseph Lindebner, Louis Goll, Florentine Digmann, Aloysius Bosch and several others all learned to speak Lakota.[156] The Jesuits learned the language quickly, and some preached sermons in Lakota by 1887.[157]

Most of the Franciscan sisters who came to Holy Rosary and St. Francis were also German, and were in the Congregation of the Sisters of

---

150. John Francis Bannon, *The Missouri Province S.J.* (St. Louis: The Missouri Province, 1977), 101-102.

151. Hereafter, "the Jesuits" refers to the Jesuits at the Holy Rosary and St. Francis missions, unless otherwise indicated.

152. Duratschek, *Builders of God's Kingdom*, 99.

153. Duratschek, *Crusading Along Sioux Trails*, 133.

154. "Golden Jubilees," *Indian Sentinel* 2 (Oct. 1922):564. BCIM 8-9-7, Jerome Hunt, O.S.B., *Katoloik Wocekiye Wowapi: Prayers, Instructions, and Hymns in the Sioux Indian Language* (Fort Totten: Catholic Indian Mission Ft. Totten, 1899). BCIM 8-9-6, Jerome Hunt, O.S.B., *Catechism, Prayers, and Instructions in the Sioux Indian Language* (Cincinnati: Jos. Berning Printing Co., c. 1900).

155. BCIM 14/1-25-19, *Sina Sapa Wocekiye Taeyanapaha* (March 15, 1908), supplement.

156. Placidus Sialm, S.J. "In Memory of Those Who Have Labored Among the Sioux." *Indian Sentinel* 1 (April 1919):37-38. SFM 7-5-(14-15), Emil Perrig, S.J., diary, May 5, 1889, Sept, 21 1890. *Indian Sentinel*, 3 (April 1923):84. BCIM 14/1-4-2, *Calumet* (Oct 1927).

157. Emil Perrig, S.J., St. Francis Mission, Feb. 15, 1887, *Woodstock Letters* 16:173-175.

Penance and Christian Charity of the Third Order of St. Francis.[158] Arriving at St. Francis Mission in 1886, they came to teach the Lakota children in the mission school. But because they were semi-cloistered, and rarely traveled to the mission chapels, none learned to speak Lakota fluently. Since both the Franciscan nuns and Jesuits were originally European, they were in the unique and difficult position of having to adapt to both American and Lakota culture at the same time as they instructed the Lakotas. Most of them stayed at these missions for life, and thus brought continuity to the mission.[159]

In addition to the other complexities of establishing missions in the Dakotas, the Jesuits and Franciscan nuns also faced a great financial burden. In this area, however, Mother Catherine Drexel came to their assistance. Drexel, an acquaintance of Bishop Marty, was a wealthy heiress who founded the Sisters of the Blessed Sacrament, an order dedicated to helping the African-Americans and Native Americans. Using her inheritance to aid African-Americans and Native Americans, she was instrumental in providing financial assistance to Holy Rosary and St. Francis. With $65,000 of assistance from Drexel, the Jesuits built the original mission schools and other buildings at the Holy Rosary and St. Francis missions.[160] They also received $108 of federal funding annually for every student who attended the mission schools.[161]

When the Jesuits at Holy Rosary and St. Francis arrived in the Dakota Territory, many of the Sioux were already predisposed to the Catholic Church since they knew De Smet, Craft, Bushman, Hospenthal, and Marty who baptized many Sioux people including several chiefs. The Jesuits were particularly familiar with De Smet's work among the Sioux, and they saw him as a hero and model. By reading collections of De Smet's published letters,[162] the Jesuits became acquainted with his mission method. They also recognized some of the Lakota chiefs to whom he referred in his letters. Like De Smet before them, the Jesuits at Holy Rosary and St. Francis concentrated on converting the Lakota chiefs since the Jesuits knew that others would follow. Actually the Jesuits had a tradition of fo-

158. Duratschek, *The Beginnings of Catholicism in South Dakota*, 96.

159. These Jesuits lived at Holy Rosary or St. Francis missions during the years indicated in parentheses: Florentine Digmann (1886-1931), Placidus Sialm (1914-1940), Joseph Lindebner (1897-1922), Louis Goll (1913-1946), Henry Billing (1886-1940), and Eugene Buechel (1903-1954).

160. HRM 2/1-1-6, "Chronicles of the Sisters of St. Francis," [Mission diary written by the nuns at Holy Rosary Mission] 1888 entry, p.1.

161. Duratschek, *Builders of God's Kingdom*, 99.

162. Pierre Jean De Smet, *New Indian Sketches* (New York: D. & J. Sadler, 1863). Pierre Jean De Smet, *Letters and Sketches with a Narrative of a Years's Residence among the Indian Tribes of the Rocky Mountains* (Philadelphia: M. Fintian, 1843). Pierre Jean De Smet, *Oregon Missions and Travels over the Rocky Mountains in 1845-46* (New York: E. Dunigan, 1847).

cusing their evangelical skills on the community leaders, and the *Constitution of the Society of Jesus* encouraged this practice:

> The more universal the good is the more it is divine. Therefore preference ought to be given to those persons and places which, through their own improvement, become a cause which can spread the good accomplished to many others who are under their influence or take guidance from them. For that reason, the spiritual aid which is given to important and public persons ought to be regarded as more important, since it is a more universal good.[163]

Applying this principle, the Jesuits of Holy Rosary and St. Francis converted several Lakota chiefs including Big Turkey, Two Strike, He. Dog, and Big Head.

Big Turkey supported the Catholic mission effort even before the Jesuits arrived. In 1885 when the government agent tried to transport a load of lumber to build a public school on Rosebud, Big Turkey and a few other Lakotas unhitched the agent's team until the agent promised to take the lumber back to the government agency.[164] Big Turkey informed the agent that he wanted a "Blackrobe" school and no other.[165] In 1890, one of the Jesuits baptized Chief Big Turkey before a whole congregation and gave him the name Peter.[166]

In 1899, Father Digmann, superior of St. Francis Mission, wrote of Chief Two Strike's conversion in his diary. When Two Strike was 80 years old, he was ill and in danger of dying. But Digmann kept after him to accept baptism, indicating that if he died before baptism, the consequences might be eternally tragic. Eventually Two Strike came to the church at St. Francis Mission, as Digmann described, dressed "in his full attire as an Indian Chief and a clean white shirt,"[167] and Digmann baptized him. After receiving baptism, his ailment mysteriously left him and Two Strike attributed his cure to his baptism.[168] Stories like this indicating a miraculous conversion with attendant signs spread among the Lakotas and led more of the Lakotas to the Catholic Church.

The Jesuits also baptized several other chiefs. Father Henry Westropp, S.J., who lived at Holy Rosary and then transferred to St. Francis, baptized Chief He Dog on Christmas, 1909.[169] Also at St. Francis Mis-

---

163. George Ganss S.J., *The Constitutions of the Society of Jesus* (St. Louis: The Institute of Jesuit Sources, 1970), 275.

164. A government agency was a distribution point for the rations that the government gave to the Native Americans. The government put an agency on both Pine Ridge and Rosebud.

165. HRM 7-14-8, Digmann, diary, 1885 entry. "Peter Big Turkey," *Indian Sentinel* 2 (Jan. 1921):237.

166. HRM 7-14-8, Digmann, diary, June 1, 1890.

167. *Ibid.*, Jan. 5-6, 1899.

168. *Ibid.*, Jan. 5-6, 1899.

169. Florentine Digmann, S.J., "The Old Guard," *Indian Sentinel* 6 (Winter 1926):44.

sion, Emil Perrig, S.J., who helped establish St. Francis in 1886, baptized Chief Big Head in 1906 when the Chief was 68 years old. Before 1906, however, Big Head had two wives, since polygyny (the practice of men having several wives) was common the Sioux. Therefore, before Perrig baptized him, the Jesuits persuaded him to give up one of his wives. After his conversion, Big Head assisted the Jesuits by accompanying them when they traveled around the mission, and by serving as a catechist to the Lakotas.[170]

As with Big Head, one of the first problems that confronted the Jesuits was the Lakota custom of polygyny. The Jesuits, however, persuaded many of the polygynous men to give up all but one of their wives, so that they could receive baptism.[171] Another problem that the Jesuits saw with the Lakotas' idea of marriage was that the Lakotas frequently left their wives. Consequently, the Jesuits tried to instill in them the Catholic tradition of marriage. For example, after converting to the Catholic faith, Chief Big Turkey wanted to divorce his wife, who was a non-Catholic, and marry a younger Catholic woman. Digmann, however, did not allow this, and told him that he had to keep his wife:

> When he could not get my consent, he got so angry that in a meeting he threw his prayerbook on the floor, and soon afterwards stampeded with the hostiles [during the Wounded Knee battle]. . . . [After the battle he met Digmann] I refused to shake [his hand] saying: "You have given scandal to all by throwing your Prayerbook away and going with the hostiles." He excused himself and wanted to go to confession. "Not before you have begged pardon from the congregation at the Church door next Sunday before Mass." He did. Then I took his hand and led him into the church. This broke him. His wife was later baptized. They renewed their contract and lived in peace until she died.[172]

Though the Jesuits were strict about sacramental matters, they were not rigorists who insisted that the Lakotas follow all the nonessential customs of the Church in America. In his diary on March 10, 1891, Digmann wrote, "[Bishop] Marty approved of my plan to go slow with the commandments of the church, insist first on keeping the Ten Commandments of God."[173] But divorce continued to be a problem that the Jesuits confronted throughout their time in the Dakotas, and they campaigned vigorously against it. Since the reservations were really a series of small communities on large tracts of land, the Church had a community atmosphere, and if a couple had a marital problem, everyone knew about it.

---

170. Alexander Cody, S.J., "Chief Big Head," *Indian Sentinel* 2 (July 1920):141-142.
171. HRM 7-14-8, Digmann, diary, Feb. 10, 1892.
172. *Ibid.*, March 15, 1891.
173. *Ibid.*, March 10, 1892.

Often, the Jesuits and other Lakota Catholics intervened when a couple had difficulties, and tried to keep them together. They also discouraged Catholics from marrying non-Catholics, and if this type of marriage occurred, they sought to convert the non-Catholics.

In many cases, however, the marriages that took place on Pine Ridge and Rosebud before the Jesuits arrived actually were a great benefit to the Catholic missions. French trappers and traders lived in the Dakota Territory since the eighteenth century, and many married Lakota women. But in the 1870's and 1880's, even more French and also Irish traveled to the Dakota Territory lured by tales of gold in the Black Hills. Also at this time many Mexican and Irish men traveled north with cattle companies to the Dakota Territory and settled there, marrying Lakota women.[174]

The government's census of Pine Ridge in 1886 indicated that 10 percent of those living on Pine Ridge were Lakotas of mixed ancestry.[175] Furthermore, Florentine Digmann, S.J., one of the founders of the St. Francis mission, wrote of the multi-ethnic character of the Reservation in 1887:

> Squaw-men: There was a number of white men, French, Canadian, Yankees, Irish, Mexican, who from their youth had lived among the Sioux, and raised large families with Indian women. They even had been incorporated into the tribe, signed as such treaties, with the government and had tribal rights. They were a good help to the missionaries to learn the language and customs of the people. . . . The French, Canadian, and Irish squaw-men had been baptized Catholic.[176]

Next to the Lakotas, the French were the largest ethnic group on the Pine Ridge and Rosebud reservations,[177] and they continued to marry the Lakotas throughout the twentieth century. Thus when the Jesuits arrived at Pine Ridge and Rosebud, many of the Lakotas of mixed ancestry had a Catholic background from their French, Mexican, or Irish heritage. When the Holy Rosary and St. Francis schools opened, most of the chil-

---

174. Joe Whiting, interview, Kyle, South Dakota, October, 1992. Joseph Zimmerman, S.J., "Flying Owl," *Indian Sentinel* 23 (Oct. 1943):127. HRM 7-17-6. Placidus Sialm, S.J., *Camp Churches*, unpublished manuscript, c. 1935. p.4. Louis Goll, S.J., *Jesuit Missions among the Sioux* (St. Francis: St. Francis Mission, 1940), 30. "Many full-bloods came into contact with the priests through mixed-bloods of French-Canadian, Irish, or Mexican descent."

175. James Bell, report, Sept. 7, 1886, *Annual Report of the Commissioner of Indian Affairs to the Secretary of the Interior for the year 1886*, 76.

176. HRM 7-14-8, Digmann, diary, May 15, 1887, p.13.

177. The following are a list of families with French background on the Pine Ridge and Rosebud reservations: LaPointe, Roubideaux, Randall, Richards, Cordier, Bordeaux, Whiting, Janis, Clifford, Boyer, Clairmont, Ferron, Antoine, LaRouche, LaLeff, Ducheneux, LeRoy, Mousseaux, Giroux, Pourier, Garnier, DuBray, LaClair, Beauvois, Flammond, Shangreau, LaDeaux, Salway, Garnette, Palmier, Peneaux. Mexican families on the Pine Ridge and Rosebud reservations: Hernandez, Giago, Martinez, Romero, Sierra, Mesteth.

dren at these schools were of mixed ancestry: Lakota/French or Lakota/Mexican.[178] Because of the marriage of French, Irish, and Mexican Catholics with the Lakotas, the Jesuits' task was that much easier.

The Jesuits who established the St. Francis and Holy Rosary missions had a good deal of success. In 1885, about 7,000 Lakotas lived on Pine Ridge, and about the same number lived on Rosebud. By 1908, about 2300 of the 7000, or 33 percent, of the Lakotas on Pine Ridge were Catholic.[179] From 1886 to 1940, the Jesuits baptized 7500 people on Pine Ridge and 8000 on Rosebud; half of these died by 1940, six percent had fallen away, and the rest were Catholic.[180] By 1940, almost half of the 15,000 people on Rosebud and Pine Ridge were Catholic.[181]

When the Jesuits arrived at Pine Ridge and Rosebud, several factors favored the success of these missions: the Catholic Church had a long historical relationship with the Sioux; several Lakota chiefs requested Catholic priests for their reservations; and many of the Lakotas on these reservations, including several chiefs, were already Catholic.[182] Moreover, in the 1880's, the Catholic Church grew in numbers on several Sioux reservations in the Dakota Territory because of newly formed missions and schools established by the Benedictines. The Lakotas on Pine Ridge and Rosebud recognized that many of the Sioux on other reservations already accepted the Catholic faith, and this also facilitated the Lakotas' acceptance of Catholicism. Furthermore, because of contact and marriage with French, Mexican, and Irish Catholics, many Lakotas had family connections with Catholics. All of these factors helped the Jesuits attract the Lakotas to the Catholic Church.

178. George Bischofberger, S.J., "Holy Rosary Turns Golden," *Jesuit Missions* 18 (June 1938):155.

179. "Holy Rosary Mission School," *Indian Sentinel* (1908):27.

180. Louis Goll, S.J., *Jesuit Missions among the Sioux*, 68-69.

181. HRM 2/1-3-1, "Report on Indian Work to Commission," July 30, 1938; "Report on Indian Work to Commission," Aug. 24, 1939; Report on Mission, April 17, 1939.

182. HRM 7-14-8, Digmann, diary, Jan. 8, 1892.

CHAPTER TWO

Economy and Education

IN THE 1870'S, THE LAKOTA ECONOMY UNDERWENT A PROFOUND CHANGE, as did their entire way of life. By 1876 the government confined the Lakotas to reservations, and thus forced them to abandon their nomadic lifestyle. The buffalo population declined severely by this time because of white people's hunting of the buffalo for skins and tongues, and because of the U.S. Army's policy of exterminating the buffalo to destroy the Native Americans' food supply. Since the Lakota economy was based entirely on the buffalo, they had no choice but to adapt to the South Dakota economy, which was based on farming and ranching.

By the 1880's, the Lakotas were no longer dependent on hunting and gathering for survival, and this also affected their religious practices. Since the Lakotas' religion was so closely tied to their hunting and gathering lifestyle, after 1880 they no longer had the occasion to practice the religious rituals connected to their traditional economy. After they stopped hunting buffalo, the rituals related to achieving a successful buffalo hunt lost some of their significance. When they hunted the buffalo, the Lakota religion and culture were bound together. But as the Lakotas moved further into the South Dakota economy, their traditional religious practices were no longer linked to their economy or lifestyle. In the past, their economy was sacred, but for the Lakotas the modern economy had no religious significance.

The Lakotas' adaptation to the modern economy led to a great deal of cultural trauma. This profound economic and cultural change resulted in great confusion, alcoholism, crime, and broken families. In response to this great turmoil, the Jesuits sought to integrate the Lakotas into the South Dakota economy, and help them find a new religious significance for their work. Describing the Jesuits' attitude toward work in 1893, Aloysius Bosch, S.J of Holy Rosary Mission wrote:

> The second glory of religion is to teach people how to work –
> steadily, regularly, honestly, and religiously. They should give
> each other mutual help, should work for their own and their chil-
> dren's prosperity in a practical way.[1]

The Jesuits at Holy Rosary and St. Francis stressed that work was an essential part of the religious life, and saw work as the charity that Christians gave to each other in their daily lives.

Eugene Buechel, a German Jesuit at Holy Rosary Mission, often encouraged the work ethic through his sermons. Fortunately, he wrote down all his sermons, and his Jesuit brothers preserved about 300 of them. Most of his sermons encouraged work in some form: either prayers, devotions, or work in the secular sense. Frequently citing the example of God's punishing Adam and Eve by making them earn their food by the "sweat of their brow," Buechel argued that work was an essential aspect of religion.[2] In his 1907 sermon titled "Idleness," he emphasized this theme:

> For God said, "Cursed is the earth in thy work; with labor and toil thou shalt eat thereof all the days of thy life. . . ." Since all men, the rich and the poor, the young and the old, the saints and the sinners are children of Adam and Eve, all must take that penance. Do you think that anybody can claim for himself a life of nothing but pleasure? Still there are many who do everything to keep away suffering and work against the sentence of God.[3]

In this sermon, Buechel emphasized that sloth was a mortal sin, which he said led to "eternal damnation for the idle man can show no good work he has done, no good fruit."[4]

Raising many of these same themes in his 1910 sermon "On Work," Buechel stressed the connection of work to religion:

> It is the *law* of God that we should work, and anyone who breaks this law habitually, constantly, a lazy man, is a criminal and will have to suffer God's punishments both in his body and in his soul.[5]

Buechel used the strongest language to convey the necessity of working diligently at all life's tasks. He added that "on work will depend everything; health, happiness, holiness, heaven."[6] The message of this sermon was that work made people physically strong, gave them a better standard of living, and kept them from sin. He also described work as both a divine and natural law. Everything in creation had to work, he claimed, and he gave the example of the earth working to bring forth life in the

1. SFM 7-1-1, Aloysius Bosch, S.J., "Indians in Council," *Sacred Heart Messenger* (1893):882.

2. SFM 7-3-8, Eugene Buechel, S.J., "Labor: A Duty," sermon, Pine Ridge, Jan, 23, 1910.

3. SFM 7-3-7, Buechel, "Idleness (Sloth)," sermon, Pine Ridge, Nov 24, 1907.

4. *Ibid.*

5. SFM 7-3-8, Buechel, "On Work," sermon, Pine Ridge, Feb. 20, 1910. "Law" underlined in original.

6. *Ibid.*

Spring. He reminded them that Christ and the apostles all had jobs such as carpentry and fishing, and that God chose Mary "from among the poor working people."[7]

Buechel gave several sermons, such as "Labor – A Duty," and "The Good Use of Time," in which he stressed that work was essential to salvation.[8] The Jesuits in South Dakota particularly stressed this theme to encourage the Lakotas to become economically self-sufficient. Yet Buechel also indicated that the work ethic applied to all aspects of life including a person's education, family life, vocation, and religious life. In several of his sermons he indicated that work was inseparably bound to the religious life. He believed that if an individual did not work diligently, he or she could not be a good Catholic.

The Ignatian approach to work was quite apparent in the Jesuits' ideas, and the *Spiritual Exercises* reinforced this emphasis on work. Explaining a passage from the *Exercises,* Buechel wrote in his notes, "that true love manifests itself not so much in words and sentiments but in deeds and works."[9] In contrast to the Protestant reformers of his time, Ignatius stressed that works were crucial to salvation. At the Holy Rosary and St. Francis mission schools that the Jesuits established, they continued this Ignatian tradition, and sought to show the Lakotas that work was a part of the sacred life.

School Funding

In the mid-nineteenth century, American Catholics believed that Catholic schools were essential because public school education was biased in favor of Protestantism. In response to this bias, Catholics built their own schools, and sought public funding for them. Successfully blocking the Catholics' attempts to obtain state funding for their parochial schools, many people argued that church and state must remain separate. But when President Grant proposed federal funding for Protestant mission schools for the Native Americans, many denominations quickly adopted a different view of church-state separation, especially since the government, in the 1870's, gave most of the funding to Protestant mission schools.

The Jesuits were wholly in favor of state support for their mission schools, and in their writings, they attempted to demonstrate that the mission schools were in the best interest of all involved. Placidus Sialm, a Swiss Jesuit who arrived at Holy Rosary Mission in 1901, called the federal funding of Catholic mission schools "a beautiful cooperation of church and state."[10] This "cooperation," however, more closely resembled

7.   *Ibid.*

8.   SFM 7-3-8, Eugene Buechel, S.J., "Labor – A Duty," sermon, Pine Ridge, Jan. 23, 1910; Eugene Buechel, S.J., "The Good Use of Time," sermon, Pine Ridge, Jan. 16, 1910.

9.   HRM 7-12-3, Eugene Buechel, S.J., "Contemplation to Obtain Love."

a long drawn out battle between the Catholic and Protestant organizations over assignments to reservations and access for missionaries to reservations. Nevertheless, the Jesuits believed that they performed a patriotic duty by educating the Lakotas[11] and saved the federal government money since the mission schools cost much less per capita than the government schools.[12] Moreover, Jesuits saw their actions in the mission schools as patriotic since they instructed the students about American democracy and taught them to respect American ideals. The government encouraged the missionaries to teach American values to the Native Americans, and the Jesuits eagerly complied with the governments' wishes. Since many Protestants at this time believed that Catholics, especially Jesuits, were opposed to American ideals, the Jesuits were anxious to show that they were patriotic Americans who believed in teaching their students their American civic duties.

When the Jesuits arrived at St. Francis and Holy Rosary, their first project was to build schools.[13] In 1886, the Jesuits built a schoolhouse at St. Francis Mission and began classes that same year. Similarly on Pine Ridge, a year after they arrived in 1887, they opened the Holy Rosary Mission School. Through the lobbying efforts of the Bureau of Catholic Indian Missions (BCIM), both of these schools acquired federal funding. Nevertheless, the Office of Indian Affairs used many different tactics to try to stop this federal aid. Despite these attempts, the Catholic mission

---

10. HRM 7-17-(5-7), Placidus Sialm, S.J., *Camp Churches*, unpublished manuscript, 104.

11. Note on historiography: Catholic historians characterized the Catholic missionaries as performing a patriotic duty by educating Native American children in the federally funded mission schools. Reacting to those anti-Catholics who accused Catholics of holding allegiance to a foreign potentate, Catholic historians emphasized that Catholic missionaries were cooperating with the government and supporting the government's policies. For example, Peter Rahill in *The Catholic Indian Missions and Grant's Peace Policy* (p.325) described the work of the Catholic missionaries and the BCIM: "Rightly did the officials glory in being able to state a couple of years later that the Catholic bureau [BCIM] had always tried to carry out fully and cordially the government's program for the benefit of the red men. This patriotic effort to cooperate with the government for the benefit of an unheeded segment of the nation's inhabitants was but one factor in the development of the Church's agency for Indians."

12. Sialm, *Camp Churches*, 104.

13. In 1885, the Episcopalians already had two mission schools operating on Rosebud with about 80 students combined, and the Government had seven schools, accommodating about 30 students each. By 1886, the government established nine schools on Pine Ridge with a combined enrollment of 500 students. In the next five years, all the mission schools closed down except Holy Rosary, St. Francis, and St. Mary's, an Episcopal boarding school on Rosebud with about 50 students. James George Wright, report, Aug. 26, 1890, *Annual Report of the Commissioner of Indian Affairs to the Secretary of the Interior for the year 1890*, 60. James G. Wright, report, Rosebud Agency, Aug 31, 1885, *Annual Report of the Commissioner of Indian Affairs to the Secretary of the Interior for the year 1885*, 42. James M. Bell, report, Sept 7, 1886, *Annual Report of the Commissioner of Indian Affairs to the Secretary of the Interior for the year 1886*, 77.

schools flourished between 1881 and 1900. By investing funds in the construction of mission schools and by successfully convincing the Native
Americans to attend, the BCIM established a number of mission schools
funded by government contracts. By 1890, Catholic schools received
more financial support from the government than all of the Protestant mission schools combined.[14]

In response to the growth of the Catholic mission schools, the Office
of Indian Affairs, many of whose officials were members of the anti-
Catholic American Protective Association (APA), decided to phase out
federal funding of the mission schools.[15] Despite the BCIM's lobbying
efforts against what they perceived was an anti-Catholic policy, the government completely cut off the Catholic mission schools from direct federal funding by 1900. The elimination of public funding for mission
schools also affected Protestant mission schools, but the Protestants did
much the same in public schools as they did in their mission schools. In
all the public schools on the reservations, ministers held compulsory "non-
denominational" Christian services, which were actually Protestant services which used the Protestant hymnals and Bible.

In the 1890's the anti-Catholic bias at the Office of Indian Affairs
was obvious. Appointed by President Harrison in 1890, Daniel Dorchester, the Superintendent of Indian Schools, was a prominent anti-Catholic
who wrote the tract *Romanism versus the Public School System* (1888), in
which he said that Catholic education was a danger to American civil lib-
erties and claimed that Catholics were the subjects of a foreign potentate.
He said that the Catholic educational system's "crying defect is that its
teaching is not only un-American but anti-American, and will remove
every one of its pupils, in their ideals, far from a proper mental condition
for American citizenship."[16] Dorchester's personal opinions may even
have influenced his actions as Superintendent. At this time, Dorchester
and Thomas Morgan, the Commissioner of Indian Affairs, were the subjects of a Senate investigation which examined charges that they discrimi-
nated against Catholics in their hiring practices and fired qualified Catholics in the government schools for Native Americans.[17]

Working with Dorchester, Morgan began a campaign of harassment
directed at the Catholic mission schools. He tried to remove Native

---

14. Joseph Gavan, "The First Word from Father Craft," *The New York Freeman's Journal*,
Jan. 17, 1891, p. 8. Of the $554,558 federal funds allocated for the Native American
missions, $347,689 went to Catholic missions.

15. Rahill, 343.

16. Francis Paul Prucha, S.J., *The Churches and the Indian Schools* (Lincoln: University of
Nebraska, 1979), 12. Sister Mary Lijek, C.S.F.N., *Relations between the Office of Indian
Affairs and the Bureau of Catholic Indian Missions: 1885-1900* (Washington: Catholic
University of America, 1965), Masters' Thesis, 11-14.

17. Lijek, 13-14.

American children from Catholic schools against their will and place them in government schools which had trouble attracting students. In a letter to an Indian Agent in Green Bay 1891, he said:

> If the government school is full it would be proper to give the [Native American] parents their choice of schools; but if the government schools be not yet filled, such choice ought not be allowed.[18]

After Morgan left the Office of Commissioner of Indian Affairs in 1893, he became a prominent speaker at A.P.A. functions, at which he said on one occasion:

> The Roman Catholics have assumed an attitude on the Indian question that is un-American, unpatriotic, and a menace to our liberties. I challenge the course they have pursued, as that of a corrupt ecclesiastico-political machine masquerading as a church, a course that has been without precedent, and is without justification. Its spirit has been that of the Inquisition, its methods those of the disreputable politician, and its agencies, intrigue, secrecy, conspiracy, falsehood, and slander.[19]

Both Morgan's and Dorchester's opinions about the Catholic Church indicated that the BCIM's perception of anti-Catholic bias was not simply an illusion.

Through the next ten years, the Office of Indian Affairs continued to harass the supporters of the Catholic mission schools and tried to reduce the number of students at these schools. Since the Native Americans were wards of the Government, the government claimed the right to determine where they went to school.[20] Succeeding Morgan as Commissioner of Indian Affairs and continuing his policies, Daniel Browning set down the rule in 1896 that only after the government school was filled to capacity were Native Americans allowed to send their children to a mission school. Realizing that the mission schools took students away from the public schools, Browning attempted to use this rule to force them into the government schools. On Pine Ridge, the Lakotas protested when the government agent there attempted to enforce this ruling. The Lakota parents who wanted to send their children to the Holy Rosary Mission school wrote letters complaining of the government's harassment. In response, Browning supported the agent and stated that "Indian parents have no right to designate which school their children shall attend."[21] Catholics were outraged by this decision and argued that the government's refusal to

---

18. Lijek, p. 34, Morgan to Charles S. Kelsey, U.S. Indian Agent, Green Bay Agency, Wisconsin, October 12, 1891.
19. Prucha, 27-29.
20. *Ibid.*, 57.
21. *Ibid.*, 58.

allow Native American parents to determine which school their children attended was an infringement on their religious liberty.[22]

At the annual Catholic Sioux Congress, the Sioux expressed their dissatisfaction with the government's policies concerning the funding of the mission schools. The Catholic Sioux Congresses, which began in 1890, were annual gatherings of missionaries and Catholic Sioux lay people. Each year in June, Sioux Catholics and their missionaries from all the reservations in the Dakotas traveled to a single site on a reservation where they all met for a council. At the Catholic Sioux Congress they held in 1897, the Sioux wrote a petition in which they requested the government to continue funding the mission schools and give Native Americans the choice to send their children to Catholic schools:

> We, Catholics of the Sioux Nation, most respectfully and humbly ask and beg of the U.S. Congress, now assembled in Washington, D.C. that you revise the late law concerning the religious schools . . . the money that is deposited for us in the U. S. Treasury is our money. For the reason that the money is ours we are of the opinion that they should let us have the choice of schools as we want them, either in our own country or in cities, Government schools (public schools), or religious or contract schools. We do not say so because we oppose Government schools or schools of a different creed; but we want you to let us have a school in which our children are taught our religion.[23]

After a vigorous lobbying campaign by the BCIM, the Roosevelt administration finally revoked the Browning Ruling in 1902.[24]

Since the Government terminated all direct federal funding for the mission schools by 1900, the BCIM had to look to other sources for financial aid. To help fund the mission schools for the Native Americans, the BCIM founded the Society for the Preservation of the Faith among Indian Children in 1901.[25] Dedicated to spreading the Catholic faith among the Native Americans, this society solicited donations of money from lay people which it used to fund the construction of schools, buy food and clothing, and cover any expenses that the mission schools might incur. The BCIM also gained support for the Society from the American bishops and priests who recommended it to their parishioners.[26]

To popularize the efforts of the BCIM and to seek funding, in 1902 the BCIM began publishing a periodical, *The Indian Sentinel*, "in the interest of the Society of the Preservation of the Faith of Indian Children."[27]

22. *Ibid.*, 57-58.

23. Editorial, *Indian Sentinel* (1905-1906): 32.

24. Prucha, 61-62.

25. William Ketcham, letter, *Indian Sentinel* (1902-1903): inside front cover.

26. Prucha, 49.

Though it began as an annual, by 1916 it became a quarterly magazine. It was the mouthpiece of the BCIM and had several purposes, one of which was to keep the missionaries and Native American Catholics informed about the policies and actions of the BCIM. *The Indian Sentinel* contained articles from Native American Catholics and Catholic missionaries at all the Native American missions. It informed readers about the life of the missionaries and Native Americans, and the challenges that they faced. Since it was also a fund raising magazine, it often contained appeals for clothing, toys for the children, blankets or anything else that the missionaries needed. Frequently the missionaries asked for funding for the construction of churches or schools. When the missionaries finished a building project that some patron funded, they usually published a photograph and description of it in the *Sentinel*. The *Sentinel* also carried stories concerning the culture and customs of the different Native American nations in all parts of the country, including Alaska. In the articles they contributed, the missionaries revealed many of their ideas and attitudes toward the Native Americans, and also their plans for their missions. Moreover, the *Sentinel* contained many articles honoring prominent Native American Catholics, including chiefs, catechists and athletes.[28]

The other main periodical concerned with the Catholic missions to the Native Americans was *The Calumet*, an annual periodical which the Marquette League began publishing in 1913. Founded in 1904 and based in New York City, the Marquette League was a society of Catholic lay people dedicated to raising funds for Catholic Indian missions.[29] Like the *Sentinel*, *The Calumet* published articles by Catholic missionaries who told of their experiences with the Native Americans and wrote letters thanking those who made some donation to their missions. The *Calumet* and *Sentinel* circulated throughout the United States, and Catholic patrons of the missions and Native Americans were the primary audience of these two magazines. In the absence of federal funding, the *Sentinel* and *Calumet* helped raise money for the missions and schools, and popularized the missionaries' causes.

But despite the termination of federal funding in 1900, the government still attempted to harass the surviving schools. In 1901, William Jones, the Commissioner of Indian Affairs, launched another offensive against the mission schools. He ruled that the children at mission schools and their parents would no longer receive the government rations promised to them under the 1876 treaty.[30] Those who attended the public schools, however, would receive rations under this plan. To support his

---

27. *Indian Sentinel*, (1902): inside cover.

28. "James Thorpe," *Indian Sentinel* (1913):48. "Andrew Sockalexis," *Indian Sentinel* (1913):48.

29. BCIM 14/1-4-2, *The Calumet* (April 1913).

30. Prucha, 65.

position, Jones argued that children who went to non-public schools were no longer wards of the government and the government had no obligation to support them.[31] Recognizing the coercive intent of this rule, Catholics opposed this ruling as an infringement of the Native Americans' religious liberty. But even after the BCIM's lobbying efforts, the government phased out rations for mission schools from 1907 to 1909.[32]

Despite the elimination of rations, the Holy Rosary and St. Francis mission schools were able to expand their enrollment during this controversy because the BCIM found another way to fund them. In 1904, the BCIM lobbied the Roosevelt administration for the right of Catholic Native Americans to use their "tribal funds," which the government held in a trust for them, to finance the Catholic mission schools on a pro rata basis. The Sioux of Pine Ridge, Rosebud, Crow Creek, and six other Native American nations sent petitions to Roosevelt requesting permission to use their tribal funds to pay the fees of the mission schools. In that year, Roosevelt granted their wishes and allowed the Native Americans of nine mission schools, eight Catholic schools and one Lutheran school, to use tribal funds for parochial education. In 1904, Holy Rosary Mission school received $21,000 from the tribal funds for its 200 students for the year, and St. Francis received $27,000 for 250 students.[33]

In 1906, however, Quick Bear, a Lakota man from Rosebud, challenged this practice. At the urging of the Indian Rights Association, he brought a suit against the Indian Office charging that the use of tribal funds for Catholic education was illegal. In 1908, *Quick Bear v. Leupp* went to the United States Supreme Court, and the court upheld the right of Native Americans to use tribal funds on a pro rata basis for mission schools.[34] Yet before the government allowed Lakota children to attend the mission schools, their parents had to sign a petition each year which indicated that they desired to send their children to the mission schools. This practice guaranteed that no Lakota children attended the St. Francis or Holy Rosary mission schools without their parents' approval.[35]

Curriculum

When the Jesuits opened their boarding school at St. Francis mission they had 40 Lakota students.[36] In the beginning, they only had an elementary school in which the Franciscan sisters and Jesuits taught the chil-

---

31. *Ibid.*, 67.

32. *Ibid.*, 80.

33. *Ibid.*, 84-87.

34. *Ibid.*, 84-95, 149-160.

35. *Ibid.*, 149-160.

36. Emil Perrig, S.J., St. Francis Mission, Feb. 15, 1887, *Woodstock Letters* 16 (1887):173.

dren biblical history, prayers, English, and math. Using Ravoux's cate-chism and other books, the Jesuits taught the children to sing hymns in Lakota and English.[37] They also used a "Magic Lantern" to show the children colored slides depicting scenes from the life of Christ and the Bible.[38] Such visual aides allowed the Jesuits to attract the children's at-tention while they explained the significance of the pictures.

At this time, the Jesuits stressed that the Lakotas were intellectually equal to the whites. In 1891, a reporter for the *New York Freeman's Jour-nal* asked John Jutz, S.J., "Are the little Indians capable of learning?" and he replied,

> Yes indeed; just as capable as white children. It is hard for them
> to learn English, but when they learn enough of it to understand,
> they go ahead just as rapidly as white children. They study the
> same books and learn very readily.[39]

But though Jutz believed the Lakotas had the capability, he said that they sometimes lacked the will to work,[40] and in their schools the Jesuits con-centrated on teaching work habits.

As soon as the Jesuits established the Holy Rosary and St. Francis boarding schools, they began a farm that supplied food to the school and provided experience in agricultural methods for the students who spent some of their time working on the farm. At this time, the Jesuits also trained the boys to be bakers, shoemakers, and carpenters. Since the stu-dents were not accustomed to the regimented working schedules that they advocated, the Jesuits gave toys to the students who performed their tasks satisfactorily.[41] As the schools grew, the Jesuits added a high school and industrial school at each mission. The enrollment increased steadily throughout the years so that by 1940 the St. Francis and Holy Rosary mis-sion schools had a combined enrollment of over 700 students, girls and boys.[42] The schools were staffed mostly by the Franciscan sisters and the priests, but by 1928 Holy Rosary had Lakota teachers and Lakota indus-trial instructors.[43]

Though the Jesuits and Franciscan sisters taught all the students the basics of reading, writing, arithmetic and religion, they stressed industrial education most of all for the high school students. Many of the older

37. HRM 7-14-8, Digmann, diary, Sept-Oct. 1886.

38. HRM 7-14-8, Digmann, diary, Nov. 1886.

39. "Forty Years among the Sioux," *New York Freeman's Journal*, Feb. 7, 1891, p.5.

40. *Ibid.*

41. HRM 7-14-8, Digmann, diary, Sept. 1886.

42. BCIM 14/1-4-3, "All Aboard for a Visit to the Missions," *Calumet* (Oct. 1940):6-7.

43. A.C. Riester, S.J., "Progress at Pine Ridge," *Indian Sentinel* 8 (Summer 1928):105.John Scott, S.J. "Sioux Boys Learn Carpentry," *Indian Sentinel* 19 (Dec. 1939):155-156.

students at the mission school served as apprentices to Brother Andrew Hartman, S.J., and Brother Joe Schwarzler, S.J., who were the carpenters and builders at the mission school. Because of the training under these men, several of the Lakota boys were able to get carpentry jobs from the government and in the private sector.[44] In the carpentry shop they learned fine wood working and built much of the furniture at the missions.[45] Moreover, Hartman and his Lakota apprentices built the chapels and school buildings on the reservation, with the help of many of the Lakota men and women who donated their time.[46] Over the years, Hartman and the Lakotas built the entire mission, over 100 buildings, with no outside help. By doing so much building, Hartman and his Lakota helpers acquired a reputation for excellence, and businesses on and off the reservation sought out their skills.[47]

By the 1920's, the Jesuits taught the Lakota boys tin smithing, shoe repair, electrical shop work, dairy farming, poultry farming, and ranching.[48] The schools were working farms and ranches which produced almost all the meat, eggs, flour and vegetables that the schools needed each year.[49] At St. Francis mission school the Jesuits had 2000 acres under cultivation, and the older students learned to operate modern farm machinery like tractors, plows and combines.[50] The school farms grew corn, wheat, oats, rye, potatoes, soy beans, clover, alfalfa and also many types of vegetables.[51] Thus the students learned first-hand farming and ranching, which were virtually the only sources of employment on Pine Ridge and Rosebud.

From the descriptions of the tasks that the students learned, the industrial education at the St. Francis Mission School was quite extensive. At the mission school, the students worked in a shoe shop where they repaired shoes for the mission students. In the blacksmith shop they

44. John Scott, S.J. "Sioux Boys Learn Carpentry," *Indian Sentinel* 19 (Dec. 1939):155-156. Brother Joe Schwarzler, S.J., interview, St. Francis Mission, May, 1992. Fr. Jones, interview, St. Francis Mission, Oct. 1992.

45. John Scott, S.J., "Sioux Boys Learn Carpentry," *Indian Sentinel* 19 (Dec. 1939):155-156.

46. Placidus Sialm, S.J., "Dedication of Kyle Chapel," *Indian Sentinel* 17 (Jan. 1937):5-6. HRM 7-17-4, Fr. F. Coffey, S.J., "Reverend Placidus Sialm, S.J. 1872-1940," p.4. HRM 7-14-8, Digmann, diary, March 18, 1889.

47. William Moore, S.J., "Preparing for Tomorrow," *Indian Sentinel* 19 (Feb. 1939):19. BCIM 1-246-3, William Moore, S.J., "The Importance Placed on Ranching, Agricultural, and Shop Training at the St. Francis Mission School, Rosebud Reservation," April 1938.

48. SFM 1/1-1-2, H.E. Bruce, Special to the *Sioux City Journal* Nov. 11, 1925, p.2. BCIM 1-246-3, William Moore, S.J., "The Importance Placed on Ranching, Agricultural and Shop Training at the St. Francis Mission School, Rosebud Reservation," April, 1938, p. 4.

49. BCIM 1-246-3, William Moore, S.J., "The Importance Placed on Ranching," April, 1938, p.4

50. Moore, 7.

51. Moore, 7.

learned to forge and weld. The students in the tin shop made buckets and feeders for the mission farms. St. Francis also had an automotive shop where the older students learned to overhaul cars and do other repairs. In their large bakery, the students and Jesuits working together supplied all the bread for the missions. In the electrical shop, the boys learned to install wiring systems. All of these skills helped them contribute to the mission farm and ranch which was virtually a self-sustaining community. In 1938, William Moore, one of the Jesuits at St. Francis, described the industrial training at the school:

> In the bakery 6300 good-sized buns and 1200 three-pound loaves of bread are produced weekly. . . . The dairy herd at St. Francis Mission consists of one-hundred high grade Holstein cows which produce one-hundred gallons of milk a day. In the big roomy dairy barn the Indian boys learn modern methods of caring for animals and sanitary precautions in the production and conservation of milk on a large scale. St Francis Mission has a ranch of 12,500 acres on the Rosebud reservation and adjoining land in Nebraska. A herd of one thousand head of high grade Herefords is maintained always. . . . Students of the St. Francis Mission school take part in the branding and vaccination of the cattle, and in the care of the calves. The Mission is glad that it has "potential Indian cattle-men" . . . who can pass from potentiality to actuality. Mission students, some from the high school department, others from the grades, have worked daily in the poultry yard, gaining extremely valuable experience.[52]

At St. Francis and at Holy Rosary, which had a similar school, the Jesuits put together a large, complex and rather successful operation. The boys acquired practical experience in jobs relevant to the economy in South Dakota. The other interesting aspect of the industrial school system was that it was almost an autonomous system. The different shops provided services for each other: the mission farm provided flour for the bakery; the carpenters built the barns, houses and even the school furniture; the blacksmiths repaired the farming equipment; the tin smiths made feeders for the chickens; and they all contributed to the production of food at the mission. On a practical level, the mission farm allowed the school to continue when government terminated their rations. Actually much of the food that the government sent the Lakotas was of poor quality, and even before the government cut the rations, the Lakotas needed food.[53]

---

52. Moore, 8-9.

53. Proceedings of Council: Sioux Delegation and House Comm. on Indian Affairs, Feb. 4, 1891, RG 48, Entry 663, Box 13, 35, Records of the Department of the Interior, National Archives in Washington D.C. p. 4. American Horse addressed the government agents saying, "In the first place the flour is wretched, dark and bad tasting. The pork is decayed, the cattle issued to us is very small, or poor quality and diseased."

In addition to the reading and writing courses at the mission school, the nuns taught the girls typing, shorthand, bookkeeping, accounting, canning, butter making, cooking, sewing and embroidery.[54] The girls and nuns also made and repaired the clothing the students wore at school. Though the Sioux received some clothing from the government at first, they complained that the clothes were of the poorest quality.[55] Thus, in regard to food and clothing, the mission industrial school provided that which the government did not.

Sewing was a skill that was also economically beneficial to the Lakota women, and the Jesuits encouraged them to use this skill. Several of the Jesuits at Holy Rosary and St. Francis sought donations of fabric and clothes through *The Indian Sentinel, The Calumet,* and their letters.[56] They then distributed the cloth to the Lakota women who sometimes made quilts out of them.[57] When Christmas approached, the Lakota women gathered in their sewing circles and sewed quilts to raise money to celebrate, buy presents for the children, or purchase statues to decorate their churches.[58] By teaching them sewing, the Franciscan Sisters gave the Lakota women a skill which benefitted them financially and provided them with some autonomy. The sewing circles were also social clubs which retained and reinforced the Catholic character out of which they grew.

In addition to providing industrial skills and education for the Lakotas, the mission boarding schools helped the Lakotas to support their families and gave them an environment that allowed the students to concentrate on their work. For several reasons, day schools were not a practical option for most students. Since Pine Ridge Reservation occupied over 5000 square miles, most children could not commute to school. Before 1930, no paved roads existed on the reservation, homes were spread out over the reservation, and travel in the winter was difficult and dangerous. The only place in which the children could study and live was in the school dorms. Since their homes had no electric lighting, no desks, often inadequate beds, the children would have found it difficult or impossible

---

54. BCIM 1-246-3, William Moore, S.J., "The Importance Placed on Ranching, Agricultural, and Shop Training at the St. Francis Mission School, Rosebud Reservation," April, 1938, p. 3.

55. Proceedings of Council: Sioux Delegation and House Comm. on Indian Affairs, Feb. 4, 1891, RG 48, Entry 663, Box 13, 35, Records of the Department of the Interior, National Archives in Washington, D.C. p. 3. American Horse, an Oglala chief, addressed the government agents saying, "The clothes which we receive are the poorest; the food is bad and we get sick, the quality of everything we get is poor."

56. John Scott, S.J., *High Eagle and His Sioux* (St. Louis, 1963), 29.

57. BCIM 14/1-4-2, Placidus Sialm, S.J., "A Trip of 200 Miles Costs Father Sialm only Ten Cents," *The Calumet* 2 (Jan. 1921):4.

58. Daisy Whirlwind-Horse, interview, Porcupine S.D., June 1992. Rosie Redhair, interview, Pine Ridge S.D., Oct. 1992.

to study at home even if they could have traveled to their homes after school. Moreover, most of the Lakotas were too poor to feed and clothe their children, and the Lakotas wanted their children in the boarding schools for this reason.

The other compelling reason for them to go to boarding school was that the Lakotas did not have enough room for their children to sleep in their houses. Furthermore, South Dakota in the winter was difficult at best: high winds and temperatures of twenty below were not uncommon. On Pine Ridge and Rosebud, most of the houses before 1940 were small log cabins with no insulation, poor heating, and little furniture. At the St. Francis and Holy Rosary mission schools, the children lived in a large dorm with beds, health care, adequate clothing, and a higher quality and greater quantity of food than most received at their homes. As late as 1938, Joseph Zimmerman, an American Jesuit and St. Francis Mission Superior from 1924 to 1930, noted that many Lakota children came back from summer vacation "emaciated" because their parents were too poor to feed them properly at home.[59]

Despite these problems with day schools, the government in the 1930's resumed its campaign to remove children from the mission schools and place them into the government day schools. But even in the 1930's, the day school option was still not practical for many because of inadequate housing. In 1933, the Superior of St. Francis Mission, Martin Schiltz, S.J., wrote a letter to BCIM Director Fr. William Hughes in which he outlined some of the disadvantages of the day schools:

> The practice of Indian parents is that when they cannot get their children into boarding schools, they pitch their tents near the day schools and there live a miserable life all year just to take care of their children over the night, and home training under such circumstances is impossible. Besides the parents are so poor that agency people and the missionaries must provide food and clothing for very many of them.[60]

Lakota parents found it difficult to part with their children, especially since the Lakotas had such strong family ties. But parents did visit the children at the mission schools. During their visit they camped for a few days in tents on the mission grounds while their children stayed in the dorms.

In 1934 John Collier, Commissioner of Indian Affairs, issued a rule that again challenged the Lakotas' right to place their children into the mission boarding schools:

---

59. Joseph Zimmerman, S.J., "Thy Kingdom Come," *Indian Sentinel* 18 (Nov. 1938):138.

60. BCIM 1-217-2, Martin Schiltz, S.J. to Fr. Hughes, Director of the BCIM, Oct. 27, 1933.

> Government and other boarding schools shall eliminate from their
> rolls those pupils who are within reasonable distance from public
> or day schools, except those pupils who are found to be institu-
> tional cases. No contract shall be entered into with a mission
> boarding school until the proposed enrollment in such boarding
> school had been approved by superintendent of Indian educa-
> tion. . . . It is understood that neither government nor mission
> authorities are to establish new schools where school facilities al-
> ready exist.[61]

Just as in 1896 with the Browning Ruling, Collier attempted to reduce
the enrollment at Catholic mission schools. In the 1930's, the government erected new day schools on the reservations and tried to induce students to attend them.

In response to this, many of the Lakota people complained to the
BCIM Director and sought aid from him. They wrote letters criticizing
the government social worker, Clara Madsen, who implemented Collier's
policy on Pine Ridge. In 1934, a Catholic Lakota woman, Mrs. Philip
Mesteth wrote BCIM Director Hughes describing Madsen's actions:

> I am a Sioux from the Pine Ridge Reservation and I want to re-
> late to you the circumstances about the school proposition. Well I
> am going to tell you just in my plain way of talking there is a
> lady out here right in this Agency. I don't know where she is
> from. But she is trying to force we Indians to send our children to
> schools we do not care for and cannot afford to either, however.
> Personally I have always attended a Mission School in my school
> days at the Holy Rosary Mission School and it is a very very nice
> school for I know it is, and I want my children to continue there
> if I can help it. The Lady who is here apparently does not know
> anything about the Indians and she is out here ordering them what
> to do with their children. I don't think that's a bit right.[62]

Similarly Laura Patton, another Catholic Lakota on Pine Ridge, complained about Madsen:

> I am writing you this letter in regards to my children I have al-
> ways sent them to the [Holy Rosary] Mission as soon as they
> were able to go to school, at least for six years, and now Miss
> Clara Madsen a social worker is trying to force us to send our
> children at the Indian day school or public schools which cannot
> be done on account of our home conditions. We haven't got the
> rooms to keep them in, we are all poor families out here and we

---

61. HRM 1/1-1-5, John Collier, "Plan of Cooperation of Indian Service School Officials
and Administrative Heads of Mission Schools in South Dakota," June 1934.

62. BCIM 1-223-14, Mrs. Philip Mesteth, letter, Pine Ridge, Aug. 20, 1934. This letter
and the following letter were not addressed specifically to Hughes, but were in with
Hughes' papers.

can't build up more rooms for the children to sleep in. . . . I am a woman of nine children and I know what it is to keep nine children well fed and dressed and how much money it takes to feed them. How could a mother keep nine children in a small home during the winter from going hungry with small wages, when they could be in the Mission well taken care of in health and in clothing and well fed and protected by the missionaries. . . . In my home condition I can't keep them home because I got a two room house. One room is 15 by 11 [feet] and the kitchen 10-15. . . . You don't know what it is for eleven of us to sleep in one bedroom during the winter when I have to put some of my children on the floor and all I have in my room are two beds.[63]

Several other families with much the same problems wrote similar letters to the BCIM Director protesting the actions of the government social worker and requesting his aid.[64] On these reservations, most of the houses were quite small since lumber was scarce and expensive. Since the Lakotas often had large families and lived in conditions similar to those at the Patton household, day schools were impractical for many of them.

In addition to writing to the BCIM, the Lakotas at the 1938 Catholic Sioux Congress composed a resolution supporting their Catholic schools:

The Catholic Congress respectfully asks the Secretary of the Interior to instruct the Commissioner of Indian Affairs to consider the wishes of the parents of Indian school children as to the school which these children are to attend. We Indians want that the Catholic Mission schools be allowed to fill to their capacities and that the contract be extended to this full number.[65]

Despite the actions of the Bureau of Indian Affairs, the St. Francis and Holy Rosary mission schools flourished in the 1930's and 40's, and each year attracted 300 to 400 students to each school. The only way that the mission schools continued, however, was through the Lakotas' signing the petitions which enabled the schools to draw on the tribal funds for support. If the Lakotas were ever dissatisfied with the mission school, they could have refused to sign the petition and could have sent their children to the public school.

The Lakotas, however, willingly undertook the programs in education and industrial training at the mission schools since they knew that they needed these skills to acquire jobs. The destruction of the buffalo made the industrial education of the Lakotas necessary, and the Lakotas

---

63. BCIM 1-223-14, Laura Patton, letter, Oglala, S.D. Aug 21, 1934.

64. BCIM 1-223-14.

65. HRM 4-1-2, Emil Afraid-of-Hawk and William Bush, "Minutes of Golden Jubilee Indian Congress: 1938," p.3.

either had to adapt to the American economy or accept poverty. The Jesuits did Westernize the Lakotas in terms of their economy, but this was unavoidable. By stressing practical industrial training, the Jesuits tried to help the Lakotas obtain jobs in the South Dakota economy so that they could become economically self-sufficient.

CHAPTER THREE

Catholic Sioux Congresses

BISHOP MARTY AND THE JESUITS WHO ESTABLISHED THE HOLY ROSARY and St. Francis missions were either from Germany, Austria or Switzerland, and in all of these countries the clergy and lay people held annual Catholic Congresses. In Germany and Austria the Catholic Congresses began in 1848 and continued through the end of the century. The Swiss held their Catholic Congresses in the 1860's. By uniting and organizing both the laity and clergy, these congresses promoted greater devotion to the Church, stimulated Catholic scholarship, encouraged the preservation of Catholic education, and supported the cause of civil rights for Catholics. During the *Kulturkampf*, the German Catholic Congresses were a means of promoting Catholic unity, and a vehicle for opposing Bismark's anti-Catholic policies.[1]

The American bishops also encouraged lay Catholic congresses. In 1889, African-American Catholic lay delegates gathered in Washington, D.C. for the first African-American Catholic Congress.[2] This Congress was an expression of unity of the African-American Catholics and a forum for discussing common concerns. In the same year, 1500 Catholic lay delegates assembled in Baltimore for a Congress to commemorate the centenary of the American hierarchy and to stimulate lay activity in the Church.[3]

Probably influenced by the lay congresses in Europe and America, Bishop Marty decided to establish a lay congress among the Sioux.[4] Beginning in 1890, the Catholic Sioux Congress was usually an annual event lasting four days. From the start, the Catholic Sioux Congresses were

---

1. Martin Spahn, "Congresses, Catholic," *Catholic Encyclopedia* (New York: Robert Appleton, 1908), 4:242-243.

2. Cyprian Davis, O.S.B., *The History of Black Catholics in the United States* (New York: CrossRoad, 1990), 163-164.

3. J.Q. Feller, "Lay Congresses, American Catholic," *The New Catholic Encyclopedia* (Washington: Catholic University, 1967), 8:577.

4. "The Great Catholic Sioux Congress of 1910," *Indian Sentinel* (1911):3.

quite successful, and 1000 to 4000 Sioux attended each year through 1938 when World War Two interrupted them.[5] Every year the Sioux held the Congress at a different mission in North or South Dakota, and many of them traveled long distances to attend. From each reservation, horse-drawn buggies with Sioux Catholics made the journey to the site of the Congress. The Congresses caught on quickly, and at the 1894 Congress at Cherry Creek, Cheyenne River Reservation South Dakota, about 2300 Sioux attended. In his diary, Emil Perrig, a Jesuit from St. Francis, recorded the number of wagons that arrived at this Congress from each reservation:

> Of the Indians there were: 200 wagons and about as many riders from Standing Rock, 42 wagons from Rosebud, 2 wagons from Pine Ridge, 7 wagons from Crow Creek, 8 wagons from Lower Brule, 9 wagons from Fort Totten, 1 from Fort Berthold, 19 from Bad River, Cheyenne River Ag[ency]; 100 from Cheyenne River, Cheyenne River Ag[ency]; 69 from Cherry Creek.[6]

Though Fort Berthold and Fort Totten were both over 200 miles from Cherry Creek, the Sioux at these two reservations still made the journey because the Congresses were important to them. Each year they made these trips to the Congresses by horse and buggy, and they continued this until the 1930's, after which they traveled by truck. When they reached the site of the Congress, they camped out in tepees or tents, a custom they continued through the 1970's.[7]

The Catholic Sioux Congress was a gathering principally of the St. Joseph's and St. Mary's societies of all the Sioux reservations, but the Church encouraged all Catholics on the reservations to attend. The St. Joseph's and St. Mary's societies were men's and women's Catholic societies dedicated to encouraging devotion to the Church. These societies had local gatherings usually every week at which the men and women gave speeches, discussed moral issues, exhorted each other to live by the rules of the Church, and organized Catholic celebrations like the Congresses. The St. Joseph's and St. Mary's societies from each reservation elected delegates from among themselves who represented them in the business sessions of the Congresses. In these sessions the delegates composed and voted on resolutions.

In devising these resolutions, the Sioux displayed their independence by opposing, on occasion, the missionaries' desires. In 1893 at the Congress at St. Francis Mission, the Sioux were even bold enough to reject

---

5.   BCIM 14/1-6-1, Fr. Paul Lenz, *An Historical Narrative of the Catholic Sioux Indian Congress: 1890-1978*, pamphlet.

6.   SFM 7-5-(14-15), Emil Perrig, S.J., diary, July 3, 1894.

7.   BCIM 14/1-6-1, Fr. Paul Lenz, *A Historical Narrative of the Catholic Sioux Indian Congress*, 1933-1934 entries. Michael Steltenkamp, S.J., interview, May 1995.

Bishop Marty's advice concerning the organization of the Congresses. Marty suggested that the Congress be held in four different places each year to reduce the traveling and expenses. The Sioux, however, rejected his proposal, and Aloysius Bosch, S.J., of Holy Rosary Mission, described how they openly spoke against Marty's proposal immediately after he presented it to them:

> [Marty] had not yet taken his seat when up stood Straight Face, police captain at Cheyenne River Agency, and the "Heiyomakipishni" (I do not like it), uttered very often during the speech, gave the whole drift of his answer. And then he always looked so triumphantly around and the whole crowd so often nodded assent, accompanying the head with the usual "How, how," that I could not help turning from time to time to the Bishop and asking him, "My lord, do you hear? Your proposal will never be accepted." After Straight Face and two other Indians spoke, and I am sure they would have talked till evening against the suggestion had not the Bishop yielded to their opposition.[8]

The Sioux did not want to be fragmented even if maintaining their national unity meant greater travel and expense. The last speaker who opposed Bishop Marty's suggestion said:

> Look at that rope! The little strings out of which it is made are very fine, and a little child might tear them; but now they are tied together and no man may pull it asunder. United we shall be strong, and these large meetings unite us.[9]

The Sioux were not so awed by the presence of the bishop that they accepted all his wishes. By rejecting the bishop's proposal, they asserted that the management of the Congress was in their hands.

Since the Sioux had gone through such a dramatic change in lifestyle, they wanted to maintain their identity as a nation, and besides, they enjoyed traveling and visiting with other Sioux bands. This expression of national solidarity was also beneficial to the Catholic life on the reservations since the Congresses created an atmosphere in which the Sioux Catholics mutually supported each other in their faith. For example, at the 1891 Congress at Standing Rock Reservation, the Lakotas learned that the Dakota Sioux on the Standing Rock Reservation already formed well-organized St. Joseph's and St. Mary's societies. After returning from this Congress, Digmann explained the effect that it had on the Lakotas:

> Our Indians of Rosebud and Pine Ridge had seen that their tribal brethren of North Dakota were far ahead of them in 'The way of the Great Spirit and in Christian civilization.' After their return

---

8. SFM 7-1-1, Aloysius Bosch, S.J., "Indians in Council," *Sacred Heart Messenger* (1893):884.

9. Bosch, "Indians in Council," 885.

they were eager to start the St. Joseph and St. Mary Societies on their own reservation.[10]

The Congresses also placed the Lakotas in positions of responsibility, and required from them a tremendous effort in labor and management skills. Commenting on the 1893 Congress, Aloysius Bosch, S.J., of Holy Rosary, recognized that the Lakotas took great pride in their positions at the Congresses. He also noted that since they all had to work together to make the Congresses a success, the organization of the Congresses had the effect of unifying them and inspiring devotion to the Church:

> The very preparations for the Congress had awakened no little activity among our people. They came in greater numbers to Church, listened more attentively to the catechetical instructions, stood much better the necessary Church drill; in short, they wanted to be as good as their brethren in other missions, who soon would come and see their progress. Then, too, the preparations, which were carried on during the whole year made the Indians feel that they were one body and were bound to help one another.[11]

Thus the Jesuits recognized that the Sioux's national unity contributed to unifying the laity and expanding the Catholic Church on the different reservations.

The Congresses were successful primarily because they encouraged Sioux national unity and built on Sioux traditions, which the Sioux integrated into the event on their own initiative. Traditionally, the seven bands of the Sioux joined together each year in June for a feast, a Sun Dance, and a council.[12] Since Marty and the other missionaries wanted to rid the reservations of the Sun Dance and also the Ghost Dance Religion that flourished on several Sioux reservations in 1890, they used the Sioux Congresses as a substitute for them.

In 1890, the Ghost Dance religion was at its peak. The Ghost Dance religion was a quasi-Christian apocalyptic religion that began forming in 1870. Some of its members believed that the messiah would return to punish or kill the white people for their sins. After this happened, they believed that the Native Americans would then gain their land back, and the dead Native Americans, the ghosts, would come to life and reunite with them. This religion was named after a dance, the Ghost Dance, which was the central ritual of this religion. During this dance, the Ghost Dancers wore ceremonial buckskin shirts which, according to their religion, were impervious to enemy bullets. By performing this dance, the Ghost

---

10. HRM 7-14-8, Digmann, diary, July 8, 1891.

11. SFM 7-1-1, Aloysius Bosch, "Indians in Council," *Sacred Heart Messenger* (1893):878.

12. Lenz, 2.

Dancers believed that they helped to hasten the apocalypse, which involved Jesus' returning to the earth. Many Ghost Dancers believed that Jesus was already on the earth, signifying that the end was near, and many of the Lakotas on Pine Ridge and Rosebud shared this belief. Writing in his diary on September 30, 1890, Digmann described the views of the Ghost Dancers on Rosebud: "they had really sent a delegation to some peak in Wyoming where Christ was said to appear," and a Ghost Dancer told Digmann that on that peak "the Son of the Great Spirit now appears and teaches people."[13]

In the winter of 1890 some of the Lakotas found the anti-white teachings of the Ghost Dance particularly welcome because they believed the government had cheated them. From 1889 to 1890, they encountered a series of misfortunes: their crops failed, diseases spread through the reservations, the government cut their rations and forced them to cede half their land.[14] In addition to this, many of the Sioux were starving. Angered by the government and afraid of being attacked by the Army, many Brules and Oglalas joined the Ghost Dancers who camped out at the "Stronghold" in the Bad Lands on Pine Ridge. Reacting to the increasing militancy among the Sioux, the government agent called in the troops.

On December 3, 1890, John Jutz, S.J., Holy Rosary Mission Superior, and Jack Red Cloud, Chief Red Cloud's son, went out to the Ghost Dancers in the Bad Lands to try to pacify them and bring them back to the mission. Later, Jutz described the meeting:

> We arrived at the Indian camp, and drove straight to the tent of the Chief. His name was "Two Strike." We alighted, and I went at once into his tent and greeted him with the customary salutation "How How," and presented him with a little package of tobacco. He returned the greeting. In a few minutes the tent was filled with Indians. . . . I told the Indians that I had come to rescue them from their sorry plight, for they could not stay where they were. Besides their food supply would soon run out, and they were not allowed to kill cattle which did not belong to them. I also told them that the soldiers had not come to wage war against them, and that the General [John Brooke] was a very kind gentleman, who would give them meat and everything else they needed. All they had to do was to come to the Agency, and from there they could quietly go back to the camp at Rosebud. They listened with great attention, and one of them stood up and said: "Father, if what you say is true, lift up your right hand and swear to the Great Spirit that it is true." I stood up and lifted up my

---

13. HRM 7-14-8, Digmann, diary, Sept. 30, 1890. Weston Labarre, *The Ghost Dance* (New York: Delta, 1970), 229-232. James Mooney, *The Ghost Dance Religion and Wounded Knee* (New York: Dover, 1973), 816-821.

14. Mooney, *The Ghost Dance Religion and Wounded Knee*, 824-842.

right hand. All the Indians arose and lifted up their hands as a token that they believed me.[15]

Assuring them safe passage, Jutz convinced 40 Lakotas, including Chief Two Strike, to hold a council with General Brooke. The 40 Lakota men returned to the mission and stayed there overnight before the meeting.[16] The next day, the Lakotas met with General Brooke. The meeting was cordial and successful in convincing several chiefs to leave the camp in the Bad Lands and return to the government agency in peace. A few days after this meeting, many of the Lakotas in the camp, some influenced by Jutz's intervention and others who lost faith in the ghost shirts' ability to protect them, left their camp, and returned to the mission.[17] A few weeks after this, on December 29, 1890, the Seventh Cavalry moved in and massacred a group of Sioux Ghost Dancers who were from the Cheyenne River Reservation. They killed about 200 Sioux men, women, and children at Wounded Knee Creek.[18] After the massacre, the nuns at Holy Rosary Mission provided medical care for some of the wounded Lakotas.[19]

Since the Ghost Dance religion expressed anti-white sentiment, tendencies toward militancy, and syncretism, the missionaries were anxious to direct the Sioux's attention to other forms of celebration. But by discouraging the Ghost Dance, the missionaries did not lead any of the Sioux from a traditional belief, since the Ghost Dance was a new religion that the Sioux adopted shortly before the massacre. After the massacre, in which the Ghost Dancers' shirts failed the crucial test, this religion vanished from the reservations.

Though the Sun Dance was neither anti-white nor apocalyptic, the missionaries wanted to eliminate this dance because of the extreme physical suffering involved in it.[20] During their traditional annual councils at which the Sioux bands gathered together, the Sioux made a large circular scaffold of pine branches to enclose the Sun Dance grounds. They left an opening on the east side of the circle through which dancers entered. In the center of the circle, they placed a cottonwood pole that a virgin girl cut down for the ceremony according to their tradition. The Sun Dance

---

15. John Jutz, S.J., *Woodstock Letters* 47 (1918):320. BCIM 1-25-12, John Jutz, S.J. to Fr. Stephan. Dec. 14, 1890.

16. BCIM 1-25-12, John Jutz, S.J. to Fr. Stephan, Dec. 14, 1890. John Jutz, S.J. "Historic Data on the Causes of Dissatisfaction among the Sioux Indians in 1890," *Woodstock Letters* 47 (1918):313-327. SFM 1/1-1-1, Affidavit of John Jutz, St. Francis Mission, Rosebud Agency, July 11, 1894.

17. SFM 7-5-(14-15), Emil Perrig, S.J., diary, Dec. 9-12, 1890. Louis Goll, S.J., *Jesuit Missions Among the Sioux*, (St. Francis Mission 1940), 11.

18. Mooney, *The Ghost Dance Religion and Wounded Knee*, 868-874.

19. SFM 7-5-(14-15), Emil Perrig, S.J., diary, Dec. 31, 1890. Jessie Crow, interview, Oglala, S.D., Oct. 1992. Mooney, 868-874.

20. William Powers, *Oglala Religion*, 95-99.

was closely related to the buffalo hunt, and during this dance, the men acted out the buffalo hunt. Many of the men also fasted and deprived themselves of water for three or four days during the dance.[21] At the central ceremony of the Sun Dance, the men pierced the front of their chests with a knife or awl, each making two incisions. Placing a piece of wood or bone below the skin, sometimes into the muscle, they attached the piece of wood or bone on both sides to a rope which they fastened to the top of the cottonwood pole. Then they danced to exhaustion. Many threw themselves backwards so that the piece of wood attached to them ripped through their flesh. The dancers who pierced themselves danced for a supernatural blessing from the Great Spirit who they believed took pity on them in their suffering. Frequently they cut off pieces of their skin and flesh offering them to the Great Spirit as a sacrifice. In return, they asked for visions, success in buffalo hunts, prosperity for their band, or even for many wives.[22]

But though the Catholic missionaries opposed the Sun Dance itself, they allowed the Lakotas to preserve some of the customs and structures of the Sun Dance and incorporate them into the Catholic Congresses. For example, two photographs of the 1911 and 1920 Congress showed the grounds at which the Sioux Catholics gathered for the speeches and other events of the Congress. These photographs showed that the Sioux constructed a large circular scaffold of pine boughs with a pole at the center. This bower and center pole were quite similar to the Sun Dance grounds. At the Congresses, however, an American flag flew at the top of the center pole, and the people put an altar for Mass on the site.[23] At most of Congresses, they constructed the same type of circular bower with the center pole.[24] Moreover, a Jesuit's description of the 1919 Congresses said that on one side of the bower "was the official entrance through which, according to Indian etiquette, everyone who wished to be present, must enter and leave."[25] Thus the Congress retained some of the forms of Sioux rituals, but changed the content.

---

21. Luther Standing Bear, *My People the Sioux* (Lincoln: University of Nebraska, 1975), 122. Original edition published in 1928.

22. Louis Goll, S.J., *Jesuit Missions Among the Sioux* (Saint Francis Mission, S.D. 1940), 15.

23. *Lakota Times*, Aug. 2, 1988, p.3. photograph of Catholic Sioux Congress at Holy Rosary July 14-17, 1911. BCIM 14/1-4-2, n.a., "Indians meet in Convention," *The Calumet*, (Oct. 1920). William Huffer, "Catholic Sioux Congress of South Dakota: Indian Hospitality and Faith," *Indian Sentinel* 3 (Oct. 1923):147-148.

24. Joseph Gschwend, S.J., "Catholic Sioux Indians in Council," *America* June 20, 1931, p.253. Paul Lenz, *A Historical Narrative of the Catholic Sioux Indian Congress: 1890-1978*, photograph of 1920 Congress. BCIM 14/1-4-2. n.a., "Catholic Sioux Congress," *The Calumet* (October 1919):1. BCIM 14/1-25-18, *Sina Sapa Wocekiye Taeyapha*, (Aug. 15, 1906), front page of supplement, column 1.

25. *Woodstock Letters* 48(1919):428.

In the Sun Dance, the participant offered his suffering and his blood to the Creator. In a symbolic sense, the Mass, celebrated in the bower, became the substitute for the Sun Dance sacrifice. The missionaries even compared the sacrifice of Christ to the Sun Dance which suggested that they hoped to use the similarities between the two to help the Sioux understand Christianity. In 1907, Digmann wrote:

> The late Bishop Martin Marty, O.S.B., then Abbot of St. Meinrad's was one of the first who preached to the Sioux, taking occasion, from the cruelties they practiced at the Sun Dance to appease the Great Spirit, to point out to them our divine Savior hanging from the tree to atone for our sins.[26]

Bishop Marty also intentionally set the date of the Congresses in June so that the Congress coincided with the traditional time for the celebration of the Sun Dance.[27] By doing this, Marty followed in the tradition of the early Church which set the date for the celebration of Christmas at the time of a traditional non-Christian feast. By retaining traditional forms and symbolism, the Congresses created an atmosphere that was in some ways similar to the Lakotas' traditional celebrations.

Another way that Marty built on the Sioux traditions at the Congresses was his appreciation of the Sioux style of oration. One of the reasons that Marty wanted to establish the St. Mary's and St. Joseph's societies and the Congresses was that they encouraged the speechmaking that was already part of the Sioux culture.[28] Traditionally, the Sioux were accomplished orators who held forth for hours at a time. They also listened with infinite patience to the long speeches. Since Marty knew that the Sioux were great orators, he established the St. Mary's and St. Joseph's societies to direct this Sioux tradition towards the lay preaching of the Gospel. His plan was quite effective. In both the local meetings of these societies and at the Congresses, the Sioux spent much of their time preaching or listening to the speeches of their orators.[29]

Throughout the history of the Congresses, the Jesuits recognized the Lakotas' oratorical skill and often lauded them for their skill.[30] George

---

26. Florentine Digmann, S.J., "The Catholic Indian Schools: St. Francis," *Indian Sentinel* (1907):21-22. HRM 7-14-8, Digmann, Diary, June 30, 1891. Marty "went to preach the Gospel to the Sioux, leading them from the victims of the sundance to our Savior hanging on the Cross."

27. "Catholic Indian Schools: St. Francis," *Indian Sentinel* (1907):24. HRM 7-14-8, Digmann, diary, June 30, 1891.

28. Duratschek, *The Beginning of Catholicism in South Dakota*, 111. Duratschek, *Crusading along Sioux Trails,* 98.

29. BCIM 14/1-5-3, Louis Pfaller, O.S.B., *The Catholic Church in Western North Dakota 1738-1960* (Mandan: Crescent Printing, 1960), 26. Harvey Markowitz, "Catholic Mission and the Sioux," in *Sioux Indian Religion*, Raymond DeMallie, ed., (Norman: University of Oklahoma, 1987), 122-123.

Prendergast, S.J., of Holy Rosary Mission, wrote an article in the *Jesuit Missions* magazine titled "Orators of the Plains" which described the 1931 Congress:

> At the Sioux Indian Congress at Holy Rosary Mission South Dakota, last Spring were gathered together the best orators of the Oglala and Brule tribes. They spoke, in their native tongue, on politico-religious questions such as the state divorce laws and Catholic higher education for their children, subjects of grave importance and worthy of the best orators. They are natural born speakers, these Indians, if ever there were such. They can speak for an hour with hardly a stop, and never hesitate a moment for a word. Their gestures are most graceful and expressive. At the same time, the Sioux orator has all the classic restraint and control which the ancients labored so steadfastly to acquire. . . . It was inspiring, indeed, to watch these men and women rise up in the assembly without the least sign of trepidation, and deliver their apparently carefully prepared but, as far as composition went, strictly extemporaneous speeches.[31]

In the same article, Prendergast, praising the Sioux for their eloquence, also suggested that Americans could learn much from the Sioux on the matter of oration. Traditionally, speeches were a central part of most Sioux celebrations, and before the Sioux learned to write, their almost total reliance on speech, rather than on writing, compelled them to develop their formidable oratorical skills. At the Congresses the Sioux continued this tradition, with the encouragement of the missionaries, and gave most of their speeches in Lakota or Dakota. Until the 1940's, the Sioux language was the primary language spoken at all the Congresses.[32] Even at most other Catholic celebrations, the Jesuits and other missionaries encouraged their oratorical traditions, and most of the Lakota celebrations began with speeches by the Lakotas and missionaries.[33]

To organize and manage the Congresses, the members of the St. Mary's and St. Joseph's societies also drew on their Sioux traditions. Joseph Luther, a Jesuit scholastic and teacher at St. Francis Mission who

30. Jerome Hunt, O.S.B., "The Catholic Sioux Congress," *Indian Sentinel* (1910):13. Fr. Paul Lenz, *A Historical Narrative of the Catholic Sioux Indian Congress: 1890-1978.* BCIM 1-250-14, Fr. Sialm to Mr. and Mrs. Poulter, Holy Rosary Mission, Nov. 23, 1939. "Great Catholic Indian Congress in South Dakota." *Woodstock Letters* 48 (1919):428. Joseph Zimmerman, S.J., "In the Bad Lands," *Jesuit Missions* 7 (May 1933):101.

31. George Prendergast, S.J., "Orators of the Plains," *Jesuit Missions* 11 (Feb. 1932):35, 46.

32. Myrtle Crow Eagle, interview, St. Francis, S.D., Oct. 1992. Fr. C.P. Jordan, interview, St. Francis, S.D. Oct. 1992.

33. Joseph Zimmerman, S.J., circular letter, Dec. 1930 in *High Eagle and His Sioux* (St. Louis, 1963), John Scott, S.J., ed., 13-14.

attended the 1924 Congress, commented on the Sioux's management practices in a letter to his provincial:

> The entire Congress was financed by the voluntary contributions of the Indians. Food and rations consisting of meat, vegetables, coffee, dried fruit, etc., were distributed to each tent and family daily. Over 1600 horses were kept in a common pasture. All the details of the Indians' life during the four days of the Congress were regulated by a sort of common tribal law and custom that was touched at once with the simple romantic traits of the old buffalo hunt days and, and now leavened with the charity, trust and peace they have found in the Gospel of Christ.[34]

Traditionally, when the Sioux bands gathered together for their national councils, they had the huge task of managing many different people, and they developed customs that governed the organization of these large gatherings. These customs determined the arrangement of the tepees, the pasturing of the hundreds of horses that came, and the distribution of food and water. When the Sioux camped out at the Catholic Congresses, they had many of the same organizational tasks, and so they simply integrated their traditional customs into the Congresses. In a *Sentinel* article, a priest visiting the Dakotas, John Woods, described the atmosphere of the 1924 Congress:

> [The Sioux] pitched their tents in preparation for three days which, in all but the significant religious exercises, closely resembled their tribal life as it was at the coming of their first apostle [DeSmet].[35]

Rather than emphasizing how much the Sioux changed, Luther and Woods emphasized that the Congress preserved many Sioux customs.

In addition to maintaining some Sioux customs, the missionaries integrated some American democratic traditions into the Congresses' structure. For instance, the business sessions of the Congresses incorporated American democratic traditions rather than the traditional Sioux social principles that concerned hierarchy and authority. For instance, the local St. Mary's and St. Joseph's societies elected delegates to represent them at the Congresses. They also elected different Congress presidents, vice-presidents, and secretaries each year. In contrast to the American democratic traditions, a Sioux band traditionally had a head chief and three or more other chiefs who held their positions for life. The head chief's word was law, and the other chiefs were counselors to the head chief. A Sioux man became a head chief usually by birth and merit, but sometimes just by merit. Often the head chief appointed his eldest son to succeed him.

---

34. Joseph A. Luther, S.J., "A Real One Hundred Percent American Convention," *Woodstock Letters* 53 (1924):351.

35. Father John Woods, "27th Annual Sioux Congress," *Indian Sentinel* 4 (Oct. 1924):147.

But if the son was not competent to rule on account of his reputation or some other factor, the head chief appointed someone else. The head chief, however, was not the only one involved in the decision. The chiefs and influential men in the community discussed the matter, and the appointment was subject to their approval.[36]

If a family or group was not satisfied with the head chief, they could leave him, break off from the band, and elect their own chief. Thus chiefs became more or less powerful on the basis of their merit. In the Sioux society, only men were chiefs, and women did not even participate in the discussions which involved appointing a chief. Men also held all the other positions in traditional Sioux government. The only exception to this was the rare occasion when a woman was appointed marshall. In Sioux society, a marshall was a type of policeman who saw that the head chief's will was obeyed, and also supervised the establishment or the leaving of a camp. Nevertheless, women did not sit on the councils, and did not make policy.[37]

At the Catholic Sioux Congresses, the men occupied the primary positions of responsibility such as president, vice-president, and secretary. Furthermore, all the catechists were men, and they played a prominent role at the Congresses as preachers. At the 1892 Congress at the Cheyenne River Reservation, Bishop Marty defined the women's role in the Congresses when he declared that women were neither allowed to vote nor to take part in the Congress's deliberations.[38] Though Marty imposed this rule, the practice of men leading the community was already the Sioux tradition.

Over the years, however, the Sioux women played an increasingly important role in the Congresses. For example, when over 4000 Sioux gathered at the 1910 Congress at Standing Rock Reservation, one of the days was designated as the "women's day" at which a member of each St. Mary's delegation addressed the Congress. Upon hearing the women's speeches, the Apostolic Delegate, Diomede Falconio who attended this Congress, approved of the speeches saying, "In all my life I have never observed women speak with such eloquence and independence, and yet with such modesty."[39] The St. Mary's Societies also had local autonomy, and women made speeches at their local meetings.[40] By 1920, the Congresses no longer observed Marty's ban, and thereafter the women participated fully in the deliberations at the Congresses.[41] Actually by the

36. Walker, *Lakota Society*, 24.

37. *Ibid.*, 23-31. Powers, *Oglala Religion*, 40-42.

38. SFM 7-5-(14-15), Emil Perrig, S.J., diary, July 5, 1892.

39. "The Great Catholic Sioux Congress of 1910," *Indian Sentinel* (1911):7.

40. BCIM 1-145-1, Digmann to Fr. Hughes, May 6, 1924.

41. BCIM 14/1-4-2, "Indians Meet in Convention," *Calumet* (Oct. 1920).

1940's the Jesuits made the case that the Catholic Church gave women more influence in the Lakota society than they had in the pre-contact times.[42] By addressing the Congresses and taking part in the business sessions, the Sioux women gained prominence in the Catholic community life.

The Jesuits also tried to improve the lot of women in the society by emphasizing the idea of a stable marriage. Often Lakota boys eloped with Lakota girls, and these marriages frequently were unstable. Both missionaries and catechists tried to discourage such spontaneous marriages, and also spoke out against the divorces that occurred on the reservations. At the 1920 Congress, the Sioux passed a resolution that they sent to the Governor of South Dakota requesting laws to make divorce more difficult.[43]

During the meetings of the St. Joseph's and St. Mary's societies both locally and at the Congresses, the delegates and catechists gave many long speeches against what they believed were the great evils of their time: alcoholism and divorce.[44] At most of the Congresses since the 1890's, the bishops, priests and catechists emphasized the danger of these practices. To combat the alcohol problem on the reservations, the Lakotas established temperance societies at the Congresses, and made pledges to abstain from drinking any alcohol.[45]

In the 1910's and 1920's, the Peyote religion gained a following on Pine Ridge and Rosebud, and this was another practice that the Jesuits saw as a great evil. They wanted to eradicate the Peyote religion completely, and often spoke against it at the Congresses. Peyote was a small cactus which was native to Mexico and which could produce hallucinogenic effects when ingested. The use of peyote in religious ceremonies was common among the Mexican Native Americans, and many used it to gain what they believed was a religious experience. In the late 1800's and early 1900's, the use of peyote spread to North America where many different Native Americans combined the beliefs surrounding the use of this cactus with Christian beliefs. Though their beliefs varied, many members of the Peyote religion believed that the ingestion of peyote and the resulting vision gave them a knowledge of the truth and the "road" to salvation. For many of them, salvation involved their meeting with Christ upon their death.[46] Since this religion, like the Ghost Dance, was a new

---

42. *Jesuit Missions* (Sept. 1943):210.

43. C.M. Weisenhorn, S.J., "Sioux Congress of Pine Ridge," *Indian Sentinel* 2 (Oct. 1920):174.

44. HRM 4-1-2, Joseph Gschwend, "Catholic Sioux Indians in Congress," *America*, June 20, 1931, p.253.

45. "The Sioux Congress," *Indian Sentinel* 1 (Oct. 1916):29. "Great Catholic Sioux Congress of 1910," *Indian Sentinel* (1911):6.

46. Weston Labarre, *The Peyote Cult*, (Hamden: Shoe String Press, 1959), 156.

quasi-Christian religion, the Jesuits' attempt to eradicate the Peyote religion was therefore not an assault on the traditional Sioux culture. But though the Lakotas abandoned the Ghost Dance shortly after Wounded Knee, the Peyote religion maintained a presence on the Sioux reservations to the present.

Writing tracts and campaigning for the prohibition of peyote in the 1920's, Louis Goll, S.J., Holy Rosary Mission Superior from 1920 to 1926, was the most outspoken on the subject. He described peyote as a habit forming hallucinogen that destroyed a user's self-reliance and eventually drove them insane. He also opposed the use of peyote because he saw it as a mockery of the Catholic faith. He wrote that members of the Peyote religion used the peyote tea as water for "baptism," and used the peyote button as a type of "communion wafer," which the Peyotists believed was the body of Christ.[47] Agreeing with Goll, Leo Cunningham, S.J., of Holy Rosary condemned the Peyote religion claiming that it "seems to be the devil's own way of mocking the Blessed Sacrament."[48] The Jesuits were also alarmed that the Peyote religion gained many converts, including many Catholic families.[49]

Because of their attitude toward peyote use, the Jesuits were especially gratified by converting the members of the Peyote religion to the Catholic faith. When they were successful at this, they spread the news around the reservation and sometimes wrote articles to the *Indian Sentinel* telling of the person's conversion.[50] In his diary, Fr. Eugene Buechel, S.J., of Holy Rosary Mission recorded that he often appealed to the members of the Peyote religion to leave their practices and join the Catholic Church. Furthermore, at the Congresses the catechists made many speeches denouncing the use of peyote.[51] At the 1920 Congress, the Sioux passed a resolution against peyote use which they sent to the U.S. Congress:

> We the representatives of the Sioux Nation, gathered together in our Catholic Congress at Pine Ridge, South Dakota, implore the Congress of the United States to grant prompt passage of a bill against the peyote evil.[52]

---

47. HRM 4-1-2, Louis Goll, S.J., "The Peyote Cult," c. 1923.

48. BCIM 1-235-11, Fr. Cunningham to Fr. Tennelly, Porcupine Feb. 4, 1936.

49. BCIM 1-229-15, Leo Cunningham, S.J. to Fr. Tennelly, June 26, 1935.

50. Eugene Buechel, S.J., "Hired at the Eleventh Hour," *Indian Sentinel* 21 (May 1941):70, 80.

51. Joseph Luther, S.J., "A Real One Hundred Percent American Convention," *Woodstock Letters* 53 (1924):349.

52. C.M. Weisenhorn, S.J., "Sioux Congress on Pine Ridge Reservation," *Indian Sentinel* 2 (Oct. 1920):173.

In addition to serving as a time to warn the Lakota people about the dangers to the faith, the Congresses were also a time for the celebration of the Catholic sacraments. The bishops confirmed the children. The priests heard thousands of confessions, administered first communion, baptized, and offered Mass every day. At all the Congresses, the priests gave sermons in English, Dakota and Lakota. The Sioux also preached and sang hymns in Dakota and Lakota.[53] From a description of their behavior at the Congresses, the Sioux apparently exhibited a reverent attitude, especially during the celebration of the Masses and sacraments. Describing a Mass at the 1908 Congress, John Stariha, Bishop of Lead, commented:

> I saw beautiful devotions in the various churches but never such as I saw here with the Indians. Their living faith made a great impression upon me and I thought to myself, such must have been the faith and devotion of the first Christians. No one moved during the entire Mass, all were on their knees with their heads bowed to the ground until the end of Mass.[54]

Because of their popularity, the Congresses attracted Native American priests and sisters from several Native American nations. Father Albert Negahnquet, who was a Potawatomi, came to the 1909 Congress at Fort Totten, North Dakota. At the opening of the Congress, he celebrated the High Mass and later addressed the Congress.[55] The first Chippewa priest, Father Philip Gordon, attended the 1915 Congress and also addressed the people.[56] These two priests came to several Sioux Congresses, and played prominent roles in the celebrations. Articles in the *Indian Sentinel* praised these two priests for undertaking ecclesiastical vocations,[57] and also covered their participation in the Sioux Congresses. One such *Sentinel* article described the 1916 Catholic Sioux Congress at the Fort Peck Reservation in Poplar Montana which Gordon attended:

> The Congress opened Saturday with a Solemn High Mass by Father Philip B. Gordon, the Chippewa Indian Priest, who represented the Bureau of Catholic Indian Missions at the Congress. Father Gordon was assisted by Father Albert Negahnequet, the Potawatomi Indian priest from Oklahoma. . . . The acolytes were Indian boys; the choir one of Indian youths and maidens, and the sermon was preached in an Indian language. . . . In the afternoon, Bishop Lenihan [of Great Falls] suggested a Eucharistic Procession after the manner of St. Anne de Beaupre and of Our

---

53. Joseph Gschwend, "Catholic Sioux Indians in Congress." *America*, June 20, 1931, p.254.

54. John Zaplotnik, *Bishop John N. Stariha,* unpublished manuscript, Archives of Diocese of Rapid City, p.36.

55. Jerome Hunt. O.S.B., "The Catholic Sioux Congress," *Indian Sentinel* (1910):13-14.

56. "Indian Congresses," *Indian Sentinel* (1916):23.

57. *Indian Sentinel* (1904-1905):3, 4, 32.

Lady of Lourdes. Under the direction of Father Negahnquet, a procession was formed and the Blessed Sacrament was borne in state around the camp. At the door of each tepee, the priest bearing the Blessed Sacrament paused and blessed the occupants. The entire procession journeyed more than two miles in order to encircle the camp.[58]

Father Gordon also went to the 1923 Congress where he urged the Sioux men to consider vocations to the priesthood.[59] Yet even though the Sioux did not produce a priest until 1985,[60] several Sioux women became nuns, and the Congresses also featured them as speakers.[61] The Sioux appreciated that Native Americans held prominent positions at the Congresses since it gave them a sense of unity with other Catholic Native Americans and increased their perception of universality of the Church.

The Congresses also served as events which encouraged the creation and display of Sioux art. When dignitaries visited the Congresses, the Sioux often gave them gifts of Sioux artwork. For example, when the Apostolic Delegate, Diomede Falconio, came to the 1911 Congress at Standing Rock Reservation, the Sioux presented him with a sacred pipe and a pipe bag.[62] Even though the sacred pipe and pipe bag were part of the traditional Sioux religion, the Sioux and the priests believed that these gifts were perfectly appropriate. At the 1916 Congress, the Sioux gave BCIM Director William Ketcham a tobacco pouch and beaded saddle bag.[63] Furthermore, a *Sentinel* article described Bishop Lawler's visit to the 1923 Congress, at which the Sioux "Indians presented [Lawler] with a magnificent Indian pipe bag and a blanket, both of which had been six months in the making."[64] The Sioux also gave presents to patrons of the missions. Joseph Luther, S.J., of St. Francis Mission, who attended the 1924 Congress at Rosebud, wrote:

> A beautiful Indian dress of buckskin, elaborately beaded and worked, was presented to two sisters of the Blessed Sacrament as

---

58. "The Sioux Congress," *Indian Sentinel* 1 (Oct. 1916):27-28.

59. William Huffer, "Catholic Sioux Congress of South Dakota," *Indian Sentinel* 3 (Oct 1923):148.

60. Fr. C.P. Jordan, a former student of St. Francis Mission, was the first Lakota priest. After his ordination in 1985, he took up residence on the St. Francis Mission where he continues to minister to the Lakotas today.

61. HRM 4-1-2, Emil Afraid of Hawk and William Bush, "Minutes of the Golden Jubilee Indian Congress: 1938," p.2.

62. "The Great Catholic Sioux Congress of 1910," *Indian Sentinel* (1911):7.

63. "The Sioux Congress," *Indian Sentinel* 1 (Oct. 1916):30.

64. Fr. William Huffer, "Catholic Sioux Congress of South Dakota," *Indian Sentinel* 3 (Oct. 1923):148.

a present from the Congress for their foundress, Mother Catherine Drexel.[65]

Thus the Congresses showcased the Sioux art and showed that the missionaries valued it.

The other form of art that the Jesuits integrated into the Congresses was drama. At several Congresses in the 1930's, the Jesuits organized plays at which the children performed. At the 1931 Congress, the children from the Holy Rosary Mission School performed *Coaina: The Indian Rose*, which portrayed the life of a pious Algonquin Catholic girl named Coaina. The play encouraged devotion to the Virgin Mary and discouraged marriage between Catholics and non-Christians.[66] The Jesuits realized that the plays placed the children in roles that aided them in learning the religious values that the Jesuits sought to instill in them.

At the 1938 Congress, the children of the Holy Rosary Mission School presented *The Princess of the Mohawks*, a play about the Mohawk woman Kateri Tekakwitha. Tekakwitha was born in New York in 1656 near a Jesuit mission. The Jesuits instructed her and when she reached the age of twenty, they baptized her. During her life the Jesuits recognized her as a model Catholic for enduring persecution from her fellow Mohawks on account of her faith. Desiring to pursue a religious vocation, she took a vow of chastity and made plans to found a convent. Even though she died at the age of twenty-four, she acquired a reputation for her sanctity.[67] The Church declared Tekakwitha venerable in 1943 and beatified her in 1980. These declarations helped demonstrate to the Sioux that the Church recognized exemplary Catholics of all nations.[68]

In *Princess of the Mohawks*, Tekakwitha endured the ridicule of her people, persevered in the faith, and died the death of a saint. After she died, she appeared to her people and assured them of God's love for them. This play also placed in stark contrast the Christian life of Tekakwitha and the life and values of the medicine man who was the prime villain in the play.[69] By portraying the life of a Native American Catholic, this play provided the Sioux with a Native American model with whom they could identify. The program for the play even stated quite clearly that Tekakwitha's virtues were worthy of imitation:

---

65. Joseph A. Luther, S.J., "Highlights from a Hundred Per Cent American Convention," *Jesuit Bulletin* 3 (Dec. 1924):13. Joseph A Luther, "A Real One Hundred Per Cent American Convention," *Woodstock Letters* 53 (1924):346, 351.

66. HRM 4-1-2, A.H. Dorsey, *Coaina: The Indian Rose* (Beatty: St. Xavier's Academy).

67. Ellen Walworth, "Our Little Sister Kateri Tekakwitha, the Lily of the Mohawks," *Indian Sentinel* (1908):9.

68. F.X. Weiser. S.J., *Kateri Tekakwitha* (Montreal: The Noteworthy Co. 1972), 164.

69. *Tom-Tom*, [Monthly journal of Holy Rosary Mission] 4 (June 1938):3-5, Holy Rosary Mission File, Archives of the Missouri Province of the Society of Jesus in St. Louis.

We present in dramatic form the life of the saintly Indian maiden, Kateri Tekakwitha, who by her virtuous life amidst countless hardships attained a high degree of sanctity and embodied in herself the highest Christian ideals. She is the noble exemplar of the virtues which Holy Rosary Mission is trying to foster in the souls of the Oglala Sioux. May the dramatization of her saintly life not only afford entertainment to all, but may it also prompt an imitation of her heroic life.[70]

In this play, as in *Coaina*, the actors and actresses wore not simply costumes but the elaborate traditional Sioux clothing, and this encouraged the children and those who attended the play to appreciate the Sioux art.

The Church actually encouraged the Native Americans to study the life of Tekakwitha thirty years before the Church declared her venerable. *The Sentinel* published several articles before 1943 which featured Tekakwitha. For instance, in her 1908 article to the *Sentinel*, Mary Walworth quoted the petition that circulated among the Catholics of several Native American nations in 1884 and which they sent to pope Leo XIII:

Though we Indians are very poor and miserable, yet Our Maker had great pity on us and gave us the Catholic religion. Moreover, he had pity on us again and gave us Catherine Tekakwitha. This holy virgin, and Indian like ourselves, being favored by Jesus Christ with a great grace, grew up very good, had a great love for Our Maker, and died good and holy, and is now glorious in heaven, as we believe, and prays for us all. This virgin, we believe, was given to us from God as a great favor, for she is our little sister. . . . We beg thee with the whole of our hearts to speak and say: "You Indians, my children, take Catherine as an object of your veneration in the church, because she is holy and is in heaven."[71]

By publishing this petition and other articles about Tekakwitha, the BCIM demonstrated that it took Tekakwitha's cause seriously and tried to raise support for it.

In their efforts to illustrate the universality of the Catholic Church, the Jesuits recounted and praised Tekakwitha's virtues. Surviving copies of the earliest sermons that the Jesuits gave at St. Francis and Holy Rosary showed that they encouraged the imitation of Tekakwitha's example at least as early as 1907.[72] Furthermore, in 1921, the Director of the

---

70. HRM 1/1-2-1, Program, "The Princess of the Mohawks," Holy Rosary Mission, presented May 19 and 20, 1938.

71. Ellen Walworth, "Our Little Sister Kateri Tekakwitha, the Lily of the Mohawks," *Indian Sentinel* (1908):5.

72. SFM 7-3-7, Eugene Buechel, S.J., "All Saints' Day: On Heaven," sermon, Holy Rosary Mission, Nov. 1, 1907.

BCIM sent Louis Goll, S.J., of Holy Rosary Mission a copy of Tekak-witha's life and referred to her saying,

> This saintly Indian maiden should be better known among the In-dians and the white people too, and we should make it our own affair to spread a knowledge of her life and virtues.[73]

Goll replied that he was eager to comply, and promised to put a large picture of Tekakwitha in the girls dormitory and name that building "Tekakwitha Hall."[74]

The children of Holy Rosary Mission also performed the play *Tekak-witha* on Easter in 1933.[75] In this play, the Jesuits used traditional Sioux symbols to communicate their message in the play. A description of the play among the Jesuits' papers said:

> The White Eagle feather in [Tekakwitha's] hair is very symbolic. Because the Indians believed that the eagle could soar higher than any other bird, they used its feathers as symbols of the closeness of the wearer to the Great Spirit. It connotes highmindedness. Only the favorite daughter of the family was given the feather af-ter an elaborate ceremony.[76]

In 1935 the Holy Rosary Mission school children performed another play about Tekakwitha. Describing the play in a *Sentinel* article dedicated to Tekakwitha, Joseph Zimmerman, S.J., of Holy Rosary Mission, wrote:

> The memory of this noble Indian maiden will not perish. Tekak-witha lives. In our Indian Mission schools her life and her vir-tues are being constantly represented to the young and old by the Indian children, when they re-enact her story in the play, "Lily of the Mohawk." This is one of the great events of the year for our 335 Sioux Indian children and their parents here at Holy Rosary. . . . Clad in the rare, beautiful old robes, once worn on great occasions by their parents, the young actors were splendid.[77]

Thus both at the Congresses and in the schools, the Jesuits emphasized Tekakwitha, and the plays allowed the children to learn about her life. The plays about Tekakwitha also gave the Lakotas a strong woman as a role model and heroine.

---

73. BCIM 1-126-2, Fr. Ketcham to Fr. Goll, S.J., June 17, 1921.

74. BCIM 1-126-2, Fr. Goll to Fr. Ketcham, June 22, 1921.

75. HRM 2/1-1-8, "Chronicles of the Sisters of St. Francis," 1933 entry. *Calumet,* (July 1933).

76. HRM 1/1-2-1, Description of pictures taken at the play "Princess of the Mohawks," Holy Rosary Mission, May 19-20, 1938.

77. Joseph Zimmerman, S.J., "Kateri Tekakwitha Still Lives," *Indian Sentinel* 15 (Fall 1935):87.

Since the children came to the Congresses, the plays and many other activities allowed the children to take part in this event. The boys served as acolytes at Mass, and both boys and girls sang in the choir.[78] At some Congresses, the priests gave them their diplomas for completing grammar school.[79] The children also received first communion, and participated in processions at the Congresses, particularly the crowning of the Queen of the Holy Rosary.[80] The mission band, composed of Lakota students and conducted by Andrew Hartman, S.J., of St. Francis Mission, was another familiar attraction which provided many musical performances throughout the Congress.

At the Congresses, certain practices became traditions. One Bene-dictine priest who attended the Congress in 1939 remarked that "three special ceremonies cannot be omitted at an Indian Congress: the hand-shaking, the visit to the cemetery, and the visit to the nearby sick."[81] Usually walking together in a procession, the Sioux visited the cemetery at which they prayed for the departed.[82] Each Congress also closed with the handshaking ceremony. In this ceremony, all the people formed a large circle and each person went around the circle shaking hands with everyone.[83] Though the precise origin of the handshaking ceremony is unclear, the circle was an important organizing symbol in Sioux ceremo-nies. Most likely they combined Sioux traditions with the Western custom of handshaking to form a new Sioux tradition.

From 1890 to 1939 the Congresses were much the same in manage-ment, structure and content. At the Congresses the Sioux participated in processions, the mission band played, the priests administered the sacra-ments, the bishop often attended, the catechists preached, the delegates voted on resolutions, the Sioux held feasts, and the Sioux managed the Congresses from the start. Even their attitude towards keeping the man-agement of the Congress in their hands was consistent. For example at the 1931 Congress, two delegates "introduced the motion that [the deter-mination of the site of] all future Congresses should be left in the hands of the Bishop and any reservation could apply for the Congress."[84] The delegates voted and denied the motion demonstrating that they wanted to

---

78. "The Sioux Congress," *Indian Sentinel* 1 (Oct. 1916):27.

79. HRM 4-1-2, Francis Bull Head (Congress Secretary), "Sioux Indian Congress – Holy Rosary Mission: May 29-31, 1931," p.1

80. Bull Head, 2.

81. Fr. Edward Berheide, O.S.B., "Crow Hill Indian Congress." *Indian Sentinel* 19 (Sept. 1939):100.

82. William Huffer, "The Little Congress," *Indian Sentinel* 3 (Oct. 1923):150.

83. Alfred Meyer, O.S.B., "The Gathering of the Sioux Clans," *Indian Sentinel* 21 (Sept. 1941):100, 110.

84. HRM 4-1-2 Francis Bull Head, (Congress Secretary) "Sioux Indian Congress – Holy Rosary Mission: May 29-31, 1931," p.5

remain responsible for the organization of the Congresses. Later in that Congress they decided among themselves where to hold the next Congress.[85] Just as they opposed Marty's proposal to hold separate Congresses, they again resisted giving the bishop the authority to determine where to hold the Congresses.

The Congress's success was due to many factors. One of the elements that made the Congresses appealing was that all of the Sioux, even the children, were actively involved. The plays, the processions, the singing, the speeches, the catechizing, the sacraments, and the meetings allowed all the people to participate actively. By emphasizing ritual, the Congresses also meshed with the traditional Sioux way of celebrating. Moreover, the Congresses incorporated aspects of Sioux tradition such as oratory, architecture, feasts, organizational customs, and the tradition of the annual Sioux council. Building on Sioux customs and sometimes transforming them, the Congresses combined Sioux, American, and Catholic customs together into one celebration. Finally, the Congresses did not simply preserve the Sioux custom of holding national councils, but they actually restored this custom to the Sioux. In the 1870's and 1880's, the government divided the Sioux bands and restricted them to different reservations in the Dakota Territory. This undermined their national unity and obstructed their ability to hold their traditional national councils. The Catholic Sioux Congresses returned the tradition of annual councils to the Sioux, and unified the Sioux Catholics on the different reservations.

---

85. *Ibid.*, 5.

CHAPTER FOUR

Lakota Catechists

REALIZING THAT THE ESTABLISHMENT OF A NATIVE CLERGY AT A FOREIGN mission always helped to spread the Catholic faith, the Church historically promoted a native clergy. In the twentieth century, several popes restated this policy in their mission encyclicals. In *Maximum Illud* (1919), Benedict XV wrote:

> Anyone who has charge of a mission must make it his special concern to secure and train local candidates for the sacred ministry. In this policy lies the greatest hope for new Churches. For the local priest, one with his people by birth, by nature, by his sympathies and his aspiration, is remarkably effective in appealing to their mentality and thus attracting them to the faith. . . . For the local clergy is not to be trained merely to perform the humbler duties of the ministry, acting as the assistants of foreign priests. On the contrary, they must be able to take up God's word as equals so that some day they will be able to enter upon the spiritual leadership of their people.[1]

Similarly, Pius XI also emphasized the necessity of a native clergy in *Rerum Ecclesiae* (1926):

> Before anything else, We call your attention to building up a native clergy. If you do not work with all your might to attain this purpose, We assert that not only will your apostolate be crippled, but it will become an obstacle and impediment to the establishment and organization of the Church in those countries.[2]

Throughout this encyclical, the pope forcefully advocated the establishment of a native clergy, stated that all peoples were equal in all ways, and warned the missionaries against any bias, condescension, or racism.[3]

---

1. J. Neuner, S.J. and J. DuPuis, S.J., *The Christian Faith in the Doctrinal Documents of the Catholic Church* (New York: Alba, 1982), 311.

2. Pius XI, *Rerum Ecclesiae. The Papal Encyclicals: 1903-1939*, Claudia Carlin, ed., (Raleigh: McGrath Publishing, 1981), p. 285, paragraph 19.

Preferring native priests to foreign missionaries, Benedict XV and Pius XI wanted a native clergy as soon as possible in all the missions because the native priests knew the culture and language better than the foreign priests. The native priests, they agreed, should ultimately serve as bishops.[4] Addressing the missionaries, Pius XI said: "You should prefer the native priests to all others for it is they who will one day govern the churches and Catholic communities founded by your sweat and labor."[5] Citing the earliest Christian communities as a model, Pius XI noted that the Apostles put converted natives in charge of their communities.[6] He added that since wars and social conflicts sometimes resulted in the expulsion of foreign missionaries, a native clergy would not be hindered by such events.[7] In short, both Benedict XV and Pius XI agreed that natives made better missionaries than foreigners. In regard to appointments to the episcopate, they advocated giving preferential treatment to the native clergy for the purpose of establishing a truly catholic or universal Church.

Pius XI, however, went even further than his predecessor in promoting a liberal interpretation of mission theology. In *Rerum Ecclesiae*, he encouraged the missionaries to

> establish entirely new Congregations, which would correspond better with the genius and character of the natives and which would be more in keeping with the needs and the spirit of the different countries.[8]

In the Dakotas, the institution of the native catechists coincided well with the Lakota culture, and the Catholic Church had long encouraged the establishment of native catechists. In addition to supporting the creation of organizations that conformed to native culture, Pius XI renewed the call for native catechists in this encyclical.[9]

Realizing that too few priests were available to serve the pastoral needs of all the Lakotas, the Jesuits at Holy Rosary and St. Francis made a concerted effort to recruit Lakota catechists. From 1900 to 1940 each mission, at all times, maintained a staff of about ten Lakota catechists.[10]

---

3. *Ibid.*, p.287-288, paragraph 26.

4. *Ibid.*, p.286-288, paragraphs 20, 21, 26.

5. *Ibid.*, p.288, paragraph 26.

6. *Ibid.*, p.286, paragraph 21.

7. *Ibid.*, p.286, paragraph 22.

8. *Ibid.*, p.288, paragraph 27.

9. *Ibid.*, p.286-288, paragraphs 21, 27.

10. This is a list of some of the catechists who served at either the Holy Rosary Mission or St. Francis Mission in the period of 1886-1945: Nicholas Black Elk, Ivan Star-Comes-Out, Emil Afraid-of-Hawk, Joe Horn Cloud, Edward White Crow, John Foolhead, Amos Fast Horse, Joe Richard, Peter Bald Eagle, Reyes Hernandez, George Apple, Silas Fills-the-Pipe, Tom Yellow Bull, Tom Fast Wolf, Ben Marrowbone, Albert Red Horn, William Red Hair, John Big Crow, Harry Bluethunder, Joseph White Hat, Dan Hollow

Most of the catechists spoke Lakota and several did not speak English. The catechists were men, and most were married elders. By appointing the elders as catechists, the Jesuits built upon the Lakota tradition of respect for elders. If the Jesuits recruited simply the young English speakers as catechists, it would have undermined their social structure. But since the elders were married, the priesthood was not open to them.

The Lakotas considered the catechists to be the community leaders, and the position was quite a time consuming job. The catechists took pride in their positions and often served for decades: Silas Fills-the-Pipe, Nick Black Elk, White Crow, John Foolhead, and Ivan Star-Comes-Out were prominent catechists, each of whom served in this position for over 20 years.[11] But even though the catechists had a great deal of responsibility on the reservations, they received only a small salary of $5-15 per month. Sometimes, however, they received compensation in the form of housing, and the Jesuits often requested donations through the *Indian Sentinel* to fund the construction of houses for catechists. Fr. Buechel of St. Francis Mission was especially successful in acquiring contributions for the catechists. By working with the Issac Jogues Mission Circle, a group of 200 women in Jersey City who supported the Catholic mission effort, he was able to acquire numerous contributions for catechists. He wrote the Mission Circle hundreds of letters concerning the progress of the mission, the catechists that they supported, and the chapels or catechists houses that the Jesuits built with their contributions.[12]

Buechel and the other Jesuits sought funding for the catechists because they realized that they were essential for the mission. Since Pine Ridge and Rosebud were such large sparsely populated tracts of land and since the horse and buggy was the only means of transportation across the reservation until the 1930's, catechists served the needs of the Lakota Catholics when the Jesuits were unavailable. The reservation was composed mostly of small groups of a few houses that were separated by large distances. To serve all these widely separated people, a few Jesuits rode

---

Horn Bear, Frank Arrowside, John Big Crow, George Moccasin Face, Leo Sharp Fish, Issac White Crane Walking, William Crow Good Voice, Noah Yankton, Joe Red Willow, Charles Giroux, Albert Long Soldier, Sam Little Bull, Louis Mousseau, Alexander Two Two, Tom Little Bull, James Grass, John Boyer, William Randall, Issac Iron Shell, Tom Larvie, Jesse Chasing Hawk, Albert Guerue, George Low Cedar, Felix Walking Eagle, Peter Red Elk, Peter Pourier, Rex Long Visitor, Oliver Lone Wolf, Jacob Kills-in-Sight, Joseph Horned Antelope, Charles Black Bear, Joseph Red Eyes, and Ben Leading Fighter.

11. BCIM 1-161-11, Sialm to Hughes, March 20, 1926. BCIM 14/1-4-2, Floyd Brey, S.J., "Fills-the-Pipe Entertains," *Calumet* (July 1934). Placidus Sialm, S.J., "White Crow: Sioux Catechist," *Indian Sentinel* 13 (Summer 1933):140. HRM 7-17-(5-7), Placidus Sialm, S.J., *Camp Churches*, p.92.

12. SFM 7-1-(6-9), SFM 7-2-(3-5), Alice Boyle and Viola Manning wrote numerous letters to Fr. Buechel.

circuits that began at the St. Francis or Holy Rosary missions. Taking a
month to complete the circuit, they traveled to each of the communities or
clusters of houses on Pine Ridge and Rosebud to offer Mass and adminis-
ter the sacraments. The Jesuits held Mass either in the small chapels in
each community, or in the homes of those who were ill, infirm, or too far
removed from the chapels to make the trip. Before they continued their
journey to the next stop, they spent the night in the Lakotas' houses.
They traveled to different people's houses bringing them gifts of bread
and vegetables from the mission, offering Mass in their house, and spend-
ing a day or a few days living with them before moving on to the next
place.[13]

Since the circuit took a month to complete, the Jesuits could offer
Mass in each community only once a month. On the other Sundays the
catechists held the service at which they preached, read the gospel, and
led the people in prayers and hymns in Lakota. During Lent, the catechists went to the houses of each Catholic family to pray and say the rosary.[14] Also in this season, they gathered the laity in the chapels, sometimes five times a week, and made the stations of the cross.[15] They also
counseled people who had marital troubles, sometimes bringing the couple
right into the St. Joseph's or St. Mary's society meeting.[16] Of course, the
catechists often taught the children as well as adults about the Catholic
Church, and also tried to convert non-Catholics.

The catechists were responsible for giving funeral services, exhort-
ing people to stay away from drink and peyote, speaking at all the gatherings, and praying with the sick and other Catholics on special occasions.
Since the Lakotas frequently asked for priests and catechists to pray over
the sick even if the illness was minor, the work of the catechists was necessary.[17] When people were quite sick or in any kind of distress, the catechist or Jesuit went over to that family, prayed with them, and often
stayed with them for several days.[18] The Lakotas especially appreciated
that the catechist or priest stayed with them since visiting was an important part of the Lakota culture.

From 1905 to 1918, the BCIM Director, William Ketcham, worked
with the Jesuits to acquire funding for the catechists and organize their
efforts. Ketcham was a strong supporter of Native American catechists in

---

13. Jessie Crow, interviews, Oglala, S.D. June and Oct. 1992.

14. *Ibid.* Jessie Eagleheart, interview, Kyle, S.D. June, 1992.

15. Alexander Cody, S.J., "Chief Big Head," *Indian Sentinel* 2 (July 1920):140-143.

16. Fr. Bernard Fagan, interview, Rosebud, S.D., May 1992.

17. HRM 7-19-10, Henry Westropp, S.J., "Bits of Missionary Life Among the Sioux," n.d.
pamphlet, p.7.

18. Leo Chasing-In-Timber, interview, Two Strikes district, Rosebud Reservation, S.D.,
Oct. 1992.

all the Catholic missions, and he continually solicited donations for their support. In a letter published in *The Calumet* he wrote:

> The native catechist is a necessary factor in propagating and maintaining the Faith among the Indians. . . . As the missionaries are so few in number . . . so the local catechist is a necessity, if the people are to have religious exercises and instructions of some sort every Sunday. The catechist becomes the teacher and the leader, and the work of the Church under his supervision goes on unremittingly. . . . It is the catechist who can do the most in the homes, encourage attendance at religious services, prepare the old and infirm for the sacraments, smooth the way for the coming of the missionary, not only among Catholics, but non-Catholics and pagans. . . . I am entirely familiar with the splendid work done by the catechists everywhere.[19]

Ketcham also worked with the Marquette League to acquire financial support for the catechists. Through their periodical, *The Calumet*, the Marquette league solicited donations from their subscribers for the support of catechists.[20] Likewise, the Jesuits wrote many letters published in the *Sentinel* in which they requested donations for the monthly salary of catechists and for funds to construct houses for them.[21] The catechists themselves also contributed to the *Sentinel* so that the readers knew of their work.[22]

One of the catechists at Holy Rosary Mission, Nick Black Elk, was especially prominent, and John Neihardt wrote a rendition of part of his life in *Black Elk Speaks*. Neihardt, however, never told of Black Elk's life as a Catholic, even though Black Elk was a Catholic from 1904 to 1950 when he died. Black Elk led a fascinating life. He fought in the battle of Little Big Horn in 1876. Later he toured the United States and Europe with Buffalo Bill.[23] At this time, he became interested in Christianity, and in a letter he dictated when he was in Europe in 1889, he quoted I Corinthians (13: 1-3): ". . . And though I bestow all my goods to feed the poor, and though I give my body to be burned, and have not charity, it profiteth me nothing." In the same letter, he also expressed a desire to see "where they killed Jesus."[24] When he returned to Pine

19. BCIM 14/1-4-2, William Ketcham, *The Calumet* (April 1917) supplement.

20. BCIM 14/1-4-2, "Indians Trained as Catechists," *The Calumet* (July 1916).

21. Leo Cunningham, "A Catholic Meeting House," *Indian Sentinel* 9 (Spring 1929):57. Otto Moorman, S.J., "Passing of the Log Chapel," *Indian Sentinel* 8 (Fall 1928):161.

22. Emil Afraid-of-Hawk, "Sam Little Bull," *Indian Sentinel* 23 (April 1943):63-64. Francis Bull Head, "Sioux Catholic Congress at Holy Rosary Mission," *Indian Sentinel* 31 (Fall 1931):173-174.

23. Fr. Joseph Zimmerman, S.J., "Catechist Nick Black Elk," *Indian Sentinel* 30 (Oct. 1950):101-102.

24. Raymond De Mallie, *The Sixth Grandfather* (Lincoln: University of Nebraska, 1984), 10.

Ridge, however, he continued his practice as a medicine man, and also was a Ghost Dancer who fought at Wounded Knee. Black Elk married Kate War Bonnet, and she had their children baptized in the Catholic Church in 1895.[25] In 1904, Black Elk decided to join the Catholic Church, and Father Joseph Lindebner, S.J., of Holy Rosary Mission baptized him. Following a common missionary practice, Lindebner named Black Elk after the saint on whose feast day he received baptism. Years later, a Holy Rosary publication described his conversion:

> According to Black Elk's daughter Lucy Looks Twice, Fr. Lindebner came upon her father during a curing ceremony for a sick boy. The priest destroyed Black Elk's instruments, told him to leave, and administered the Last Sacraments to the boy whom he first baptized. When Fr. Lindebner was through, he found Black Elk sitting outside dejected as though he had lost all his power. Black Elk accepted the priest's invitation to come to Holy Rosary Mission. After two weeks of preparation, Black Elk asked for baptism, and received it on Dec. 6, 1904, the feast of St. Nicholas.[26]

Lindebner and the other Jesuits vigorously opposed the *yuwipi*, a ceremony which the Lakota medicine men used for the purpose of healing people. Often they tried to convince the Lakotas that these ceremonies were evil, and they also attempted to stop these ceremonies when they encountered them. But though Lindebner did desecrate Black Elk's ceremony, he did not force Black Elk into the Catholic Church. Black Elk was already predisposed to the Catholic Church because his family was Catholic. He could have ignored the Jesuits and retained his traditional beliefs as some medicine men chose to do.

From the Jesuits' point of view, Black Elk's conversion was especially significant since he was a medicine man, which in the Jesuits' eyes made him an arch-infidel. Shortly after his baptism, Black Elk became a catechist, and this was especially helpful to the Jesuits since he was the ideal candidate to persuade the Lakotas to refrain from participating in the ceremonies the medicine men performed. As a catechist, Black Elk was a great help to the Jesuits, and they recognized him as a model Catholic.

Black Elk was also a zealous missionary who traveled long distances to spread the Catholic faith, and both the BCIM and the Jesuits supported his missionary work. Convinced of the value and potential of the catechists, Ketcham planned to use Sioux catechists to act as missionaries to other Native American nations. In 1908, Ketcham and Father Henry Westropp, S.J., of Holy Rosary Mission, sent Lakota catechists, including

---

25. *Ibid.*, 13.

26. HRM 5-1-4, Fr. Seminara, S.J., Fr. Manhart. S.J., Cassidy, Steinmetz, S.J., and Simurdiak, *Canku Wakan (Sacred Road): The Story of Holy Rosary Mission*, pamphlet, Holy Rosary Mission, 1981, 9-10.

Black Elk, to evangelize the Arapahos in Wyoming.[27] On May 31, 1908, the *Sinasapa Wocekiye Taeyanpaha: Catholic Sioux Herald* published Black Elk's letter describing his trip:

> We [Black Elk and Joe Red Willow, a Lakota catechist on Pine Ridge] are invited by a majority of people, and we had a really big meeting with the Arapahos and what they want to know about is the St. Joseph and St. Mary's Societies. So we did the best we can. We told the Arapaho people that we, too, are very poor, and that there is no difference between them and us because we are both Indians. And they asked me to say a few words to the members there, so I told them about the St. Joseph and the St. Mary's organization. First how to conduct a meeting, and then I told them about the order of the meeting: that you've got to have a president, vice-president, secretary, treasurer, a critic, and a doorkeeper. And they were all so enthused that they are going to start their own St. Joseph and St. Mary Society there. And then they asked me how to pray, so this is what I said to them. When you say the Our Father, remember that there is one Father and one Son. This is what you've got to believe. And after my talk, they were so interested so they want us to go back to the land of the Arapahos again, in the near future. . . . They had a big election of officers [of the St. Mary's and St. Joseph's Societies] while we were there. [The names of the elected officers followed]. . . . The next Catholic Congress is in Rosebud. These officials are planning to come there and to get more ideas while the meeting is going on.[28]

The correspondence between Ketcham and Westropp indicated that Black Elk was quite a traveler and was willing to undertake these missionary expeditions. Later that year in November, Ketcham and Westropp also financed Black Elk's month-long expedition to the Winnebagos.[29]

In 1908 Westropp wrote Ketcham that Black Elk was anxious to travel spreading the faith among the Shoshones:

> An Arap[aho] catechist wants you to help him put up a log-cabin chapel among the Shoshones. Bl. Elk wants to go there and Fr. [?] has just applied for Joe Red Willow. I will try to get Joe to go. I am certain that the Indians can get Indian converts quicker than any white priests.[30]

---

27. BCIM 1-55-3, Ketcham to Westropp, Dec 11, 1907. BCIM 1-58-26, Westropp to Ketcham, April 2, 1908; Ketcham to Westropp, Oct. 8, 1908. In his letter to Westropp, Ketcham refers to a letter he wrote to Nick Black Elk. BCIM 1-67-16, Westropp to Ketcham, Feb 2, 1910.

28. Michael Steltenkamp, *No More Screech Owl,* unpublished manuscript Marquette University Archives, 259-260.

29. BCIM 1-58-26, Westropp to Ketcham, Nov. 8, 1908; Ketcham to Westropp, Dec. 12, 1908.

Because of their Native American heritage, the Lakota catechists, Westropp believed, were ideal lay missionaries and were able to influence the Native Americans whom the Jesuits were not able to approach as easily. Black Elk also demonstrated his willingness to work as a missionary in a letter he wrote to Ketcham in 1909:

> The Assiniboins in Canada want the prayer [the Catholic faith]. They want to see me very much. The other thing is this: I want to take care that many children in North and South Dakota join the Society for the Preservation of the Faith. Therefore I want to go round for 2 or 3 months.[31]

Black Elk's mission to other Native American nations and different Sioux bands demonstrated his dedication to these missions since he had to remain with them for long periods of time.

Westropp believed that Black Elk accomplished a great deal among the Lakotas and the other nations he visited, and he often complimented Black Elk for his work (c.1909):

> I would say that Nick is a very faithful fellow and when he travels he always has the spread of the faith in view, even if he goes in business. He has been a close friend of mine for 3 years and I don't know if it is any praise to say of him that we both have exactly the same ideas. It was always my idea to get him to travel among the tribes and make them lean toward the faith.[32]

Westropp also credited Black Elk with many conversions (c.1910):

> One of the most fervent of [the catechists] is a *quondam* [onetime] ghost dancer and chief of the medicine men. His name is Black Elk. Ever since his conversion he has been a fervent apostle and he has gone around like a second St. Paul, trying to convert his tribesmen to Catholicism. He has made many converts.[33]

Several Jesuits including Westropp often compared Black Elk to St. Paul since Paul once opposed the Church and then became a zealous missionary. Westropp also noted that Black Elk had the Lakota talent for oratory, and wrote that "on a moment's notice he can pour forth a flood of oratory holding his hearers spellbound."[34] Black Elk often traveled with

---

30. BCIM 1-58-26, Westropp to Ketcham, Sept. 15, 1908.

31. BCIM 1-63-3, Nick Black Elk to Ketcham, Pine Ridge, Sept. 7, 1909.

32. BCIM 1-63-4, Ketcham to Westropp, Oct 14, 1909. Westropp's response to the above letter was written on that same letter.

33. Henry Westropp, S.J., "In the Land of the Wigwam," pamphlet, c.1910. p.12, Holy Rosary Mission folders, Missouri Province Archives of the Society of Jesus in St. Louis.

34. HRM 7-19-10, Henry Westropp, S.J., "Bits of Missionary Life Among the Sioux," N.D. c. 1910, p.8.

Westropp and in 1910, they traveled together to the Sisseton Reservation in South Dakota to evangelize the Sioux people there.[35] Moreover, in 1913, Westropp arranged for Black Elk and Ivan Star-Comes-Out to help start a mission to the Sioux on the Yankton Reservation, located in South Dakota and Nebraska, since no priest could be found.[36] Through his years as a catechist Black Elk traveled hundreds of miles to spread the Catholic faith, visited several different reservations, attended numerous Congresses, dictated over a dozen letters to a Catholic newspaper, and served as a missionary to several Native American nations.

Father Ketcham organized several missionary expeditions in which he sent Sioux catechists to different Native American reservations. In 1908, he spent so much time and effort organizing and financing the catechists' trips that he wrote, "to an onlooker it would appear that I have become a bureau for traveling Indians."[37] The catechists also worked and traveled with the Jesuits of St. Francis and Holy Rosary when they visited other Native American nations. In 1910, Digmann wrote that he sent a Lakota man to the Winnebago Reservation to assist Westropp, who was already there.[38] When traveling to Oklahoma in 1910, Westropp also took two catechists with him.[39]

In some cases Ketcham even wanted to send Lakota catechists great distances to start missions. Realizing the problems involved in sending married men on missionary expeditions to distant reservations, Ketcham tried to interest an unmarried Lakota man in moving to the Mescalaro/Apache reservation to start a mission. In a letter to Digmann in 1910, Ketchem suggested that a Lakota catechist "might find a wife among the Apaches. This would give him rights in the tribe. . . . It would be a planting of Catholicity where we have only a nominal adherence."[40] After trying for a year, Ketcham and Digmann could find no one willing to go to the Mescalaro/Apache reservation.[41] Although the Lakota catechists enjoyed traveling, they were reluctant to move to other reservations. In the Lakota society, family ties were strong and they were loath to break them. The catechists' life, families, and extended families were on Pine Ridge and Rosebud, and though they were happy to visit other reservations, usually they did not want to remain at them for long periods of time.

35. DeMallie, *The Sixth Grandfather*, 21.

36. HRM 7-17-(5-7), Placidus Sialm, S.J., *Camp Churches*, manuscript, p.84. DeMallie. *The Sixth Grandfather*, p.24.

37. BCIM 1-58-26, Ketcham to Westropp, Dec. 1908. DeMallie, 19.

38. BCIM 1-67-16, Digmann to Ketcham, Aug. 6, 1910.

39. BCIM 1-67-16, Digmann to Ketcham, Sept 28, 1910 and Oct 5, 1910.

40. BCIM 1-67-16, Ketcham to Digmann, Nov 5, 1910.

41. BCIM 1-73-1, Secretary of BCIM to Westropp, Oct. 9, 1911.

In 1918, Ketcham also tried to find a Lakota catechist for the Klamath Reservation in Oregon where the Klamaths, the Modocs and the Paiutes, lived. Since only two Catholics lived on this reservation, Ketcham wanted to send a Lakota catechist there to evangelize these Native Americans and establish a Catholic community.[42] He was willing to entrust to the catechist the responsibility of attracting these Native Americans to the Catholic Church, converting them, and founding a new mission with little or no help from the clergy. In 1919, Ketcham and Henry Grotegeers, S.J., Holy Rosary Mission Superior at the time, sent Charles Giroux, a Lakota catechist, to the Klamath Reservation and funded his transport and expenses.[43] Though Giroux stayed four months at Klamath and returned to Pine Ridge, he desired to return to this mission at a later time.[44]

The problem that Ketcham faced was that he found it difficult to obtain a commitment from a catechist to remain for a long time at another reservation. When discussing the possibility of sending Lakota catechists to Klamath Falls and Warm Springs Reservations, he wanted a commitment of eight months to a year.[45] Giroux, however, was married and the mission to the Klamaths separated him from his wife, who stayed on Pine Ridge. Most if not all of the catechists were married and often had children, so Ketcham's idea to send the catechists to other reservations for a long time was not realistic in most cases.

By sending Lakota catechists as missionaries to other reservations, the Jesuits at Holy Rosary and St. Francis competed with Protestants who successfully did this on several reservations. In 1918, Fr. Placidus Sialm, S.J., of Holy Rosary commented on this situation:

> Father Westropp's idea to evangelize the Indians through Indians has some truth in it. If we can get "the right man" – it will be a success in many ways. The Protestants followed that plan of sending catechists from other reservations in many cases. And many of them "stick like flies". . . . I met the same system in Montana and Wyoming. If their Indians can do it why should ours not be able?[46]

The Episcopalians also had several Lakota catechists on the Pine Ridge and Rosebud reservations who competed with the Catholics.

To prepare the Lakota catechists to defend the Catholic Church and teach Lakota Catholics and non-Catholics about the Church, the Jesuits provided them with rigorous training. Beginning in 1922, 10 to 20 catechists underwent the Spiritual Exercises of St. Ignatius when they went on

---

42. BCIM 1-109-18, Ketcham to Louis Mousseau (catechist) Porcupine, S.D., August 6, 1918.

43. BCIM 1-114-15, Groteegers to Ketcham, Oct. 29, 1919.

44. BCIM 1-119-8, Grotegeers to Ketcham, May 11, 1920 and March 30, 1920.

45. BCIM 1-109-18, Ketcham to Sialm, S.J. June 28, 1918.

46. BCIM 1-109-18, Sialm to Ketcham, July 1, 1918.

their annual three-day retreats. To accompany his presentation of the exercises at the first retreat, Fr. Sialm showed them 60 pictures which illustrated the religious teachings he gave them. Sialm also reported that "the method of the examination of conscience especially pleased them, and they demanded that I should give it in writing so that they would not forget it afterwards."[47] Since the retreat had such an impact on them, the catechists asked the Jesuits to continue it.[48] Willingly, the Jesuits complied, making the retreat an annual event.

Like others who completed Ignatius's Spiritual Exercises, the catechists felt that the Exercises were a powerful experience. In 1923, Sialm recorded the reactions of the catechists to the exercises:

> "What I know," said Alexander Two Two, a few weeks ago, "I chiefly learned in the retreat last year." On the third day of that retreat, Nick Black Elk came to me with this very worthy resolution: "We catechists resolve never to commit a mortal sin. . . ." Nick Black Elk wished to invite all the Sioux catechists to the coming retreat.[49]

The retreats impressed the catechists and Nick Black Elk went on the annual retreat eight times.[50] The Jesuits were especially gratified that Ignatius's exercises appealed to the catechists, and they considered these exercises an effective way to deepen the spirituality of the catechists. In 1926, Sialm described the retreats:

> Undoubtably the Retreat is the best school for Catechists. It makes them intelligent Christians and zealous and content besides. The wealth of our Holy Catholic Religion becomes clear to them. . . . The Retreat makes them think and gives them arguments and reasons to defend the faith. They get their ammunition to fight the good fight for themselves and against the enemies of our church – the Protestant sects.[51]

In addition to illustrating the animosity between the Protestants and Catholics on the reservation, this passage showed that the Jesuits found the Spiritual Exercises to be a highly effective method for producing zealous catechists who were willing to defend and promote the faith. Thus the Exercises also were a course in apologetics for the catechists.

In their letters and articles, the Jesuits often wrote of the catechists' retreats and they described the catechists as devoted Catholics whose zeal and patience were admirable.[52] In 1918, in one of Sialm's letters to

---

47. Placidus Sialm, *Woodstock Letters* 51 (1922):305.

48. *Ibid.*

49. Placidus Sialm, S.J., "A Retreat to Catechists," *Indian Sentinel* 3 (April, 1923):78.

50. HRM 1/1-1-5, Nick Black Elk, Holy Rosary Mission, Pine Ridge, Jan 26, 1934.

51. BCIM 1-161-11, Fr. Sialm to Hughes, Director of the BCIM, March 20, 1926, p.2.

52. Eugene Buechel, "Joe White Hat," *Indian Sentinel* 17 (May 1937):79. Eugene Buechel,

Ketcham, he praised the abilities of his former catechist: "I had a very good catechist, Mr. Garfield, who did very much to prepare the Indians for my next coming, so much that I could baptize some almost at every visit."[53] Moreover, in his letter to BCIM Director J.B. Tennelly in 1929, Albert Riester, S.J., Holy Rosary Mission Superior from 1926 to 1932, also expressed his admiration for the catechists' work:

> We have at present twelve Indian Catechists on this Reservation.
> We need more. These catechists are paid ten dollars a month. . . .
> The Catechist is a very necessary person out in this Indian coun-
> try. . . . One can notice a difference in a district where there is a
> Catechist and where there is none.[54]

In 1939, Sialm wrote of his catechist Ivan Star-Comes-Out:

> Our faithful catechist, Ivan Star-Comes-Out, was really a model
> Christian Indian. He was honest industrious and dependable, a
> good husband and father, and active and loyal Catholic, the right
> hand man of the missionary of his district, and a respected leader
> among his own people, the Oglala Sioux. . . . He knew very little
> English, but he read and wrote his native language perfectly and
> was a fluent and effective speaker. He was in constant demand at
> Indian gatherings, even at non-Catholic meetings, where he had
> the opportunity, and used it, to explain our holy Faith to Indi-
> ans who would never have listened otherwise to Catholic doc-
> trine. . . . The catechists' inside knowledge of the temperament
> and needs of their own race helps them greatly at the Sunday
> service which they must conduct when the priest is not present.[55]

The Jesuits wrote many such letters praising the catechists' abilities, and describing them as diligent and charitable. They appreciated the Lakota catechists' knowledge of their own culture and realized that this knowledge helped the catechists convert the Lakotas.

Stephan McNamara, S.J., Holy Rosary Mission Superior from 1934 to 36, had similar words of praise for Black Elk, and described him as "having a rare gift of making clear and persuasive the teachings of his new faith."[56] In 1940, Fr. Joseph Zimmerman, S.J., from Holy Rosary, also attested to Black Elk's missionary diligence:

"Frank Arrowside," *Indian Sentinel* 16 (Sept. 1936):122. Placidus Sialm, "White Crow: Sioux Catechist," *Indian Sentinel* 13 (Summer 1933):140. Placidus Sialm, "Sioux Catechists' Retreat," *Indian Sentinel* 6 (Fall 1926):171-172. Placidus Sialm, "A Retreat to Catechists," *Indian Sentinel* 3 (April 1923):78.

53. BCIM 1-109-18, Sialm to Ketcham, July 1, 1918.

54. BCIM 1-186-9, Riester to Tennelly, Oct 4, 1929.

55. Placidus Sialm, S.J., "Ivan Star-Comes-Out," *Indian Sentinel* 19 (March 1939):44.

56. Stephan McNamara, "Black Elk and Brings White," *Indian Sentinel* 21 (Nov. 1941):139.

[A Jesuit] gave baptism to [Black Elk] and trained him for his many years as a catechist to his race – twenty-seven years on the Pine Ridge Reservation – two years at Yankton Agency – one year at Sisseton Agency [a Sioux reservation] – one year at St. Stephan's Wyoming among the Arapahos.[57]

But even though Black Elk served as a catechist, missionary, and member of the St. Joseph's society for such a long time, John Neihardt in *Black Elk Speaks* characterized Black Elk even in his later years as a non-Christian. Moreover, even though Neihardt wrote about the Ghost Dance in this book, he failed to point out that Christian beliefs had a large influence on the Ghost Dance Religion, and that the Ghost Dancers identified their messiah as Jesus. Describing a vision he had while he was a Ghost Dancer, Black Elk told Neihardt: "it seemed as though there were wounds in the palms of his hands. It seems to me on thinking it over that I have seen the son of the Great Spirit himself."[58] Neihardt, however, did not put this in *Black Elk Speaks*. Though he wrote down a rendition of Black Elk's life, Neihardt provided a distorted view because he failed to show that Christianity had a great impact on the Ghost Dancers, and also failed to report Black Elk's conversion to Catholicism.

Desiring to set the record straight about his life, Black Elk wrote several letters affirming his Catholic faith. In 1934 Black Elk was sick, and he thought he might be dying. Fortunately he recovered from his illness and lived until 1950. After recovering, he dictated a letter to his daughter Lucy Looks Twice in January, 1934, and she and Father Zimmerman both signed as witnesses. In this letter, Black Elk said:

> I shake hands with my white friends. Listen, I speak some true words. A white man made a book and told what I had spoken of olden times, but the new times he left out. So I speak again, a last word. I am now an old man. I called my priest to pray for me and to give me holy oil and the Holy Food, (the *Yutapi Wakan*). Now I will tell you the truth. Listen my friend. In the last thirty years I am different from what the white man wrote about me. I am a Christian. I was baptized thirty years ago by the Black-gown priest called Little Father (*Ate-ptecela*). After that time all call me Nick Black Elk. Most of the Sioux Indians know me. I am now converted to the true Faith in God the Father, the Son and the Holy Ghost. I say in my own Sioux Lakota language: *Ateunyanpi:* – Our Father who art in heaven, hallowed be thy name – as Christ taught us to say. I say the Apostle's Creed and I believe every word of it. I believe in seven holy Sacraments of the Catholic Church. I myself received now six of them; Baptism, Confirmation, Penance, Holy Communion, Holy

---

57. Joseph Zimmerman, S.J. published newsletter, Holy Rosary Mission, Pine Ridge Educational Society, Feast of Christ the King, 1940, p.2.

58. Steinmetz, *Pipe, Bible and Peyote*, 180-181.

Marriage, and Extreme Unction. I was for several years a regular companion of several missionaries going out campaigning for Christ among my people. I was nearly twenty years the helper of priests and acted as a Catechist in several camps. So I knew my Catholic Religion better than many white people. For eight years I made the regular Retreat given by the priest for Catechists and I learned much of the faith in those days. I can give reasons for my faith. I know Whom I have believed and my faith is not vain. My family is all baptized. All my children and grand-children belong to the Black-gown church and I am glad of that and I wish that all should stay in that holy way. I know what St. Peter said about those who fall away from the holy Commandments. You white friends should read 2 Peter 2: 20-22. I tell my people to stay in the right way which Christ and His church have taught us. I will never fall back from the true faith in Christ. Thirty years ago I was a real Indian and knew a little about the Great Spirit – the *Wakantanka.* . . . I was proud, perhaps I was brave, perhaps I was a good Indian: but now I am better. St. Paul also turned better when he was converted. I now know that the prayer of the Catholic Church is better than the Sun-dance or the Ghost-dance. Old Indians danced that kind for their own glory. They cut themselves so that the blood flowed. But Christ was nailed to the Cross for sin and he took away our sins. The old Indian prayers did not make people better. The medicine men looked for their own glory and for presents. Christ taught us to be humble and to stop sin. Now I hate sin. I want to be straight as the Black-gown church teaches us to be straight to save my soul for heaven. This I want to do. I cheerfully shake hands with you all.[59]

Just as the Jesuits, Black Elk condemned the medicine men, the Sun Dance and the Ghost Dance, but still he did not reject the Lakota religion as being wholly evil.

In another letter he wrote in September 1934, Black Elk complained that Neihardt did not send him half the proceeds from the sales of *Black Elk Speaks* as he promised.[60] In that letter, Black Elk said that he asked Neihardt to include in his book that he was a Catholic:

I also asked [John Neihardt] to put at the end of this story that I was not a pagan but have been converted into the Catholic Church in which I work as a Catechist for more than 25 years. I've quit all these pagan works.[61]

Though the Jesuits were successful in recruiting many Lakota catechists, they were never able to attract any of the Lakota men to the priesthood. The Jesuits or the nuns, however, were successful in recruiting a

59. HRM 1/1-1-5, Nick Black Elk, letter, Holy Rosary Mission, Pine Ridge, Jan 26, 1934.
60. HRM 1/1-1-5, Nicholas Black Elk, letter, Oglala, S.D. Sept 20, 1934.
61. *Ibid.*

few Lakota sisters, and by 1940 three women from Holy Rosary mission became nuns.[62] The Lakotas, however, had to wait until 1985 for their first priest, Fr. C.P. Jordan, to be ordained. Explaining the paucity of vocations in 1904, Digmann wrote:

> Bishop Marty has tried four Indian boys and the Church wished it, the door to the priesthood is open to any who have the vocation, but it is not given to all and many 'do not take the word.' So far none has been found.[63]

Here Digmann indicated that the absence of Lakota priests was not, at least solely, due to lack of effort on the part of the Church. Several factors might have contributed to the lack of the Lakotas' interest in that vocation.[64] Celibacy was never a Lakota tradition and single Lakota men were rare. Additionally, to become a priest, a Lakota man would have had to live off the reservation for years, and study in a Western academic setting. The Lakotas, however, found breaking their ties to the reservations quite difficult. Even the young Lakotas felt that attending college off the reservation was a great and often insurmountable strain. Though the Lakotas were formidable orators, seminary study focused on reading and writing in English and Latin, and was an environment that was foreign to their culture.[65] Besides, the Lakota men did not have any immediate desire to become priests, and most were married. Those who wanted to serve the Catholic Church became catechists and they took pride in these positions.

Despite the success of the Lakota catechists, the greatest flaw in the Holy Rosary and St. Francis missions was the Jesuits' inability to establish a native clergy. In *Rerum Ecclesiae*, Pius XI wrote that unless missionaries built up a native clergy their "apostolate [would] be crippled."[66] Whether the Jesuits, the Lakota traditions, or some combination of the two was responsible for the lack of vocations is difficult to determine. Never-

---

62. Louis Goll, S.J., *Jesuit Missions among the Sioux*, 69.

63. HRM 7-14-8, Digmann, diary, April 6, 1904.

64. *The Woodstock Letters* [51 (1922):309-310] has an interesting note on the topic of Native American vocations, but does not positively identify the author of the letter. It indicated that this passage was written by Jesuits among either the Native Americans of South Dakota or Wyoming: "The Indians have thus far shown little inclination to follow vocations to the priesthood or the sisterhood. Perhaps this is partly due to lack of opportunity. When a boy asks to go to college, the money question frightens him. He will then go to Haskell, Genoa, or some other Indian government school, where he does not need to pay. The missionaries assign the following reasons for this disposition. In the first place the old Adam is still strong in the Indian. Sometimes the beginnings of a vocation appear, but unfavorable surroundings smother it before it matures."

65. Bernard Flood, interview, Okreek, Rosebud Reservation, South Dakota, October 1992.

66. Pius XI, *Rerum Ecclesiae. The Papal Encyclicals: 1903-1939*, Claudia Carlin, ed., p. 285, paragraph 19.

theless, the Jesuits actively recruited a group of Lakota catechists who were instrumental in spreading the Catholic faith. By sponsoring the catechists' missionary expeditions to different Native American nations, the Jesuits and BCIM Director showed their confidence in the catechists' abilities.

CHAPTER FIVE

Language and Legend

THROUGHOUT THEIR HISTORY, JESUITS LEARNED FOREIGN LAN-
guages to advance their missions, and wrote many of the early dictionar-
ies of non-Western languages. Continuing this tradition, the Jesuits at
Holy Rosary and St. Francis made significant efforts to learn Lakota and
encourage its use. The Jesuits, however, induced students to speak English in the mission schools so that they learned English more quickly and
acquired employment more easily. But by banning Lakota in the mission
schools they were actually following a government policy which advocated that the Native American students be compelled to speak English.[1]
Since few jobs were available on the reservations, the Lakotas often had
to seek jobs off the reservation where English was a necessity. For Lakotas who wanted to attend a college, graduate school, or to run any type
of business, English was essential. Even though the Jesuits insisted on
the use of English at the mission schools, and did scold the children for
using Lakota, they did not try to eradicate Lakota. On occasion they
even made speeches in Lakota at the mission school.[2]

Outside the mission school, the Jesuits encouraged the use of Lakota
in many ways. At the Catholic Sioux Congresses, the participants primarily spoke either Lakota or Dakota, and both Jesuits and catechists
preached in Lakota.[3] The Jesuits also encouraged the Lakotas to write
articles in Lakota to spread the faith. The Lakotas contributed these articles to the four- to six-page monthly periodical called the *Sina Sapa Wocekine Taeyanpaha*, *The Catholic Sioux Herald*.[4] The Benedictines of
Devil's Lake, under the guidance of Jerome Hunt, O.S.B., published this

---

1. H. Price, Commissioner of Indian Affairs, "Report of the Commissioner of Indian
Affairs," *Annual Report of the Commissioner of Indian Affairs to the Secretary of the
Interior for the Year 1881*, p. XXXIV.

2. HRM 2/1-1-6, "Chronicles of the Sisters of St. Francis," Dec. 25, 1907, p.30; 1915
entry, p. 81; 1928 entry, p.121.

3. SFM Series 7, boxes 2-3, Eugene Buechel, S.J. diary, 17 volumes, 1893-1954.

4. BCIM 14/1-(boxes 25-26).

periodical from 1893 to 1936. About 80% of the periodical was in the Lakota and Dakota dialects, and the rest was in English. Most of the authors of the articles were Sioux catechists or members of the St. Mary's and St. Joseph's societies who used this periodical to exhort each other to lead a Catholic life and to keep each other informed about these societies' activities on the different Sioux reservations. The articles discussed Church History, the lives of saints, temperance, honesty, and anecdotes about leading a Christian life. Even though most of the writers were Sioux, occasionally the Jesuits and Benedictines contributed articles in Lakota or Dakota. Usually the catechists from Pine Ridge and Rosebud each month contributed two or three articles which varied in length from a paragraph of text to over 700 words. Just as the Sioux had a tendency to make long speeches, they were quite prolific writers. The Jesuits created an environment through the Catholic Congresses, the St. Mary's and St. Joseph's societies, the Lakota newspaper, and the prayerbooks that fostered the use of the Lakota and Dakota dialects.

The BCIM also encouraged the missionaries to learn the indigenous languages and often published in the *Sentinel* translations of the Lord's Prayer and Hail Mary in the various Native American languages.[5] Advocating the study of the native languages, a *Sentinel* editorial of 1917 said:

> The key to an Indian's heart is his mother tongue. It appeals to him with a directness of which the English, or any other language is utterly incapable. The visitation of the Indian missions will disclose the fact to any inquirer that the successful missions and the good Catholics are to be found only where the priests make use of the Indian languages for religious instruction and devotional exercises.[6]

The popes at this time also encouraged the study of native languages. In his letter *Maximum Illud* (1919), Pope Benedict XV reemphasized the Church's longstanding policy that missionaries learn indigenous languages:

> Among the attainments necessary for the life of a missionary, a place of paramount importance must obviously be given to the language of the people to whose salvation he will devote himself. He should not be content with a smattering of the language, but should be able to speak it readily and competently. For in this respect he is under an obligation to all those he deals with, the learned and ignorant alike, and he will soon realize the advantage a command of their language gives him in the task of winning the confidence and sympathy of a people.[7]

---

5. "Eskimo Hymn and Prayer," *Indian Sentinel* 1 (Jan. 1917):13. "Choctaw Hymn and Prayer," *Indian Sentinel* (July 1916):11. "The Lord's Prayer (in Papago)," *Indian Sentinel* 1 (July 1917):7. "The Lord's Prayer in Navajo," *Indian Sentinel* 1 (April 1918):25.

6. Editorial, *Indian Sentinel* (Jan. 1917):20.

7. Benedict XV, *Maximum Illud*, in *The Christian Faith*, J. Neuner, S.J. and J. Dupuis, ed., 321-313.

In the 1920's, the Jesuits and Lakotas of Holy Rosary and St. Francis produced several books in Lakota that encouraged Catholic devotions. Fr. Sialm recruited Emil Afraid-of-Hawk to translate into Lakota George Schurhammer's life of St. Francis Xavier. In 1925, Afraid-of-Hawk published a 64-page version of this work entitled *Watakpeya Tanka, St. Francis Xavier.*[8] Furthermore, Father Eugene Buechel, S.J., was an expert on the Lakota dialect who spent most of his life working at the St. Francis and Holy Rosary missions. Buechel wrote and distributed two works in Lakota which greatly aided the Lakotas' study of the Catholic religion. In 1924, Buechel published *Wowapi Wakan: Bible History in the Language of the Teton Sioux Indians*, a work of over 300 pages all in Lakota.[9] It contained a condensed version of the Old Testament and translations of New Testament texts. He made the book available to catechists, other lay people, and those who were not able to read English, which also included many of the catechists. By using these books, the Lakotas learned to read the Scriptures in their own language. The catechists also used this book to instruct the other Lakotas. In 1925, Buechel had 3500 copies of his *Bible History* produced and he distributed them on Pine Ridge and Rosebud.[10]

To accompany this book, Buechel wrote *Lakota Wocekiye na Olowan Wowapi: Sioux Indian Prayer and Hymn Book* which he published in 1927.[11] He distributed at least 5000 of these prayerbooks across the reservations.[12] Written mostly in Lakota, this 380 page book was a collection of Bible passages, hymns, and prayers. He translated into Lakota all the weekly Bible readings and sixty hymns, ten of which were hymns to Mary: "O Mary My Mother," "Hail Queen of the Heavens," "Ave Maria Bright and Pure," "Daughter of a Mighty Father," "O Heart of Mary Pure and Fair," and several others. Encouraging devotion to the Sacred Heart, Buechel translated into Lakota seven hymns which related to this devotion: "O Sacred Heart that on the Cross," "O Sacred Heart! O Love Divine," "O Sacred Heart what shall I Render Thee" and others. Also in the book were Lakota hymns for Advent, Christmas, Lent, Easter, and Pentecost.[13] He translated into Lakota the Creed, Salve Regina, Angelus, Agnus Dei, Gloria, Pater Noster, the Stations of the Cross, prayer before a

---

8. HRM 7-17-6, Placidus Sialm, S.J., "Camp Churches," St. Agnes Church, Manderson entry, 51. BCIM 8-11-9, Emil A. Hawk, *Watakpeya Tanka, St. Francis Xavier* (New York: Catholic Book Publishing Co., 1925).

9. Eugene Buechel, S.J., *Wowapi Wakan* (Chicago: Benziger Brothers, 1924).

10. BCIM 1-153-1, Buechel to Lusk, Feb 5, 1925, p.2.

11. The Jesuit Fathers of St. Francis Mission (Eugene Buechel, S.J. was the primary author), *Lakota Wocekiye na Olowan Wowampi* (St. Louis: Central Verein of America, 1927).

12. SFM 7-1-4, Director of Central Verein to Buechel, Feb. 4, 1927.

13. For Advent "See He Comes"; Christmas "Angels we Have Heard" and "Silent Night;" Lent "At the Cross;" Easter "Today He's Risen;" Pentecost "Come Holy Ghost."

Crucifix, prayers to St. Michael and St. Joseph and many others. The prayerbook included an Examination of Conscience and also several litanies and novenas: the Novena of Grace in Honor of St. Francis Xavier, Novena to the Holy Spirit, Litany of Loretto, and the Litany of the Sacred Heart.

Recognizing the centrality of prayer in the Lakota culture,[14] the missionaries encouraged this tradition and directed it towards Catholic prayers. The prayerbook had prayers and readings for the sick, the dead, morning prayer, night prayers, prayers before Mass, prayers before and after confession, and many others. The prayerbooks allowed the catechists to pick the appropriate prayer for the occasion.[15] For example, when Lakota Catholics were sick or dying, instead of seeking out a shaman or medicine man[16] to pray over them, they asked for a catechist. Retaining the custom of praying over the sick, the catechist referred to his prayerbook for a suitable prayer.

Buechel's primary purpose in writing the *Bible History* and *Sioux Indian Hymn and Prayerbook* was to help the Lakotas, especially those who did not speak English, understand Catholic doctrine. But he also wanted to preserve the Lakota language. In 1939, Buechel completed his book, *A Grammar of Lakota*, and in the preface, he stated his commitment to preserving the Lakota language:

> In time, however, [the Lakotas] would yield to the white man's ways and gradually adopt his language. And the day would come when the Indians would know but little or nothing of their own mother tongue. But blood asserts itself. The Indians have again become race-conscious and want to speak the language of their forefathers. But who was to help them? In order to assist them, the author has prepared this book which may aid to preserve their speech for posterity.[17]

Buechel's exhaustive grammar (375 pages) was the standard of excellence in the study of Lakota.[18]

---

14. Paul Manhart, S.J., interview, Wanblee, South Dakota, June, 1992.

15. *Ibid.*

16. Shamans and medicine men were distinguished in Lakota religion. A *pejuta wicasa*, which translates "medicine man," was primarily concerned with healing through the use of herbs. A *wicasa wakan*, "holy man" or shaman, was a mystic who spoke to the spirits. One could however be both a medicine man and a shaman. See Walker *Lakota Belief and Ritual* p. 91-94.

17. Eugene Buechel, S.J., *A Grammar of Lakota* (Chicago: John Swift, 1939) p. iv.

18. Buechel received numerous requests for his book from scholars, and these letters are in his correspondence file SFM 7-1-8. Among these were letters from the noted anthropologists Franz Boas and Ella DeLoria who thanked him for sending them a copy of his *Grammar of Lakota*; Ella Deloria to Buechel, July 31, 1939; Franz Boas to Buechel, Aug. 13, 1939.

During his life, Buechel also collected tens of thousands of Lakota words and phrases which he wrote down on notecards. Although he was unable to finish his dictionary of the Lakota language during his life, Paul Manhart, S.J., collected Buechel's notecards and published *A Dictionary of the Teton Dakota Sioux Language* in 1970. This massive book with over 10,000 entries was used in colleges and universities to teach the Lakota people their language.[19]

To compile his dictionary, Buechel sought the help of the Lakotas, including the students at the Holy Rosary Mission School. During recess he sat with his notepad and asked the students the meaning of certain Lakota words and phrases.[20] Thus Buechel at least was not rigorous about the enforcement of the ban on the Lakota dialect at the school. Others at the mission school also noticed this. Jessie Crow, a Lakota woman who went to Holy Rosary Mission School as a child in the 1930's, even then recognized the irony of the situation: the nuns scolded the students for speaking Lakota and Father Buechel spoke Lakota with them at recess.[21]

In addition to undertaking an exhaustive study of the Lakota dialect, Buechel appreciated the Lakota legends and took great pains to collect them. Using his catechist Ivan Star-Comes-Out as a source, Buechel recorded 100 Lakota legends, wholly in the Lakota language, which were published posthumously and called *Lakota Tales and Text*.[22] Even though these legends were an essential part of the Lakota religion, Buechel wanted to preserve them and clearly did not feel that they were a threat to the Catholic faith. If Buechel really believed that the Lakota religion was simply devil worship, he would not have taken such pains to collect and preserve the Lakota's religious stories.

The BCIM had much the same view of Native American legends as did Buechel. Quite often the *Sentinel* printed Native American legends from many different native groups to educate and interest their readers. In the April, 1924 issue of the *Sentinel*, they printed a Sioux creation story.[23] The *Sentinel* also recounted legends from the Coeur d'Alene, Cheyenne, Umatilla, Pima and other nations.[24] In retelling these stories the *Sentinel*

---

19. Francis Apple, interview, Kyle S.D., June 1992.

20. William Moore, S.J., "Black Eagle on Sioux Syntax," *Jesuit Missions* 8 (Nov. 1939):262.

21. Jessie Crow, interviews, Oglala, S.D., May and Sept. 1992. William Moore, S.J., "Black Eagle on Sioux Syntax," *Jesuit Missions* 8 (Nov. 1939):262.

22. Eugene Buechel, S.J., *Lakota Tales and Text* (St. Louis: John Swift, 1978).

23. Vincent Frech, O.S.B., "The Creation of Man: As Told by the Sioux," *Indian Sentinel* 4 (April 1924):91.

24. "Legend of the Chipmunk," *Indian Sentinel* 2 (Oct. 1920):179. "The Stolen Fire," *Indian Sentinel* 2 (Oct. 1921):385-386. "Indian Legend: The Creation of the World," *Indian Sentinel* 2 (July 1921):339. A. Van der Velden, "A Cheyenne Legend," *Indian Sentinel* 2 (July 1920):147-148.

articles did not in any way indicate that these legends were evil, but simply retold them as they would tell any interesting folktale. The legends in the *Sentinel* told of the deeds and exploits of supernatural beings and anthropomorphic animals. The authors who recounted these legends sometimes found comparisons with Catholic figures, which indicated that they were searching for some natural virtue in the characters. For example, in one legend published in the *Sentinel*, the author called one Native American heroine an "Indian Joan of Arc." In that legend the heroine stopped a fire because of her devotion to the Great Spirit.[25]

The Catholic missionaries and the BCIM believed that the Native American legends, or at least many of them, were a harmless aspect of the Native American cultural background. Like the Greek myths or Grimm's Fairy Tales, the Lakota legends, from the point of view of the missionaries, were not a threat to the Catholic faith. Fr. Zimmerman clearly stated his opinion of the Lakota myths in a 1927 *Sentinel* article when he referred to "the beautiful mythology of the Lakota, or Western Sioux."[26] In 1931, Sialm also wrote of his appreciation of the traditional Lakota legends:

> I was out in a Sioux Indian camp when Left-Hand Heron, the old story teller, came over to tell his wonderful tales. . . . The old stories are as vivid as a stage drama. In telling them the story teller imitates everything: gestures, voices, sounds. Ever so often his listeners burst into a hearty laugh. Then all are quiet again, curious to know how the funny incident turned out. Places, animals and people are described in detail with perfect knowledge and the skill of a clever playwright. . . . [The elder Lakota's] imagination preserves the memory of old customs and recalls vividly the sayings and doings of other days until the present gives way to the past.[27]

Yet even though many of the early European Jesuits like Sialm had a deep knowledge of the Lakota legends, culture and language, some of the American Jesuits at the missions in the 1920's and 30's were less interested in learning Lakota. American Jesuits began to fill positions at Holy Rosary and St. Francis after the Jesuit order detached Holy Rosary and St. Francis from the German Province and annexed it to the California Province in 1907. Though little conflict between the American and European Jesuits was apparent, the older European Jesuits may have believed that the younger generation was not as diligent as they were. In his diary (c. 1925), Buechel criticized his Jesuit brothers who were lax in their studies saying:

---

25. "Indian Legend," *Indian Sentinel* 1 (July 1919):18-19.

26. Joseph Zimmerman, S.J., "Great Sioux Chief Passes Away," *Indian Sentinel* 7 (Fall 1927):180-181.

27. Placidus Sialm, S.J., "Left-Hand Heron: Sioux Story Teller," *Indian Sentinel* 11 (Spring 1931):54.

It was better to try to speak Lakota and win the people than to cut out Indian and introduce all sorts of petty devotions. Get the commandments before you have the Apostleship of Prayer [a devotional society].[28]

Similarly, Buechel's sister, Alice Boyle, once wrote to him saying: "And so you are teaching Lakota. So often I have heard you stress the importance of teaching this to the younger Jesuits."[29] By the 1930's, the German Jesuits, because of their advancing years, gave control of the mission to the American Jesuits. At this time, most of the Lakotas spoke English. Since transportation and housing for the Jesuits had improved, the Jesuits also no longer lived with the Lakotas when they went on their mission circuits. Therefore, the younger Jesuits did not experience the close contact with the Lakotas that the older Jesuits had. Though speaking Lakota was a necessity for the early German missionaries, the younger American Jesuits viewed it as more of an option. Some American Jesuits at Holy Rosary and St. Francis, however, did learn Lakota well, and the Lakota elders appreciated such efforts. But those Jesuits who did not learn Lakota often had difficulties communicating with many Lakota elders. In the 1950's even the Jesuit Provincial said to one young Jesuit whom he sent to Holy Rosary that he need not learn Lakota at all.[30] Nevertheless, before the 1950's, the Jesuits created an atmosphere that fostered the use of the Lakota dialect; the *Sina Sapa Wocekine Taeyanpaha*, the Lakota prayerbooks, bible histories, devotional books, Congresses, and sermons all encouraged the use of the Lakota dialect.

Wakantanka

Though the missionaries thought that the various Native American religions had many "superstitious beliefs," they believed that even before contact with the missionaries, the Native Americans possessed many virtues and had some notion of monotheism. A *Sentinel* article in 1903 illustrated the common attitude shared by most of the Jesuits toward the Native American religion:

[A Catholic missionary's] discerning eye found in [the Native Americans] many noble qualities that endeared them to him, their naturally religious spirit, their recognition of one eternal Supreme Being, the Great Spirit, whom these poor people worshipped with many degrading superstitions, it is true, but whom they still worshipped, gave them a distinction over other savage men. As was

---

28. SFM 7-2-7, Eugene Buechel, S.J. diary, vol. 7, 1925-1928, list of Missionary Statements, 5 and 30.

29. SFM 7-1-7, Alice Boyle to Buechel, Aug. 15, 1934.

30. Paul Manhart, S.J., interview, Wanblee, South Dakota, Sept. 1992.

the case with De Smet, he admired their simple sincerity and steadfast honor when their promise was given, their reverent submission to the priestly authority and other virtues which shone out among them when they were separated from contact with the hideous barbarity that was taught them by contact with the low ruffians who play so large a part in border life.[31]

The author of this article and the priests at the BCIM who published it clearly recognized a ray of truth in the Native American religions. The BCIM and the missionaries believed that the Native Americans' recognition of "one eternal Supreme Being" was a sign that their religion had some virtue. The author's premise that Native American religion was more advanced than that of other non-Christians indicated that he believed that Native American religion had a greater degree of virtue than other religions. Since the author of this article expressed that non-Christian Native Americans possessed some, however obscure, knowledge of God and ascribed to a religion that was more advanced than that of other non-Christians, the author implicitly acknowledged that some continuity existed between the Catholic faith and these religions. Furthermore, the attitude that this article expressed toward non-Christian religion was actually similar to that expressed by Paul when he commented on the Athenians' practice of worshipping at the altar of the unknown god: "What therefore you unknowingly worship, I reveal to you (Acts 17:23)." Thus the belief that Native Americans acknowledged one supreme deity in some fashion even before contact with the West was an idea that was not inconsistent with the Church's teaching.

Not all the missionaries, however, believed that all the Native American religions had virtue. For example in 1909, Aloysius Vrebosch, S.J., a missionary to the Crows, had no respect at all for the Crows' religion:

> And what is the religion of these Crow Indians? It can be comprised in a single word, "Indian Medicine." They have absolutely no idea of the Great Spirit, which we know some other Indians have. No, the Crows' religion is only a mass of the most stupid superstitions keeping parallel with the most fantastic imaginations of their medicine men.[32]

Though Vrebosch condemned the Crow religion, he still recognized that other Native American religions had some idea of the Great Spirit. By elevating the religions of other Native Americans above that of the Crows, he acknowledged that some virtue existed in those Native American religions that accepted the Great Spirit.

---

31. "Monsignor Stephan," *Indian Sentinel* (1902-1903):4.

32. Aloysius Vrebosch, S.J., "The Crow Indians," *Indian Sentinel* (1909):30. He did not identify the Native American groups which he said had an idea of the Great Spirit.

The Lakotas were one native group which the missionaries recognized as having a belief in the Great Spirit. In Lakota, the term "*wakan*" meant holy or sacred, and Lakotas believed in supernatural beings that were *wakan*. In their efforts to teach the Lakotas about the Catholic faith, the Jesuits used the term "*wakan*" to translate Catholic doctrines and ideas into terms that the Lakotas understood. The Jesuits often combined *wakan* with other Lakota words to express Catholic concepts: the Jesuits used *yutapi wakan*, meaning "holy food," to signify the Eucharist. A church was *tipi wakan* or "sacred house." A guardian angel was *oglige-wakan*, "holy messenger."[33] As a translation for the word "devil," the Jesuits used the term *wakansica*, which in the Lakota religion were the "evil mysteries" or "evil spirits."[34] The Jesuits used *wakansica* as a translation for "devil" since it conveyed the idea of supernatural evil. Even though the term *wakan* came out of the traditional Lakota religion, the Jesuits often used it.

In his writings, Buechel showed that he respected the Lakota religion and the Lakotas' idea of God. In his *Prayerbook* and *Bible History*, he translated the word "God" into the Lakota as *Wakantanka*, meaning the "Great Spirit." In doing so, he followed in the tradition of Jerome Hunt, O.S.B., who also used *Wakantanka* as a translation for God in his catechism.[35] In their sermons, catechisms, and articles in the *Sentinel*, the Jesuits at Holy Rosary and St. Francis used the term *Wakantanka*, or *Wakan Tanka*, interchangeably with "God" to indicate to the Lakotas that continuity existed between their traditional religion and the Catholic faith.

The Jesuits believed the Lakota religion had some virtue, and believed that the Lakotas were monotheists. In 1940, Louis Goll, S.J., wrote that

> the Sioux tribes even prior to the advent of the Catholic missionaries believed in God, in one God only. There is among them no trace of real polytheism, no trace of idolatry. . . '. In the belief of the Sioux, *Wakantanka* is the Giver of everything. He formed man; He gave life.[36]

Since the Jesuits believed the Sioux were monotheists, they regarded the Sioux as more theologically advanced than polytheists. In his explanation of the nature of *Wakantanka*, Paul Radin, a noted anthropologist, supported the Jesuits' belief that the Sioux were monotheists:

> *Wakan Tanka*, the Great Mystery, has four essences to be regarded as one – the Chief God, the Great Spirit, the Creator, and the Ex-

---

33. Buechel, *A Dictionary of the Teton Dakota Sioux Language*, 370, 663, 730.

34. *Ibid.*, 689. Buechel, *Bible History*, 273. Walker, *Lakota Belief and Ritual*, 94, 129, 140.

35. BCIM 8-9-7, Jerome Hunt, O.S.B., *Katholik Wocekiye Wowapi*. (Fort Totten: Catholic Indian Mission at Fort Totten, 1899).

36. Louis Goll, S.J., *Jesuit Missions and the Sioux*, 14.

ecutive. . . . Clearly this is explicit monotheism avowedly mystical."[37]

Radin explained that the Sioux believed that all the different essences and supernatural beings of the Sioux religion were really parts of *Wakantanka*, a single mysterious reality. *Wakantanka*, as described by some Sioux, was the sixteen benevolent beings who were also one.[38] Describing Lakota religion, Black Elk referred to the Six Grandfathers who he understood to be all unified in one Grandfather, *Wakantanka*.[39] Similarly, Oglala Chief Little Wound in 1896 also spoke of the oneness of Wakantanka: "The *Wakan Tanka* are many. But they are all the same as one."[40] The Lakotas also referred to *Wakantanka* as *Tunkasila*, meaning grandfather, or *Ate* meaning father; this was similar to the Catholic practice of referring to God as "Father."[41]

Because the Jesuits saw the Lakota religion as being relatively advanced,[42] they were able to use *Wakantanka* as a translation for "God."[43] In his *Sentinel* article in 1928, Leo Cunningham, S.J., of Holy Rosary used *Wakantanka* interchangeably with God. He said that at the Holy Rosary Mission boarding school "367 Sioux Indian boys and girls are being taught to know and love *Wakan Tanka*, the Great Spirit."[44] Similarly, Fa-

---

37. Paul Radin, "Monotheism Among American Indians," in *Teachings from the American Earth*, Tedlock and Tedlock ed., (New York: Liveright, 1975), 235-236. The question of whether the traditional Sioux religion was actually a monotheism is not particularly relevant to this study. What is relevant to this study is the Jesuits' belief that the Sioux were monotheists.

38. Raymond DeMallie, *The Sixth Grandfather*, 81.

39. *Ibid.*, 94.

40. Walker, *Lakota Belief and Ritual*, 70.

41. *Ibid.*, 140.

42. HRM 7-19-10, Henry Westropp, S.J., "In the Land of the Wigwam," c. 1910, p.2. *Indian Sentinel* (April 1919):36.

43. In his account of his first meeting with Fr. De Smet, a Lakota man recalled: "His name was Father De Smet and he had come a great distance across the eastern 'Big Water' to work among the red men. For many nights I watched him as he talked to our leaders and old men. He spoke of a Supreme Being like our Great Mystery, Who had come among the white men to save them from His angry Father. The white men killed this Supreme Being and nailed Him to a tree. We could not understand how they could have done this or why they would want to. It took a brave man to come alone among our people and live with us at a time when the reputation of his race could not have been worse. We knew that he also went to our enemies, the Crows, but we could see that he wanted nothing from us but our hearts. I asked him many questions. I wanted to know if his '*Wakan*' (God) was the same as ours and he assured me they were the same."(HRM 8-7-5, David Stroud, Jr. "We Wore Our Feathers High," pamphlet Jan. 16, 1958, 25 pages, p.7.) The reliability of this particular account is uncertain.

44. Leo Cunningham, S.J., "The Great Spirit," *Indian Sentinel* 8 (Spring 1928):60. Leo Cunningham, S.J., "A Catholic Meeting House," *Indian Sentinel* 9 (Spring 1929):57. "At present the missionaries of Holy Rosary Mission, South Dakota, are doing their utmost to build a meetinghouse at each chapel and to put a Catechist in every district so that the faithful

ther Riester, S.J., of Holy Rosary, also used *Wakantanka* as a translation for God. In 1930, he wrote, "Please pray that by the grace of God we may lead many of these poor Sioux Indians to the knowledge, love and service of *Wakan Tanka*, the Great Spirit."[45] Sialm also stressed the continuity between the two religions (c.1935):

> Red Cloud learned to read the great open book by the Great Spirit – The *Wakantanka*. He was in the great school building of God [a reference to nature]. . . . He received good thoughts from the Great Spirit, from God, who had chosen him like David. . . . "*Sina Sapa owapinklala.*" I'll belong one day to the Blackgowns – I'll be Catholic. This was now his religious conviction. In [Red Cloud's] heart stood the Deposit of Faith like the hidden gold in the Black Hills – his true love for God – his respect for the Great Spirit who had now manifested himself more clearly to him.[46]

By saying that God "manifested himself more clearly," Sialm indicated that Red Cloud had some prior knowledge of God.

In 1940, John Scott, S.J., who taught at Holy Rosary, wrote that at a religion course at the Holy Rosary Mission School, the children

> learn more and more about *Wakan Tanka*, the Great Spirit. . . . They return [to their homes] with the knowledge that they are sons and daughters of the Great Spirit, brothers and sisters of Christ, and children of Mary. *Wakan Tanka* has fulfilled a dream nobler than that ever dreamed in the tepee of Sitting Bull, the dream of man's brotherhood with Christ, the great and only Messiah.[47]

In an article he wrote for the periodical *Jesuit Missions*, Scott again indicated that continuity existed between the two religions:

> Thanks to the untiring efforts of the Blackrobe, the faith of the Sioux in *Wakan Tanka*, the Great Spirit, was not crushed under the wheels of invading *Wasichu* [white people].[48]

Rather than trying to obliterate the Lakotas' faith, the Jesuits, in Scott's opinion, preserved the Lakotas' faith in the Great Spirit. Similarly Joseph Zimmerman, S.J., of Holy Rosary commented that among the Lakotas

---

Indians will be instructed in their Faith, those who have drifted away will be brought back, and the Sioux who are not as yet in the true Fold of Christ will be taught to know and love *Wakan Tanka*, the Great Spirit."

45. Albert Riester, S.J., "Sioux Trails all lead to Big Road," *Indian Sentinel* 11 (Winter 1930-31):7-8.

46. HRM 7-17-(5-7), Placidus Sialm, S.J., *Camp Churches*, 125-127.

47. John Scott, S.J., "Where Summer Trails End," *Indian Sentinel* 20 (Sept. 1940):108.

48. John Scott, S.J., "Sun Dance in Dakota," *Jesuit Missions* 15 (June 1941):167.

"there is almost universal acceptance of the God of Christianity as the Great Spirit, *Wakan Tanka*, in whom the race has always believed."[49]

Missionaries on other reservations also shared the Jesuit view of *Wakantanka*. At a Catholic Sioux Congress in 1936, Daniel Madlon, O.S.B., heard Bull Man's speech on the meeting between Craft and Chief Spotted Tail, and he summarized it in the *Sentinel*:

> One day [fifty years ago, the Lakotas] had a visitor, Father Craft. He looked like an Indian. He was riding a horse and he had a feather in his hat. He came during the [sun] dance. Afterwards he spoke to the big chief, Spotted Tail, and told him he had respect for the Indians because they worshipped the Great Spirit.[50]

Madlon's article as well as the Jesuits' articles above indicated that the missionaries saw some virtue in the traditional Lakota religion.

The Jesuits' use of the Lakota word for God was actually a sign of a rather liberal pastoral theology, since the Church, during the Chinese rites controversy, condemned the Jesuits in China in 1742 for their use of the name of a Chinese divinity, "*Shangti*," as a translation for "God."[51] Ironically, in 1659 the Sacred Congregation for the Propagation of the Faith encouraged the Jesuits to conform to the Chinese culture before this controversy arose:

> Do not in any way attempt, and do not on any pretext persuade these people to change their rites, habits and customs, unless they are openly opposed to religion and good morals. For what could be more absurd than to bring France, Spain, Italy, or any other European country over to China? It is not your country but the faith you must bring, that faith which does not reject or belittle the rites or customs of any nation as long as these rites are not evil, but rather desires that they be preserved in their integrity and fostered.[52]

The Jesuits in China, however, soon found themselves enmeshed in a controversy concerning their translation of "God" into Chinese and their participation in the Confucian and ancestor veneration ceremonies. Eventually the Holy See decided that the Jesuits' participation in these rites was contrary to the Catholic faith. In 1742, Pope Benedict XIV is-

---

49. BCIM 14/1-4-4, Joseph Zimmerman, S.J., "The True Faith Versus Paganism," *Calumet* (May 1944):16-17. Even though this article has a provocative title, Zimmerman specifically identified Peyotism and the "superstitions" concerning the medicine men as the "paganism" that he was contrasting with Catholicism.

50. Daniel Madlon, O.S.B., "Fifty Years Progress," *Indian Sentinel* 16 (Sept 1936):111.

51. F.A. Rouleau, "Chinese Rites Controversy,"in *Catholic Encyclopedia* (Washington: Catholic University, 1967), 3:613.

52. Sacred Congregation of the Propagation of the Faith. Instruction to the Vicars Apostolic of Tonkin and Cochinchina. J. Neuner, S.J. and J. Dupuis, S.J., *The Christian Faith*, 309.

sued *Ex quo singulari* which censured the Jesuits for partaking in these rites,[53] and by doing so he more clearly defined the line that the Catholic Church drew between syncretism and missionary adaptation.

From the point of view of the Catholic Church, missionary adaptation was the legitimate use of the symbols, art, and language of a culture to translate accurately Christian truth into the language of those being evangelized. In contrast, syncretism was the mixing of Catholic doctrines and practices with non-Christian beliefs and practices in a way that obscured and corrupted Catholic teaching. The hierarchy believed that the Jesuits' participation in the Chinese rites and their use of *Shangti* as a translation for God was syncretism.

Despite this historical controversy, the American hierarchy, however, did not condemn the use of *Wakantanka* as a translation for God, and they gave the prayerbooks written by Jerome Hunt and Buechel the *imprimatur*.[54] If the bishops or priests thought that the Lakota religion was simply devil worship,[55] they obviously would not have allowed the term *Wakantanka* in their catechisms. Nevertheless, the Chinese rites controversy forced later missionaries to be more careful about their participation in the religious aspects of native culture, and drew their attention to the problems of translating religious ideas from one language into another.

In a series of pronouncements in 1935 and 1936, however, Pius XI revoked the ban on priests' and lay Catholics' participation in the Confucian and Shinto rites.[56] By this act of toleration, the pope took a liberal approach to mission theology since the rites themselves had not been adapted by missionaries to coincide more closely with Catholic doctrine and practice. By this act, Asian Catholics were able to participate in already existing rites which the pope believed were not contrary to the Catholic faith. This pronouncement of toleration was significant because it sent a signal to all missionaries that the Holy See supported the practice of missionaries' adapting to indigenous cultures and taking part in native ceremonies that were not contrary to the Catholic faith.

In his mission encyclicals, Pius XII went even further than mere toleration of certain non-Christian rites. Pius XII supported the idea that certain Asian civic rites that had been influenced by non-Christian religion had virtue.[57] In 1939, he wrote a major mission encyclical titled *Summi*

---

53. F.A. Rouleau, "Chinese Rites Controversy," in *Catholic Encyclopedia* (Washington: Catholic University, 1967), 3:611-617.

54. Eugene Buechel, S.J., *Lakota Wocekiye na Olowan Wowapi* (St. Louis: Central Verein of America, 1927), cover page, Imprimatur Archbishop Joannes J. Glennon.

55. Both Harvey Markowitz and Raymond DeMallie believed that the Jesuits considered Lakota religion to be "devil-dominated heathenism" (Markowitz) or "devil worship" (DeMallie). Raymond DeMallie, *The Sixth Grandfather*, 63-66. Harvey Markowitz, "The Catholic Mission and the Sioux," in *Sioux Indian Religion*, 124, 136.

56. F.A. Rouleau, "Chinese Rites Controversy," in *Catholic Encyclopedia*, 3:615-616.

Pontificatus, which clearly advocated the preservation of all native culture that was not contrary to Catholic teachings:

> And the nations, despite a difference of development due to diverse conditions of life and of culture, are not destined to break the unity of the human race, but rather to enrich and embellish it by the sharing of their own peculiar gifts and by the reciprocal interchange of goods which can be possible and efficacious only when a mutual love and a lively sense of charity unite all the sons of the same Father and all those redeemed by the same Divine Blood. The Church of Christ . . . cannot and does not think of deprecating or disdaining the particular characteristics which each people, with jealous and intelligible pride, cherishes and retains as a precious heritage. . . . All that in such usages and customs is not inseparably bound up with religious errors will always be subject to kindly consideration and, when it is found possible, will be sponsored and developed.[58]

Respect for one's cultural traditions, the pope indicated, was good as long as these traditions were not contrary to Catholicism and as long as one's admiration for one's own traditions was not so excessive as to detract from the universal nature of the Church.[59]   In this encyclical, Pius XII made the clearest statement that he supported the preservation of indigenous culture and believed that many indigenous non-Christian customs were good.

57. Sacred Congregation for the Propagation of the Faith, "Instructio circa quasdam caeremonias et iuramentun super ritibis sinensibus," *Acta Apostolica Sedis*, (Rome: Typis Polyglottis Vaticanis, 1940) annus XXXII, series II, vol. VII, p.24-26. F.A. Rouleau, "Chinese Rites Controversy," in *Catholic Encyclopedia*, 3:616.

58. Pius XII, *Summi Pontificatus. The Papal Encyclicals* in (Raleigh: McGrath Publishing, 1981), Claudia Carlin, ed., p.11, paragraphs 43, 44, and 46.

59. *Ibid.* p.12, paragraph 49.

CHAPTER SIX

Missionary Adaptation

THE JESUITS OFTEN ADAPTED LAKOTA CUSTOMS SO THAT THEY MESHED with Catholic practices, and also adapted Catholic ceremonies to fit into Lakota culture. On Pine Ridge and Rosebud reservations, the Jesuits also lived in such a way that their lifestyles meshed with the Lakota culture. Those Jesuits who traveled the reservation on their mission circuits lived with the Lakotas, ate with them, traveled with them, celebrated with them, mourned with them, and slept in their houses.[1] Lakota hospitality impressed them, and the Lakotas accepted the Jesuits as part of their extended family.

On their own initiative, the Lakotas preserved their customs or sometimes transformed them to make them consistent with Catholic practice. But some customs, like the *yuwipi* (a traditional Lakota healing ceremony that the medicine men performed), they discarded because they were too closely tied to religious practices to which the Jesuits objected. Nevertheless, in the traditional Lakota culture, most aspects of their culture were related to their religion in some way. Hunting, harvesting, feasting, smoking, fighting, mourning, telling stories, practicing medicine, seeking visions, and performing acts of charity all were connected to their religion. The buffalo hunt, for example, was not simply a means of acquiring food, but was an elaborate ritual which was related to the Sun Dance. Certainly some Lakota practices like the games they played or the food they ate were not as religiously significant as the Sun Dance, but even the games indicated something about their ethics and ideals. The Jesuits, however, did not condemn those aspects of the Lakota culture that they saw as being indifferent to Catholic ethics. But the Jesuits also permitted Catholics to participate in certain Lakota ceremonies which traditionally were religious rituals.

Since Lakota customs and religion were bound together, the Jesuits did not attempt to ban all activities related to the Lakota religion since this would have meant developing an entirely new culture. They also did

---

1. Jessie Crow, interview, Oglala, S.D., Oct. 1992.

not try to replace the Lakota culture with the American culture, because they saw the American culture as being fraught with errors. By building on what they believed was good in Lakota culture, they sought to perfect the good tendencies with Catholic teaching. By introducing the Lakotas to what they saw as the positive aspects of American culture and condemning its negative aspects (e.g., divorce and drinking), the Jesuits tried to insulate them from what they saw as the sin of the age.

Yuwipi

The Jesuits, however, did oppose the medicine men because they believed that the religious ideas and practices perpetuated by them were contrary to the Catholic faith, and hence they forbade the Lakota Catholics to participate in the *yuwipi*. The Jesuits opposed the medicine men because they believed that they were influenced by the devil and were deceptive charlatans who conspired to cheat the Lakotas out of their money and possessions.[2] But though they believed the medicine men were practicing rituals that were inspired by the devil, they did not believe that the medicine men's actions meant that the entire Lakota religion was evil.

In an entry he made in this diary in 1892, Digmann provided his opinion of the medicine men and explained the techniques that they used in their curing ceremonies: "Dog Ghost, a medicine man, owned up that [medicine men] put flesh or blood in their mouth and then after sucking, spit it out, saying that they had sucked it out of the sick patient."[3] In 1887, Digmann also recorded in his diary the example of a medicine man who stole a man's horses and later charged the man a fee for locating the "lost" horses by divination.[4] In the same year, Digmann came upon a medicine man and his followers who tried to cure a sick child by means of the *yuwipi*. Interrupting the ceremony, Digmann said to one of them, "Give up your devil's work. This child is baptized and belongs to the Great Spirit."[5] Here, he clearly distinguished between the "devil's work" in the *yuwipi*, and the worship of the "Great Spirit." Even in the 1940's the Jesuits still believed that the *yuwipi* ceremonies were inspired by the devil. For example, in *Jesuit Missions Among the Sioux* (1940), Louis Goll, S.J., of Holy Rosary Mission, described the medicine men's techniques:

---

2. Louis Goll, S.J., *Jesuits Missions Among the Sioux*, 15-16. HRM 7-14-8, Digmann, diary, Sept. 1, 1887. For a complete treatment of the *yuwipi* consult William Powers, *Yuwipi: Vision and Experience in Oglala Ritual* (Lincoln: University of Nebraska Press, 1982).

3. HRM 7-14-8, Digmann, diary, Jan. 26, 1892.

4. *Ibid.*, Sept 1, 1887, p.10.

5. *Ibid.*, July 23, 1887, p.8.

Their reputation once established, the medicine men acted as powerful, mysterious physicians who would drive out sickness by incantations and the beating of a drum – naturally for a considerable remuneration. That now and then tricks alone did not suffice, but that the father of lies had a hand in the game to help his faithful servants can scarcely be doubted.[6]

Yet though the Jesuits opposed the *yuwipi*, they did allow the former medicine men to attempt to heal people using their herb-lore. The Jesuits distinguished, even within non-Catholic rituals, between the aspects of the practice that were acceptable and those that were not. Referring to the medicine men, Digmann wrote (c.1888),

> We did not forbid them the use of their medicines, which the Great Spirit gave to them as well as the white man. . . . For wounds, fractures, and other common exterior ailings [the Lakotas] had very efficient medicines, taught by the experience of generations. For interior maladies, however, [for?] consumption, they had recourse to their superstitious belief in the power of the Medicine man. . . . We did not forbid them to use their herbs and roots and natural medicines but forbade them the use of all superstitious practices accompanying their conjurations.[7]

Forty years later, Digmann had the same positive assessment of Lakota medicine:

> The medicine man had a practical knowledge of medicinal herbs and roots. But [the Lakotas] claimed that they had received that knowledge in a dream. . . . One day . . . I was approached by Black Thunderbird, a medicine man. He shook hands with me and asked, "Did you baptize my children?" "Yes," I answered, "they are all baptized now. You are the only black crow in the family. When will you come around? He answered, "You know that I am a medicine man, and by my practice I get many a blanket, ponies and money. But I know that before you pour the water on me, you will forbid me my practice. I am not yet prepared for that." "You may continue to give medicine," I told him, "but you must give up all superstitions and pagan ceremonies. . . ." It was several years before he would make up his mind to give up his superstitious practices. But Thunderbird kept his word and was baptized.[8]

Digmann acknowledged that the Lakotas' medical and herbal knowledge was effective and useful. He was in favor of retaining the Lakotas' herb-

---

6.   Louis Goll, S.J., *Jesuit Missions Among the Sioux,* 15.

7.   HRM 7-14-8. Digmann, diary, c. 1888, p.8.

8.   Fr. Florentine Digmann, S.J., "Thunderbird keeps his Word," *Indian Sentinel* 8 (Spring 1928):67.

lore, even though he sought to eradicate the *yuwipi* ceremony in which the medicine men used these herbs. The Lakotas also appreciated the distinction between the *yuwipi* and the medicines. At one time, Nick Black Elk was a medicine man, and though he no longer performed the *yuwipi* after he converted, he still used the medicinal herbs that he used as a medicine man.[9]

Other missionaries like Buechel shared this approach toward Lakota healing remedies. In the 1920's, Buechel performed a study of the flora in the Dakotas in which he collected and cataloged almost 300 different varieties of indigenous plants. Published posthumously, his study was called *Lakota Names and Traditional Uses of Native Plants by Sicangu (Brule) People in the Rosebud Area, South Dakota.*[10] In this study he noted not only the common names of the plants, but also the traditional Lakota names and medicinal uses of the plants. He too realized that the Lakotas were accomplished herbalists and he wanted to preserve their herb-lore. Even though he realized that some of this knowledge came from the medicine men and was connected with their religion, he rejected only the *yuwipi* and the paraphernalia associated with it.

Since the Jesuits saw the medicine men and the members of the Peyote religion as a bad influence on Catholics, the Jesuits were persistent in pursuing them and campaigning for their conversion. They believed that their conversion would set an example for other Lakotas. Sometimes they published letters or wrote to the *Sentinel* about the conversion of a prominent medicine man to spread the word of their successes.[11] In an article to the *Sentinel*, Digmann described the conversion of a medicine man named Otapela Kills Plenty. In 1887, when Digmann tried to convert Otapela, he even relaxed some of the Catholic conventions to make Otapela's conversion easier for him. At this time Otapela was dying and Digmann approached him frequently asking if he would accept baptism. But Digmann explained that he refused baptism, at first, because he believed that if he was baptized, he would have to be buried underground:

> The Sioux custom was to place the dead in a box raised on poles, or in tree trunks on the highest part of a hill. I have seen them wrap an infant in swaddling clothes and hang the bundle to the limb of a tree. "You may be buried in Indian fashion," I assured Otapela. "But be baptized before you die. It will make you a friend of the Great Spirit. It will open for you the gates of His house. . . ." [a while later] Otapela suddenly raised himself up saying, "Hurry baptize me. I want to see the Great Spirit. . . ."

9. Olivia Pourier, interview, Sharp's Corner, S.D., June 1992.

10. Dilwyn Rogers, ed., *Lakota Names and Traditional Uses of Native Plants* (St. Francis: Rosebud Educational Society, 1980).

11. BCIM 1-260-11, Joseph Zimmerman, S.J., circular letter, Feast of Christ the King, 1941.

Presently his soul was cleansed in the regenerating waters of baptism.[12]

To some the practice of a priest hovering over a dying, unbaptized person may seem insensitive, especially since the priest indicated, implicitly or explicitly, that the ailing person was in danger of eternal damnation. The Jesuits, however, believed that they helped to save the souls of those dying. So often did the Jesuits baptize the Lakotas near death that some resisted baptism thinking it would kill them.[13] Nevertheless, the example of Otapela's conversion showed that the Jesuits were not rigorists who insisted on following all the European burial customs. Rather than slavishly following practices that were inessential to Catholic rituals, Digmann allowed Otapela to be "buried in Indian fashion" above ground. In many such cases, the Jesuits concentrated on the essentials of the Catholic faith and allowed innocent or morally neutral Lakota customs to continue.

Funeral Customs and Patriotism

In addition to their flexibility about modes of burial, the Jesuits allowed the Lakota custom of wailing over the graves of their dead. When Father Bosch, S.J., of Holy Rosary Mission, died in 1903, a group of wailing Lakota women accompanied his funeral: "One old Indian woman began the death song, and as the procession left [Fr. Bosch's] grave many women joined her."[14] Similarly, in 1910 after giving the rite of extreme unction to a dying Lakota man, Digmann described the same type of mourning ritual:

> At our arrival he was actually dying; gave him absolution, Extreme Unction and scapular. The house was full of Indians. During his agony I said all the prayers for the dying. They respectfully kept quiet. After I had finished one asked: "Are you through?" Upon my "Yes" the whole crowd began their mourning howl, in and outside of the tipi, nearly all night long.[15]

Clearly the Jesuits believed this ritual was perfectly acceptable, and on occasion may have participated in it. For example, comparing the Lakota funeral rites with the Irish wake, Father Westropp, S.J., of Holy Rosary wrote (c. 1910):

---

12. Florentine Digmann, S.J., "I Want to See the Great Spirit," *Indian Sentinel* 4 (Jan. 1924):26. HRM 7-14-8, Digmann, diary, Sept. 1, 1887, p.12.

13. "Catholic Indian Schools: St. Francis," *Indian Sentinel* (1907):22.

14. HRM 2/1-1-6, "Chronicles of the Sisters of St. Francis," 1903 entry, p.18.

15. HRM 7-14-8, Digmann, diary, Feb. 27, 1910.

> Like the Irish of old, the Indians have a custom of wailing over the dead. One day [Joe Big Head] said to me: "Little Owl (my Indian name) when I die I want you to come to my grave and to cry, "Ha hoo hoo hoo, Ha hoo hoo, mi-ta-ko-la te-wa-hi-la qon, Ha hoo hoo hoo!" Like a good Irishman, I of course promised. "And if you die before, I will do the same for you," he said.[16]

Though the Lakota Catholics adopted the Catholic funeral rites, they also integrated their own customs into them.

Yet even though the Jesuits appreciated many Lakota customs, they tried to discourage certain Lakota practices that they believed were either contrary to Catholic doctrine or harmful to the Lakotas' well-being. All the Jesuits who spoke of the "give-away" ceremony objected to it on the grounds that it damaged the Lakotas' financial well-being. When a Lakota person died, his or her family gave away most of the family's possessions, including their furniture and sometimes even their house. Thus, the give-away was a part of the traditional mourning practices. The Lakotas, however, also performed the give-away at dances, adoption ceremonies, coming of age ceremonies, or at other significant events. While this practice was not so drastic in the pre-contact days when the band took care of everyone and possessions were more communal, in modern times life was often more complicated.

Even though the give-away was related to Lakota religious beliefs, the Jesuits did not believe it was contrary to the Catholic faith. The Jesuits certainly approved of generosity, but they thought that the give-away was excessive. Digmann explained his opposition to this custom in an 1889 entry in his diary:

> the customary "giving away" at their dances is a drawback to civilization. It is their pride to beat their neighbor in generosity, and not seldom leave the dance hall poor and broke, stripping themselves of what they would need for their own family.[17]

Sialm shared Digmann's opinion of the give-away, and called it a "foolish" custom and "one of the worst Indian customs to pauperize them at the occasion of a death in the family."[18] Yet one of Sialm's catechists, John Foolhead, gave away almost all his property upon the death of his daughter. Interestingly enough, on the same page in his book where Sialm chided Foolhead for practicing the give-away, he praised his devotion to the Catholic faith:

---

16. Henry Westropp, S.J., "In the Land of the Wigwam," (Pine Ridge: Oglala Light Press, c.1910), pamphlet, p.12, Holy Rosary section 4, Archives of the Missouri Province Society of Jesus in St. Louis.

17. HRM 7-14-8, Digmann, diary, Nov. 21, 1889.

18. HRM 7-17-(5-7), Sialm, *Camp Churches*, p. 92.

Foolhead was baptized early and remained a faithful Catholic
with a deep and sincere faith. The first catechist [at Holy Angels
Chapel] soon died and Foolhead took his place for twenty years.
There is no Catechist so faithful and on the spot as Foolhead all
these years.[19]

Though Sialm objected to the give-away, his praise of Foolhead indicated
that he did not think this practice was detrimental to his Catholic faith.
He also did not condemn the give-away as sinful. Furthermore, Foolhead's determination to follow this custom, despite Sialm's opposition,
showed that the Lakota Catholics on their own initiative preserved their
traditional customs.

The Lakotas integrated their customs into the Catholic funeral ceremonies in several other ways. Traditionally, the Lakotas were quite concerned with honoring the memory of their ancestors, and the Jesuits encouraged this tendency. At the mission cemeteries and the Congresses,
the Jesuits and Lakotas often performed elaborate and solemn ceremonies
to honor the dead, which combined Lakota, Catholic and American customs.

Unlike many Natives of North America, the Lakotas did not have a
great fear of the dead. According to their traditional religion, they had to
tend the spirit of the dead for two years after the person had died, in a
ritual known as ghost keeping. During this time, the spirit of the departed
did not leave the world but lingered around the family. To ensure that the
spirit of the deceased achieved the proper afterlife, the Sioux conducted
several rituals. The family took a lock of the deceased's hair, placed it in
a buckskin bag making a "ghost bundle," and constructed around it a
small tepee, a *wanagi tipi* or "spirit house." According to tradition, they
had to tend this bundle for two years and offer it food every day. After
two years, they provided the spirit with a last meal, after which the spirit
walked to the afterworld on the Milky Way, which they called the *wanagi
tacanku*, the "ghost road."[20] At the end of the road, the spirit met the Old
Woman, who determined if that person/spirit lived a good life. If she recognized that the spirit was evil, she pushed the spirit off the cliff, and the
spirit fell back to earth to wander as a ghost. But if the person lived a
good life, he or she walked into paradise, a land of plenty. The Lakotas
believed that if they did not perform the ghost keeping rituals, the spirits
of the dead lingered on the earth and did not arrive at their paradise.[21]

The Lakotas' concern for the dead was in some ways similar to that
of Catholics. After a Catholic person died, friends and relatives offered

---

19. *Ibid.*

20. William Powers, *Oglala Religion* (Lincoln: University of Nebraska, 1975), 93-95.
Joseph Epes Brown, *The Sacred Pipe*, 10-30.

21. Powers, *Oglala Religion*, 53.

Masses and prayed for him or her, because they believed that these acts benefited the deceased by reducing the time that the person may have had to spend in purgatory. Both Catholics and Lakotas felt a sense of responsibility for the ultimate destiny of the dead person and both believed that by performing ceremonies, the living affected the destiny of the dead. Even though the Lakota Catholics abandoned the traditional ghost keeping ceremony, the Catholic rituals fostered their tradition of ministering to the needs of the dead.

In his article "Indian Belief in Purgatory and Prayers for the Dead" (1890), Fr. Craft noted the similarities between the Sioux and Catholic rites and beliefs concerning the afterlife. First he described in detail the Sioux beliefs and rituals: the rite of ghost keeping, the Milky Way road, and the judgment of the souls. He also noted that the Sioux said prayers and made sacrifices when they released the spirit to help it on its journey to the afterworld. In the conclusion to his article, he argued that the Sioux beliefs and rituals concerning the afterlife were so similar to Catholic beliefs that the Sioux must have picked up these beliefs from Catholic missionaries whom he thought they may have encountered over 700 years earlier.

> It seems evident that these traditions and customs were taken in part from what was remembered of the instructions of early missionaries. The Indians themselves maintain this, and history seems to confirm their statement. They say that several hundred years ago their ancestors were instructed by a "Chief of Black Robes," or Bishop, who came to them from the East.[22]

The idea that Catholic missionaries contacted the Sioux 700 years ago and influenced the Sioux conception of the afterlife is doubtful. Nevertheless, Craft's statement showed that he believed that some ray of truth was present in Sioux religion.

Other Catholics at Holy Rosary also made the comparison between the Lakota and Catholic funeral rites. Ben Marrowbone, who was a Catholic catechist at Holy Rosary in the 1930's, said, "visiting the church was like visiting the *wanagi tipi*. Care for the soul and praying for the dead were not new things to us."[23] For the Lakotas who converted to Catholicism, the similarity of the Catholic and Lakota idea that people influenced the destiny of the dead by practicing rituals allowed the Lakotas to understand more easily the Catholic beliefs concerning the afterlife. Certainly significant differences remained, but the two religions had structural similarities that eased the Lakotas' transition to the Catholic faith.

---

22. HRM 8-4-3, Francis Craft, "Indian Belief in Purgatory and Prayers of the Dead," *Poor Souls Advocate* 2 (June 2, 1890):194-196.

23. Michael Steltenkamp, S.J., *Black Elk: Holy Man of the Oglala* (Norman: University of Oklahoma, 1993), 142.

Catholic and Lakota rituals concerning the dead were similar in several other ways. For example, each year the Jesuits and Lakotas gathered together on Decoration Day to honor their departed ones. On this day, they went to the cemetery, prayed, and decorated the graves with flowers, often leaving offerings of food and fruit at the graves. These gifts of food and decorations were a way of caring for the grave site which was similar in some ways to the Lakota tradition of tending the ghost bundle and maintaining the "house" of the dead. One of the Franciscan nuns at Holy Rosary recorded the event in 1910:

> Decoration Day is always celebrated by the Indians. Men, women, and children walk in an orderly procession, reciting the Rosary from the meeting house to the cemetery. They carried wreaths, crosses, flower bouquets made out of colorful paper. In the cemetery, they had speeches in their own language mostly given by catechists. Then they decorated their graves and offered sacrifices. They put food, clothing, money on the graves of their relatives which can be taken by the children of other people.[24]

During the Congresses, the Lakotas also decorated the graves after walking in a long procession to the cemetery. Francis Bull Head, the Congress Secretary, described the procession at the 1931 Congress:

> More than a thousand Indians were in that parade carrying many beautiful flowers of every hue and color that their loving hands made for their beloved dead. Up the cemetery hill they came. . . . Bill Randall talked in Lakota in which he told the people what they should call to mind on Decoration Day. He told them not only to place flowers on the graves of their dead but to remember to pray for the souls of the departed. . . . The cemetery was brilliant with color – flowers and American flags. The band played the STAR SPANGLED BANNER as the parade stopped at the graves of Mr. Willes Brown and Mr. Alfred Richard who were killed in action in the World War. Mr. High Eagle gave a talk on "Indian Heroes past and present." He spoke of Chief Red Cloud the greatest of all Indian Chiefs."[25]

In addition to providing an expression of the traditional Lakota concern for the dead, the ceremony encouraged American patriotism and Catholic prayers. These ceremonies also called to mind the Lakota heroes like Red Cloud whose devotion to the Catholic Church served as an example to be followed.

---

24. HRM 2/1-1-6, "Chronicles of the Sisters of St. Francis," 1910 entry, p. 42. This document was a mission diary written by one or more of the Franciscan sisters.

25. HRM 4-1-2, Francis Bull Head, "Sioux Indian Congress – Holy Rosary Mission, May 29-31, 1931," p.2-3. Francis Bull Head, "Sioux Catholic Congress at Holy Rosary Mission," *Indian Sentinel* 11 (Fall 1931):173-174.

At Holy Rosary and St. Francis, the Jesuits carried their instruction of patriotism into many of their celebrations including the funeral ceremonies. Even though the relationship between the government and the missionaries was often unfriendly, the government officials nevertheless encouraged the Jesuits to teach American values to the mission students and to the Lakotas. In this area, the Jesuits eagerly complied with the government's wishes since they were anxious to prove that they were upstanding American citizens. Throughout American history, many Protestants accused Catholics of being unamerican, and of owing their allegiance to a foreign monarch, the pope. Sensitive to such charges, the Jesuits took every opportunity to emphasize that they taught patriotism at the Dakota missions, and that their schools produced citizens willing to support their country in the wars. During World War I and World War II, the Jesuits often wrote articles praising the Lakotas for their military service.[26] In a 1938 article, William Moore, S.J., summed up the intentions of the Jesuits in the mission schools and stressed the importance of learning American democratic traditions:

> For the purpose of St. Francis Mission training is to develop the young Indian's mental powers, to train him or her to think; to inculcate convictions of morality and justice; to instill sentiments of patriotism towards our democratic institutions; to impart a sense of obligation to prepare for the duties of citizenship; and with all this, side by side and coextensive, to equip the young man or woman with such technical, commercial, or special skill as will enable him or her to earn an honest, respectable living.[27]

But though the Jesuits taught the Lakotas about American values, they did not try to eradicate the unique qualities and values that the Lakotas possessed.

Two Roads

In their efforts to teach Catholic doctrine to the Lakotas, the Jesuits often built on the symbolism in the Lakotas' own traditions. One of the instructional devices that did this effectively was *The Two Roads* catechism. Referring to this catechism, Louis Goll, S.J., wrote that in the

---

26. Joseph Zimmerman, S.J., "The Sioux Taste War," *Indian Sentinel* 23 (Jan. 1943):12-13. Joseph Zimmerman, S.J., circular letter in *High Eagle and His Sioux*, John Scott, S.J. ed., (St. Louis, 1963):60-67. *Indian Sentinel* 1 (April 1919):35. The Indian Sentinel also published many articles which outlined the contributions of the Native American Catholics to the war efforts. See "Catholic Indians and the War." *Indian Sentinel* 1 (July 1918):15-33.

27. BCIM 1-246-3, William Moore, S.J., "The Importance Placed on Ranching, Agriculture, and Shop Training at the St. Francis Mission High School, Rosebud Reservation," April 1938, p.3.

Jesuits' efforts to convert the Lakotas "talking in the abstract did little good. To their great relief they heard of a picture catechism called *The Two Roads*."[28] *The Two Roads* was a picture made in the 1880's by Father Albert Lacombe, a French missionary to the Blackfeet in Canada. Since the 1840's, Canadian missionaries used pictures similar to *The Two Roads* to help explain Catholic doctrine to the Native Americans.[29]

The Two Roads was a picture about three feet long and a foot wide which had drawings of biblical scenes and two roads running along the length. One road led to heaven and the other to hell. Along the road to heaven were a list of the virtues, the principle doctrines of the Catholic Church, and significant events in Church history represented pictorially. Along the road to hell were a list of the vices and the heretics. This method of teaching through pictures appealed to the Lakotas since traditionally they recorded their history through the use of pictures painted on buckskin.

In the Jesuits' papers was a description of how *The Two Roads* catechism should be used. The instruction provided a simple plan for explaining the Trinity, the Fall, Adam and Eve, Cain and Abel, Noah, Jesus, the passion, the Ten Commandments, the seven sacraments and the seven deadly sins. It emphasized that those who followed the good road went to heaven, while those who did not "suffer[ed] forever with the devil."[30]

The image of the two roads appealed to the Lakotas and they often used this metaphor in their speeches. For example, in 1891 and 1892 Digmann recorded several such statements: Bearshield said, "For fifty years I have been looking for the road I should walk. Now I have found it, the Blackrobes have shown it to me;" Big Turkey said, "Let us listen and walk now on the road of the Great Spirit and his Prayer" and "We meet to learn the laws of the Great Spirit and the road to heaven."[31] Since the Lakotas already believed that the Milky Way or "ghost road" was the road to heaven, the *Two Roads* meshed with their traditional symbolism and they quickly adopted this symbol.[32]

Protestants on the reservations, however, strongly objected to the use of the *Two Roads* because in this picture, Martin Luther was on the road to hell accompanied by flying demons. In 1897, the government agent at Pine Ridge Reservation, Captain W.H. Clapp voiced his objections to the catechism and provided his own description of its use:

---

28. Louis Goll, S.J., *Jesuit Missions Among the Sioux*, 29.

29. John Webster Grant, *Moon of Wintertime* (Toronto: University of Toronto Press, 1984), 124.

30. HRM 7-21-28, "Instruction by Means of the Two Roads," 8 pages, p. 3.

31. HRM 7-14-8, Digmann, diary, Nov. 15, 1891; Nov. 27, 1891; Dec. 19, 1992.

32. Powers, *Oglala Religion*, 53.

Father Bosch is evidently one of the nonprogressive Catholics, quite without a trace of liberal spirit, and one who deems it essential to obtrude the harshest, most illiberal views regarding other Christian teachings than his own. To this end he carries about with him a chart or a scroll, assuming to represent the experience of mankind since the creation, upon which are delineated two roads, along the sides of which are pictured leading historical and religious events. One road walked by all except the Catholics, leading by tortuous ways to an illuminated hell with the usual assortment of active attendants fully equipped with pitch forks, and guarded by nondescript reptilian devils, apparently of the Pterodactylian order. Into the care of these monsters those who walk over that trail, including Luther, and all others whom the church branded as heretics.[33]

Defending himself against these accusations, Bosch wrote his own letter to the Commissioner of Indian Affairs in which he maintained that he had no bias against other denominations and did not spread such bias.[34] Nevertheless, *The Two Roads* catechism was one of the devices that the Jesuits used that provoked indignation on the part of the Protestants, and tended to strain the already tense relationship of the Protestants and Catholics on the reservation. Despite this criticism, however, the Jesuits used *The Two Roads* through the 1940's because they found it to be an effective teaching device.[35]

Children's Retreats

In several other ways the Jesuits used the similarities between Lakota and Catholic ideas and practices to help the Lakotas understand Catholic teachings. An example of this was their comparison of the Catholic retreats to the Lakota vision quest. Even as early as 1895 the Jesuits, usually Sialm, Buechel, or Digmann, took the students at the mission schools on three day retreats,[36] and they continued this tradition through the 1940's. Digmann described a retreat in his diary:

Dec. 5-7 [1895] First Retreat of pupils. Seventy four made it. They kept silence better than our pupils in colleges, though it was left free to them. We adopted their word "*hamble iciyope*" for retreat, when they used to retire in solitude for three days on a

---

33. BCIM 1-35-22, Captain W.H. Clapp to Commissioner of Indian Affairs, Pine Ridge Agency, April 29, 1897.

34. BCIM 1-35-22, Father A. Bosch to the Commissioner of Indian Affairs, June 4, 1897.

35. BCIM 1-119-8, Grotegeers to Ketcham, Feb 8, 1920. Louis Goll, S.J., *Jesuit Missions Among the Sioux*, 30.

36. "St. Francis Mission, Rosebud Agency, South Dakota," *Woodstock Letters*, 34 (1905):106-107. HRM 7-14-8, Digmann, diary, Dec. 5-7, 1895.

hill to pray to the Great Spirit to obtain some favor or to thank for a favor obtained.[37]

In traditional Lakota religion, young men went on a vision quest called the *hamble iciyope* or *hanble ceyapi,* "crying for a vision."[38] By using the Lakota term for the vision quest to signify the retreat, the Jesuits drew on Lakota traditions to help them understand the significance of the retreat. To ease the Lakotas' transition to living as Catholics, the Jesuits emphasized the similarity between Lakota and Catholic practices. Even though the vision quest was a non-Catholic ritual, the Jesuits did not see the identification of the two customs as dangerous. Most likely, the Jesuits respected this Lakota ritual of extended contemplation and prayer since the Jesuits had a similar tradition in Ignatius's *Spiritual Exercises.* The Jesuits themselves even used this Lakota term to describe their own retreats. For example in 1892 Digmann wrote in his diary, "Began my Retreat and put a notice on my door: '*Hanmble iciya.*'"[39]

Lakota Art

The Jesuits and the BCIM also made an effort to integrate Native American art into the Catholic churches so that the churches would have an atmosphere that more closely meshed with their cultural sensibilities. Fr. J.B. Tennelly, BCIM Director, advocated that the missionaries preserve Native American culture, and include Native American art in Catholic structures. Describing a Pima chapel in 1939, Tennelly wrote:

> The soft-toned walls and ceiling are decorated, really decorated, with Pima designs, in red and blue, in artistically planned arrangements. The frieze running along the borders is made up of intricate, dynamic, graceful patterns such as you see on the Pima women's baskets. The ceiling is studded with patterns borrowed from the designs on the Pima war shields. . . . That an Indian should feel at home here is the intention. The aim of the Pima missionaries has been to make the Catholic religion understood, appreciated, and loved by the Indians. They have sought to make it appeal to the eye and ear, mind and heart. They have lived with the Pima Indians, learning their language and their modes of thought like one of them. They have studied how to assimilate the truths and practices of the Catholic Faith to the Pima in such as way that he becomes a Catholic Indian, that is a real Catholic in thought and feeling, while remaining what he wants to remain, an Indian.[40]

---

37. HRM 7-14-8, Digmann, diary, Dec. 5-7, 1895.

38. Powers, *Oglala Religion,* 56. This term is spelled in various ways: *hanblecheyapi, hanbleceya, hanbleyapi.*

39. HRM 7-14-8, Digmann, diary, Aug. 2, 1892.

Tennelly clearly advocated that the missionaries teach the Catholic faith in such a way as to encourage the Native Americans to maintain the positive aspects of their traditions. Tennelly also admired Native American art and, on another occasion in 1938, praised a missionary to the Kiowa, Fr. Aloysius Hitta, for establishing a Kiowa craft shop and making efforts to preserve their art. First describing their chapel, he said:

> The walls and the ceiling of the chapel are decorated with Indian designs in bright Indian colors, daringly and skillfully harmonized, as the best Indian artists know how to do. . . . When [Fr. Hitta] saw the old Indian arts and industries dying out, he felt that something wholesome was being lost. For he realized that the intention as well as the effect of the Indian arts is to give dignity to the common things of life, such as tools, dress, and dwellings. He also saw that their perpetuation would help to brace up a disinherited people by giving them a legitimate pride in their racial heritage.[41]

On Pine Ridge and Rosebud, the Jesuits also made an effort to preserve Lakota art. Realizing that the Lakota art was in danger of being lost or sold, Father Buechel, over a period of fifty years, collected a large number of Lakota art works. At St. Francis Mission, he established a museum of Lakota art and artifacts which continues today. In his collection were many fine examples of beadwork including beaded saddle bags, pipe bags, and clothing. He also collected many of the Lakotas' tools.

Several examples exist in which the Jesuits encouraged the production of Lakota art. In 1929 at a dedication ceremony of a Catholic chapel on the Holy Rosary Mission, a Lakota artist presented to the bishop a painting of Our Lady of Lourdes in the form of a Native American.[42] The Jesuits also had a Lakota artist paint the church at Holy Rosary with Lakota designs in 1935.[43] The use of Native American art in churches and in other Catholic celebrations like the Congresses made the Lakotas feel more comfortable in the Catholic Church. By encouraging Lakota art, the Jesuits indicated that Lakota art was an important cultural tradition that should be fostered.

---

40. J.B. Tennelly, S.S., "Place of the Cottonwood Trees," *Indian Sentinel* 19 (June 1939):83.

41. J.B. Tennelly, S.S., "The Romance of Anadarko." *Indian Sentinel* 18 (Jan. 1938):4.

42. HRM 2/1-1-6, "Chronicles of the Sisters of St. Francis," 1929 entry, p.123

43. HRM 2/1-1-8, "Chronicles of the Sisters of St. Francis," 1935-1936 entry. HRM 1/1-2-2, Fr. Coffey, S.J., "The Church at Holy Rosary Mission," June 24, 1940.

Processions

In their efforts to convert the Lakotas, the Jesuits often stressed those aspects of Catholicism that were similar to the Lakota traditions. They developed a pastoral ministry that stressed ritual, which was also a central aspect of the Lakota religion. Each year in May the Jesuits and laity celebrated the Rogation Days by processing through the mission farms, and praying for a good harvest.[44] The Rogation Days was a Catholic celebration which took place on the three days preceding Ascension Thursday. Beginning in the fifth century, the Rogation Days celebration originally took the place of an ancient Roman ritual, celebrated in late April, which also involved a procession and prayers dedicated to achieving a good harvest.[45] Though the Lakotas traditionally did not farm, they prayed and performed rituals for the purpose of accomplishing a successful hunt. The Rogation Days celebration showed the Lakotas that Catholics had similar ideas concerning the relationship of religion to the natural world. In other words, Catholics and Lakotas believed that prayers and rituals could affect the natural world, the harvest or the hunt.

The most popular procession at these missions, however, was the one held on the feast of *Corpus Christi*, which the Jesuits and Lakotas performed each year from 1889 through the 1940's.[46] Celebrated in the Church since the thirteenth century, the solemnity of the *Corpus Christi* was the feast of the Blessed Sacrament, a day dedicated to honoring Christ's presence in the Eucharist. During this celebration, the priests carried the Blessed Sacrament in a monstrance accompanied by a procession of the laity and clergy. Usually the processions took place outdoors. Often the laity carried banners in these processions and threw flowers in the path of the Eucharist. The Church set the date of this feast on the Thursday after Trinity Sunday, which was usually in June.

At St. Francis and Holy Rosary missions some *Corpus Christi* processions were small and just involved the people who went to a local chapel. But occasionally the Jesuits and Lakotas organized large and elaborate processions to which they invited the entire Catholic community on the reservation. In June, 1923, the Jesuits organized a *Corpus Christi* procession of about 1000 people. The procession itself lasted two hours, and an article in the *Jesuit Bulletin* described the scene:

> Having arrived at the top of the hill where the altar was erected, the people knelt in a large double circle all around the Blessed Sacrament. . . . Two large United States flags, and banners and

---

44. HRM 2/1-3-7, Sunday Announcements: 1903-1932, entries May 28, 1905, p.20; May 20, 1906, p.25.

45. Robert Broderick, ed., *The Catholic Encyclopedia* (Nashville: Thomas Nelson, 1987), 528.

46. HRM 7-14-8, Digmann, diary, June 20, 1889, p.18.

flags without number, were joyfully floating around the *Corpus Christi*. A number of Indians headed the procession in their glorious Indian bead-dresses. All the sodalities were in their regalia. The good Indians had brought all their paraphernalia to do honor to Christ.[47]

Similarly in June 1926 at Holy Rosary, the *Corpus Christi* procession "was headed by Nick Black Elk with his troop of Indians dressed in skins, and beads and profusely decorated with feathers."[48] This procession was elaborate and had floats, the mission band, banners of the Blessed Virgin, people wearing beaded Lakota clothing, and horseback riders. The catechists and the sodality members all took part. Similarly, in June, 1927, the newsletter for the Sodality of the Blessed Virgin Mary at Holy Rosary Mission described the arrangements for the procession: "Come for *Corpus Christi* men, women, and children. Come all. Bring your best Indian dresses and moccasins too. Nic[k] Black Elk will lead the Indian dress company right in front of the procession."[49] In these events the Lakotas used their traditional clothing as formal ceremonial attire for celebrating the Catholic rituals. The mission school children also participated in the event, carrying flags and banners. Dressed in white, the young girls carried baskets holding flowers which they threw in the path of the Eucharist.

The Jesuits also organized *Corpus Christi* processions at the Catholic Sioux Congresses and sometimes one or two thousand Lakotas participated.[50] Whether or not the Jesuits intended it, the *Corpus Christi* processions were similar in some ways to the native dances. Many Lakota dances themselves were a kind of procession, a long line of dancers who danced behind one another as they moved forward. In some dances they entered the dance grounds in a line then continued dancing in a circular manner. Thus, the *Corpus Christi* processions and Lakota dances were both elaborate outdoor celebrations that involved processions. The celebration of this type of ritual was appealing to the Lakotas since it was similar in some ways to their traditions.

In his notes, Sialm described the significance of the use of ritual, including the *Corpus Christi* processions, in the Jesuits' pastoral ministry:

> External ceremonies, well guided gatherings, regular festivities
> and processions will help to draw the children of nature to Christ

47. "Corpus Christi Procession at Holy Rosary Mission," *Jesuit Bulletin* 3 (March 1924):14.

48. "Corpus Christi at Holy Rosary Mission," *Jesuit Bulletin* 5 (Sept. 1926):6-7.

49. BCIM 14/1-9-9, "Sodality Newsletter," Holy Rosary Mission, Pine Ridge S.D., Sodality of the Blessed Virgin Mary, June, 1927.

50. Joseph Gschwend, S.J., "Catholic Sioux Indians in Council," *America*, June 20, 1931, p.254. John Woods, "27th Annual Sioux Congress, St. Francis Mission, S.D," *Indian Sentinel* 4 (Oct. 1924):148.

and to this Church. Our great Popes Pius X and Pius XI have some beautiful words which can give a direction also in establishing Catholic missions amongst pagans. Says Pius X, "Active participation in the most holy mysteries and the solemn and public prayer of the Church is the primary and indispensable source of the true Christian spirit." "Do not pray in the Mass, but pray the Mass." Pius XI in his great encyclical *Quas Primas*, promulgated on the Feast of Jesus Christ the King, [1925] says: "The annual celebration of the sacred Mysteries is more effective in informing people in the Faith and in bringing the inward joys of life to them, than the solemn pronouncements of the teaching Church. Documents are often read only by a few learned men: feasts move and teach all the faithful. The former speak only once, the latter every year and forever. The former bring a saving touch only to the mind, the latter influence not only the mind but the heart and man's whole nature. Being composed of body and soul, man needs to be aroused by external solemnities so that, through the variety and beauty of the Sacred Liturgy, he may receive the divine teachings in his soul and then changing them into his substance and blood, use them to advance the spiritual life. . . ." What makes an everlasting impression are undoubtedly the great processions where the congregations take part. . . . The *Corpus Christi* Procession on several occasions gathered more people than any sermons with great deliberations and orators. Indians wish to be ceremonial.[51]

The Jesuits at Holy Rosary were well-informed about papal teaching, and in this case their practices meshed perfectly with papal teaching. Referring to the Lakotas' *Corpus Christi* processions, Francis Coffey, S.J., of Holy Rosary Mission, wrote in 1942 that the "Indians were always deeply impressed by these dramatic expressions of the ritual of the Church."[52] Similarly Zimmerman believed that traditional Lakota religious tendencies aided their transition to the Catholic Church: "The simplicity and reverence in worship is edifying. Age-old love of ceremony enables [the Lakotas] to fit into our Catholic practices."[53] Both the Catholic and Lakota religions emphasized elaborate rituals, so the Jesuits built on these similarities and organized Catholic ceremonies that appealed to the Lakotas.

---

51. HRM 7-17-9, Placidus Sialm, S.J., "Notes On Indian Character," p. 2-3.

52. Francis Coffey, S.J., "Frolic and Festival," *Indian Sentinel* 22 (June 1942):91.

53. BCIM 1-217-1, Joseph Zimmerman to Mr. and Mrs. Poulter, May 1, 1933.

Buechel's Sermons

In their sermons and many other ways, the Jesuits tried to convince the Lakotas that the Catholic faith was an ancient tradition which other Native Americans accepted long ago. By doing this they built on the solidarity that Native Americans often felt for each other and on the respect they had for their ancestors. In his sermon, "The Last Day of May," Buechel referred to the appearance of the Lady of Guadalupe saying, "So your ancestors [believed that Mary was deserving of honor] 300 years ago when they once knew her."[54] About one-forth of his sermons principally concerned inspiring devotion to Mary, and he indicated that she had great compassion for Native Americans.[55] In a sermon he delivered in 1903 entitled "The Lady of Guadalupe," he described Mary's concern for Native Americans:

> No doubt Lourdes is a great favor for France; but it is not France alone that has such sacred places. In fact, wherever the holy gospel has been preached and faithfully received, there are certain chapels or churches in which the mother of God likes to bestow a greater abundance of graces on all those who come there with a childlike confidence. No wonder that the mother of all Christians showed her motherly love and care also to the Indians, when zealous missionaries had come to them and were trying to make them good Catholics. Let me tell you today how she erected her first throne of grace among the Indians at Guadalupe down in Mexico. . . . [after telling the story, he said] Countless are the favors our Lady of Guadalupe has done the Indians during those 362 years. She has been, indeed, the good mother of your ancestors as she is yours too.[56]

Stressing the universality of the Church, Buechel taught them that Mary appeared to Native Americans long ago, and stressed the Lakotas' ethnic connection to the Mexican Native Americans. The idea that Mary appeared to people related to them, "ancestors" as Buechel said, indicated to them that Mary cared for Native Americans just as much as she did for other peoples.

In several of his sermons, Buechel gave examples of pious Native Americans Catholics to provide the Lakotas with models from their ethnic group.[57] In his sermon "Exemplum Marianum: On the May Devotion,"

---

54. SFM 7-3-8, Eugene Buechel, S.J., "The Last Day of May," sermon, Holy Rosary Mission, May 31, 1909.

55. SFM 7-3-(7-9).

56. SFM 7-3-7, Eugene Buechel, S.J., "Our Lady of Guadalupe," sermon, St. Francis Mission, May 6, 1903.

57. SFM 7-3-8, Eugene Buechel, S.J., "The Desire of the Old Testament for the Savior and Our Desire for Holy Communion," sermon, Holy Rosary Mission, Dec. 5, 1909.

which he gave in 1904, he described the devotion to Mary that a group of Native Americans exhibited, indicating that he hoped the Lakotas would follow their example:

> Some time ago, I read a letter of an Indian missionary of another reservation that was written about 20 years ago. In that he tells how his Indians celebrated the month of Mary. They had their devotions in church of course, like we. But they did more. "During the month," he says, "the Indian camp puts on an almost Sunday appearance. Past quarrels are forgotten and old friendships are renewed. Frequent visits to the Bl. Virgin are made, and for the love of her they often give up their little recreations, and nothing seemed hard to them when there was question of doing her honor."[58]

In a 1907 sermon "All Saints Day: On Heaven," Buechel spoke of Tekakwitha as a model for them to follow and indicated that the Church taught that the different ethnic groups were equal in the eyes of God:

> Again we see not only old and young people in heaven but also different nations. The color of the face and the strange language do not make any difference with God, if they only love God and serve him. And thank God there [in heaven] we also behold many Indians. Hardworking missionaries and zealous sisters have lived among them in the past 300 years, have taught them to know and love God. And many became good holy Christians. Oh, how glad they are now to have listened to the priest and carried out the commandments of God. How richly they are rewarded for their service. One of them I hope will even soon be canonized i.e. we will call her a saint and have altars for her in churches. I suppose you have heard of her, the holy virgin Catherine Tekakwitha who died in 1680. And mingled with the Indians we see the millions of whites and colored people, and the inhabitants of China and Japan.[59]

In several of his sermons, Buechel said that Mary watched over the Native Americans and sometimes appeared to them. In his 1903 sermon titled "Mary the Friend of Children," he read De Smet's account of a Flathead boy to whom the Virgin Mary reputedly appeared several times. The boy in the account said:

> "Her garments were as white as snow; she had star over her head, a snake under her feet and near the snake a fruit which I did not recognize. I could see her heart from which rays of light burst

---

58. SFM 7-3-7, Eugene Buechel, S.J., "Exemplum Marianum. On the May Devotion," sermon, Saint Francis Mission, May 4, 1904. The Native Americans to whom he referred is unclear.

59. SFM 7-3-7, Eugene Buechel, S.J. "All Saints' Day: On Heaven," sermon, Holy Rosary Mission, Nov. 1, 1907.

forth and shone upon me. . . . She told me that she was pleased
that the first village of the Flatheads should be called St. Mary's."
No, [Buechel commented] it was no illusion. It was the Blessed
Virgin Mary.[60]

In the same sermon, he provided an example from the *Jesuit Relations* of
a pious Huron girl who also had a vision of Mary.[61] Buechel's sermon
indicated that he believed that these visions were genuine. In relating
these accounts, he taught the Lakotas that Native Americans were not
second-class citizens in the Church since Mary appeared to them as well
as whites.

Both Catholics and Lakotas believed that people had visions and
also that supernatural beings appeared to people. This was another point
of similarity that helped ease the Lakotas' acceptance of the Catholic
faith. Traditionally the Lakotas believed that dreams and visions carried
supernatural messages that had to be interpreted and followed. Though
the Jesuits may have been more cautious about interpreting dreams and
visions than the Lakotas, they recognized that miraculous dreams were
also part of Christian tradition. For example, writing in his diary in 1942,
Buechel told of the conversion of a Peyote leader:

> Silas Eagle Elk told me that he wanted to come back to the
> Church, that he was through with the peyote. His motive was a
> dream: he was on a road that led uphill. There he saw his father
> who died last summer – who stood on top of the hill. Silas was
> very anxious to go to him but felt it physically impossible to walk
> on. Then he heard a [?] back of him and he turned and saw a
> "little girl." She said, "If you throw that (peyote) drum (which he
> had under his arm) away, and follow that other road, you will
> reach your father." Thereupon Silas threw the drum away and
> woke up. Maybe this was an inspired dream.[62]

The Jesuits tended to accept as inspired those dreams and visions that led
people to the Church.

In many of his sermons, Buechel sought to show the Lakotas that
God and Mary helped those who prayed to them. Drawing examples from
the *Jesuit Relations*,[63] Buechel often spoke of Mary's intercession on behalf of Native Americans. In a 1903 sermon, "Confidence in Mary," he
told the story of a captive Huron man who sought Mary's help:

> Louis, a Christian Huron, was taken by the Iroquois Indians and
> was damned to the stake, i.e. to be burned. After the first torture

---

60. SFM 7-3-7, Eugene Buechel, S.J., "Mary the Friend of Children," sermon, St. Francis
Mission, May 27, 1903.

61. *Ibid.*

62. SFM 7-3-2, Eugene Buechel, S.J., diary, Jan 8, 1942.

63. Thwaites, 46:23-31.

he was securely bound with stout cords to await the preparations for death. Seemingly there was no hope of escaping death. But he did not give up his confidence in Mary and invoked her, and the bonds of his right hand began to relax. How fervent then rose his prayer of thanksgiving and petition, as they fell, leaving his hand free to unloose the rest of the cords that bound him. Guided by her he passed unharmed amid the large band of sleeping Iroquois and amid countless dangers, where the Queen of Mercy seemed to make him invisible to his enemies, he reached a safe place.[64]

In the same sermon he provided examples from the *Jesuit Relations* of two Native American women who asked Mary to heal their sick children. In these stories, the women prayed fervently to Mary, and their children were miraculously healed while they said their novenas. When he gave this sermon in 1903, many Lakotas still believed in the power of the medicine men and shamans. Buechel wanted to show them that it was through prayer and faith in God and Mary, rather than faith in the medicine men, that one might find healing or assistance.

In another sermon entitled "Our Lady of Loretto in Canada" which he gave in 1903, Buechel told other stories of Native Americans who were healed by their piety and devotion to Mary. In this sermon, he sought to substitute faith in Mary for their earlier belief in the efficacy of the medicine men's ceremonies: he said, "As soon as [the Canadian missionaries] could, they built a chapel in [Mary's] honor and taught the Indians there to apply for help instead of going to the medicine men."[65] By giving examples of Mary's intercession on behalf of Native Americans, Buechel reassured the Lakotas that Mary looked after them, and that prayers to her were effective. He also stressed in his sermons that a person came closer to God not so much through great intellectual learning, but rather by becoming humble and innocent like children. Instead of emphasizing Western academics as a way to knowledge of God, Buechel's sermons were more in the tradition of Thomas á Kempis than Aquinas. In short, Buechel's sermons stressed prayer, devotion, simplicity, humility, piety and obedience as the way to God, and reassured the Lakotas that salvation was open to all peoples.[66]

---

64. SFM 7-3-7, Eugene Buechel, S.J., "Confidence in Mary," sermon, St. Francis Mission, May 20, 1903.

65. SFM 7-3-7, Eugene Buechel, S.J., "Our Lady of Loretto in Canada," sermon, St. Francis Mission, May 13, 1903.

66. SFM 7-3-7, Eugene Buechel, "Mary the Friend of Children," sermon, St. Francis Mission, May 27, 1903.

Heroes and History

Another way that the Jesuits demonstrated the universality of the Church was to adapt to the Lakota culture. In the *Jesuit Bulletin* in 1939, Fr. W.P. Donnelly S.J., though not one of the Jesuits in the Dakotas, wrote an article in which he portrayed De Smet as an example of the model Jesuit missionary:

> In imitation of [Jesus'] great exemplar who became "to the Jews, a Jew" that he "might gain the Jews," so Father De Smet became to the Indians, an Indian that he might gain the Indians for Christ. So true is this, that no other title can be found which so aptly describes De Smet as the *White Indian.*[67]

Similarly, some of the Jesuits at Holy Rosary were so comfortable with the Lakota culture they became a part of it. For example Buechel often referred to himself as an "Indian." After Buechel's death, Joseph Karol, S.J., of St. Francis mission described him as one who adapted himself totally to the Lakota culture:

> Through his missionary work, his language study, and his artifact collection, Fr. Buechel gradually so identified himself with the Sioux that he unconsciously got into the habit of saying, "We Indians would say or do that this way."[68]

Praising Lakota habits, in 1931 Buechel wrote, "I like the oldtimers for their genuinely Indian ways, their fearless frankness, and child-like simplicity."[69] Moreover, in *The Jesuit Missions Among the Sioux* (1940), Fr. Goll indicated that Lakotas saw the Jesuits as a unique class of people who fit into their culture. After criticizing the government for unjustly stealing the Lakotas' land, Goll indicated that the Lakotas always distinguished between the government officials and the missionaries: he said "up to this day the Indians refrain from calling a Catholic priest a white man."[70]

The Jesuits were quite sympathetic to the struggles of the Lakotas through history and often found themselves in the position of speaking for the rights of the Native Americans and criticizing the injustice of the government. Often in their articles, the Jesuits pointed out that the government was at fault for breaking its treaties with the Native Americans, and turning its back when whites seeking gold, encroached on Sioux lands. In his account of the events leading to the Wounded Knee massacre, which

---

67. W.P. Donnelly, S.J., "The White Indian – A Century After," *The Jesuit Bulletin*, 17 (Jan. 1938):1-2.

68. SFM 7-1-2, Joseph Karol, S.J. "Chicken Feathers to War Bonnets -Fr. Buechel, S.J.," *Rapid City Journal*, Feb. 13, 1955, p.15.

69. Eugene Buechel, S.J., *Indian Sentinel* 11 (Spring 1931):56.

70. Louis Goll, S.J., *Jesuit Missions Among the Sioux*, 10.

he wrote in 1918, Fr. Jutz, S.J., accused the government of routinely cheating the Lakotas by failing to provide them with the beef promised to them by treaty. This situation, Jutz noted, led to the famine before the outbreak of violence at Wounded Knee and further eroded their faith in the government. Often, Jutz said, government workers stole the Native Americans' beef rations and sold them for profit.[71]

Fr. Goll also held the view that the government betrayed the Sioux on many occasions and he bitterly condemned the Army for slaughtering the Sioux people. In *The Jesuit Missions Among the Sioux*, he noted that on several occasions generals deliberately ventured on the Native Americans' lands to provoke them. He specifically denounced General Harney's actions in 1855 when the general lured the Sioux into a ambush by initiating a supposedly peaceful meeting with a chief.[72] In contrast, at the end his chapter on "Violations of Treaties," Goll praised Chief Red Cloud and, quoting him, acknowledged his determination to keep his word:

> [Red Cloud said] "I have signed the treaty of 1868 and I intend to keep it." [Goll added] In point of honor he towered above the five generals mentioned [Harney, Sherman, Sanborn, Sheridan, and Terry]."[73]

In many of their articles, the Jesuits mentioned Red Cloud's conversion and praised him as a Lakota hero who honored his treaty commitment to live in peace with the whites. The Jesuits also constantly reminded the Lakotas that Red Cloud sought to secure a Catholic school for the mission. In honor of Red Cloud's memory, in 1922 the Jesuits named one of the mission school buildings Red Cloud Hall.[74]

Ethics and Natural Law

No doubt the Jesuits had high regard for many of the Lakotas, but this does not mean that they were not condescending to the Lakotas at times. Sometimes the Jesuits referred to the Lakotas in terms that described them as children. In doing so, they indicated that they believed that the Lakotas were uneducated in the ways of the world and needed to be taught how to provide for themselves.

Even though they believed that the Lakotas had many good qualities, the Jesuits knew that the Lakotas had some violent customs even before they had contact with the West. Sometimes this violence was directed at

---

71. John Jutz, S.J., "Historic Data on the Causes of Dissatisfaction Among the Sioux Indians in 1890," *Woodstock Letters* 47 (1918):314-315.

72. Louis Goll, S.J., *Jesuit Missions and the Sioux* (St. Francis Mission, 1940), 4-5.

73. *Ibid.*, 7.

74. Placidus Sialm, S.J., "Holy Rosary Mission, South Dakota," *Jesuit Bulletin* 1 (Dec 1922):12.

their wives. Lakota men traditionally had several wives. The Lakotas, however, allowed women only one husband, and her fidelity to her husband was of paramount importance. According to their traditions, a Lakota man who found out or suspected his wife of committing adultery mutilated her as punishment by cutting off her braid, nose, or ear. A Lakota man could also kill his wife for this transgression.[75] The Lakota culture, as all cultures, had a violent side. The Jesuits at Holy Rosary and St. Francis learned of many such practices from a collection of De Smet's published letters and from the *Jesuit Relations*. These writings provided many examples of Native Americans cannibalizing captives of other Native American bands and Jesuit missionaries, after putting them through prolonged and excruciating torture. Since some of their brethren suffered brutal torture at the hands of Native Americans, the Jesuits believed that traditional Native American ethics left something to be desired.

Nevertheless, even though the Jesuits knew that the Lakotas traditionally had some violent customs, they also understood that the Lakotas did have some moral beliefs that were exemplary. For example, the Jesuits often praised the honesty of Lakotas like Red Cloud. In fact, they often blamed the whites for teaching the Lakotas many bad habits. In a sermon he gave in 1912 called "The Devil of Cursing," Buechel said, "Although I know that the Indians have no word for cursing, they will learn it from wicked white people. . . . Cursing is the Devil's language."[76] Recognizing the many vices of the white culture of the frontier, the Jesuits sought primarily to Christianize the Lakotas rather than Americanize them completely. Since the Jesuits believed that the American culture of the frontier was too secular and was fraught with problems like frequent divorces and alcoholism, they encouraged the Lakotas to embrace only what they saw as the positive aspects of American culture. They emphasized and praised certain American values like democracy, but did not try to eradicate Lakota culture and in place substitute American culture.

In a letter to his provincial in 1920, Father Charles Weisenhorn, S.J., of Holy Rosary, adopted much the same attitude as Buechel, and blamed many of the problems in Lakota society on contact with whites. He also praised the traditional Lakota beliefs concerning generosity and even said that some of their values were superior to those of many whites:

> No people is more generous than the Indian and gladly does he put all he has at the disposal of his guest, no matter at what hour of the day or night the latter may show up. And the missionary must perforce accept or go on record as a man without the semblance of courtesy or good breeding. . . . Reference to good

75. Royal Hassrick, *The Sioux* (Norman: University of Oklahoma Press, 1964), 48. Thwaites, 45:237. Walker, *Lakota Society*, 42.

76. SFM 7-3-9, Eugene Buechel, S.J., "Palm Sunday: The Devil of Cursing," sermon, March 31, 1912.

courtesy and good breeding may seem strange in speaking of these so-called savages. Yet I feel oftentimes the white man may learn a lesson from them in this respect. For the Indians have a rigid etiquette of their own, which is carefully observed, especially among the older generation, who have not been spoiled by too much contact with Protestantism and the van of white civilization. There is no such thing as a curse in the Indian language; the Red man will never take the name of God in vain, unless he has heard the expression from such as are civilized.[77]

Weisenhorn's attitude toward Protestants was not uncommon among the Jesuits in the Dakotas. Rather than blaming the Lakotas for the problems on the reservations such as divorce and drinking, the Jesuits placed the blame primarily on what they saw as being the bad influences of white Protestant culture.

The Jesuits had a high regard for the Lakotas' hospitality and often praised their traditional emphasis on generosity. In a *Sentinel* article in 1938, Sialm spoke of their charity:

It is an old Indian custom for the more prosperous to share with the needy. "We Indians," they say, "are not like the white people. We feed our visitors when we have something to eat in our house." Back of this I seem to hear One who says "give and it shall be given to you."[78]

Similarly, in 1940, Joseph Zimmerman, S.J., of Holy Rosary commented on the natural virtue of generosity in the Lakota community:

No one holds on to food or other necessities when others are in need, but everything is shared willingly and gladly. There is a genuine feeling of neighborly responsibility among our Indians here and elsewhere. But this is not altogether new. The old Sioux way of living was based upon mutual help rather than upon selfish individualism. Generosity was esteemed as a great virtue and was ostentatiously practiced. The missionaries have sought to make it Christian charity, and there is a display of real charitableness among our people.[79]

Zimmerman's attitude was an example that the Jesuits, rather than trying to eradicate the Lakota culture, actually desired to build on the virtues that the Lakotas already possessed, and perfect these virtues with Christianity. Similarly, discussing a new Boy Scout troop in 1940, Zimmerman said that the Lakotas possessed several virtues before the arrival of the missionaries:

---

77. Charles Weisenhorn, S.J., "A Missionary Trip in South Dakota," *Woodstock Letters* 49 (1920):157.

78. Placidus Sialm, S.J., "Dakota News," *Indian Sentinel* 18 (April 1938):64.

79. Fr. Joseph Zimmerman, S.J., "Sioux Virtues," *Indian Sentinel* 20 (Jan. 1940):11-12.

The appeal of the Scout oath is not new to the boys. Many of the ideals have come to them from the aboriginal tribal teachings of the campfire where bravery, truth, and generosity were named among principle primitive virtues.[80]

Fr. C.P. Jordan, a Lakota priest who as a child attended the St. Francis Mission School in the 1930's, also supported the idea that the Jesuits in 1930's and 40's saw virtue in the Lakota religion:

I think [the Jesuits] believed that there could be – without being a Catholic – there could be a thread of divinity working within the Indian. They had all that religion before the Jesuits came and they had a word for it *wakan*: mysterious, powerful.[81]

In many of their writings, the Jesuits demonstrated that they accepted the idea that the Lakotas perceived some truth through their traditional religion. From the Jesuits' perspective, the Lakotas' generosity and charity were examples of their perception of the natural law. In 1896, Digmann indicated in his diary that some of the Lakota traditions were derived from the natural law: "if the Lakota customs are from the Great Spirit, stick to them, but you can not serve two masters."[82]

Aquinas's approach to natural law indicated that non-Christians had some idea of God through the natural law which was engraved on the consciences of all people. God's law could also be perceived by examining nature. In the *Summa Theologica*, Aquinas wrote that "the natural law is nothing else than the rational creature's participation in the eternal law."[83] Through proper reasoning and examination of conscience, Aquinas believed, all people followed the eternal law to some extent when they did good acts. Since all good, from the point of view of the Church, comes from God, the Jesuits believed that all the good that was present in the Lakota culture also came from God.

The Jesuits were familiar with Aquinas especially since Leo XIII inaugurated the Thomistic Revival in 1879 with the encyclical *Aeterni Patris*. Reacting against the liberalism of the time, Leo XIII recommended the study of Aquinas' theology to combat the errors of that time. In this encyclical, he acknowledged that even non-Christians perceive the light of truth through the natural law, and quoted Romans 2:14-15 to support his statement:

---

80. Joseph Zimmerman, S.J., (catalogued under Zimmerman's name) letter, feast of St. Joseph, 1940, Missouri Province Archives of the Society of Jesus in St. Louis.

81. Fr. C.P. Jordan, interview, St. Francis, S.D., June, 1992.

82. HRM 7-14-8, Digmann, diary, Sept. 8, 1896.

83. Thomas Aquinas, *Summa Theologica* (London: Burns, Oates, and Washbourne, 1915) vol. 8, p. 11, question 91, art. 2.

Hence it is that certain truths which were either divinely proposed for belief, or were bound by the closest chains to the doctrine of faith, were discovered by pagan sages with nothing but their natural reason to guide them, were demonstrated and proved by becoming arguments. For as the Apostle says, the invisible things of Him, from the creation of the world, are clearly seen, being understood by the things that are made: His eternal power also and his divinity; and the gentiles who have not the Law show, nevertheless, the work of the Law written in their hearts.[84]

The attitudes of the Catholic Anthropological Conference (CAC) also expressed the Catholic Church's tolerant attitude toward non-Christian religions and customs. Founded in 1926, the CAC was a group of Catholic scholars, anthropologists, and missionaries who worked together to study and preserve the ethnologic, historic, religious, social, and artistic knowledge of non-Western cultures. Realizing that the missionaries had direct knowledge of the cultures, the CAC considered them to be ideal sources of ethnological data. The purpose of the CAC was to gather knowledge about non-Western societies to study and preserve, and also to help the missionaries who evangelized these societies. The Director of the BCIM was on the Executive Board of the CAC to show his support of the effort. In 1926 the Secretary/Treasurer of the Catholic Anthropological Conference (CAC), John Cooper, corresponded with Buechel and asked him to record any ethnological data about the Lakotas that was of scientific value.[85]

Primarily the CAC was a scientific organization that felt a certain urgency about collecting data on archaic cultures because it recognized that they were "becoming extinct."[86] The CAC also saw no inconsistency about its zeal to study non-Christian cultures. In his papers, Buechel had a CAC pamphlet which described its purpose:

> Our missionaries are in a position to make valuable original contributions to science. They should have the credit for giving such scientific data to the world and for adding to the sum of human knowledge. . . . We are gradually getting in a position to reconstruct the early unwritten history of man, and the growth of his arts, his social institutions, his moral codes and his religion. Naturally theology is deeply interested in this reconstruction as are ethics and apologetics. . . . We are specially encouraged, moreover by the sympathetic interest of the present Holy Father. Pius XI has cordially blessed a similar movement in Europe. . . . [He] contributed 50,000 lire to the support of the Catholic anthro-

---

84. Pope Leo XIII, *Aeterni Patris* in *The Papal Encyclicals*, Claudia Carlin, ed., p.18, paragraph 4.

85. SFM 7-1-4, John Cooper to Buechel, July 5, 1926.

86. SFM 7-1-4, "The Catholic Anthropological Conference," pamphlet, 1926, p. 2-3.

pological periodical, "Anthropos". . . . [He also] founded a new
ethnological museum in Rome as the outcome of the Mission
Congress of 1925.[87]

The Church supported study of anthropology, and these remarks indicated
that it saw anthropology as a valid science that aided in studying religion
and cultures. Furthermore, in this passage, the statement that "theology"
was interested in the development of religion and ethics indicated that
the theologians wanted to examine the non-Christian religions for evidence of natural law. If the members of the CAC believed that non-
Christian religions were wholly demonic, then they would have believed
that theologians would have had no reason to study these religions. Cooper actually believed that all peoples had some kind of religion and most,
in his words, had

> some idea, clear or hazy, of a Supreme or Superior Being. . . .
> Beneath all the unending variations of moral codes there runs a
> certain uniformity of ethical standard corresponding roughly to
> the Decalogue taken in its most literal sense.[88]

Even before Cooper contacted him in 1926, Buechel proved to be a
formidable scholar of the Lakota culture, and in addition to collecting the
Lakota legends, he carefully took notes on all aspects of the Lakota way
of life. Among his unpublished papers, Buechel wrote a 40 page document titled "Ethnological Notes" (1915). In these notes he carefully recorded the physical and cultural aspects of Lakota religious ceremonies
from his catechist, Silas Fills-the-Pipe and other Lakota informants.
Buechel recorded the practices that took place in the pipe smoking ceremony, adoption ceremony, menstrual ceremony, vision quest, and Sun
Dance.[89] He drew pictures of the clothing worn,[90] recorded the prayers in
the Lakota rituals, and described the Lakota games, dances, and ritual
clothing. In addition to his identity as a missionary, he also saw himself
as a scientist and folklorist who sought to study and preserve knowledge
about the Lakota culture. The fact that the CAC and the pope supported
anthropological endeavors to understand archaic cultures was an even
greater boost to his efforts.

---

87. *Ibid.*, 3-5.

88. John Cooper, "Present-Day Anthropology: Its Spirit and Trend," *Primitive Man*
(Washington: Catholic Anthropological Conference) 1 (Jan. 1928):4.

89. HRM 7-4-3, Eugene Buechel, S.J., "Ethnological Notes," 1915.

90. *Ibid.* HRM 7-4-3, Eugene Buechel, S.J., "Indian Games and Sports." notes, 63 games
recorded.

Lakota Dances, Games and Food

Though Buechel was interested in Lakota culture including the traditional dances, many of the Jesuits, from the 1890's to the 1910's, tended
to discourage Lakota Catholics from taking part in Lakota dances. For
years after the emergence of the Ghost Dance, the Jesuits were cautious
about the Lakota dances, and also tried to discourage the practice of the
Sun Dance. The Jesuits wanted to eradicate some dances like the Ghost
Dance and the dances associated with the *yuwipi* because they saw them
as being contrary to the Catholic faith. Nevertheless, they believed that
some of the other Lakota dances in themselves were perfectly acceptable.
In 1899 in his diary, Digmann stated his opinion of the dances:

> The Indian dances in themselves are innocent and moral. Their
> so-called Omaha dance is a war dance, mimic imitation of their
> Indian warfare. The sexes are strictly separated. Men and
> women have their own dance. The bad features about their
> dances are that they start only at dark and dance the whole night
> till daybreak. The young folks stand outside the hall and are left
> to themselves. Also the customary "giving away" at their dances
> is a drawback to civilization.[91]

Digmann did not oppose all the Lakota dances, and did not see all of
them as being contrary to the Catholic faith. He did, however, oppose
the behavior that he believed accompanied these dances. He also distinguished between the "moral" and the "bad features" of the entire event.
Fearing that licentious behavior might occur, Digmann did not like to see
young people "left to themselves" all night at the dances. He also opposed the give-away that occurred at the dances.

In 1891 before an Omaha War Dance, in which the Lakotas of the
Omaha society painted their bodies with various designs, a Lakota dancer
asked Digmann if the dance was "bad." Digmann replied, "I would not
say it is a sin but it is foolish what you do."[92] Though he certainly discouraged the dancers, Digmann did not condemn the Omaha dance as being contrary to Catholic religion. He even saw the Omaha society, which
sponsored the dance, as having the potential to be beneficial to the Lakotas. Traditionally the Omaha society was a Lakota men's fraternity, which
encouraged bravery and honesty.[93] A Lakota man, Thomas Tyon, explained the rules of this society (c. 1911):

> Whoever is an Omaha member is commanded to think nothing
> bad. And when they hear anything bad about people they pay no
> attention to it. They are commanded not to fight with anyone.

---

91. HRM 7-14-8, Digmann, diary, Nov. 21, 1889.

92. *Ibid.*, Nov. 27, 1891.

93. Walker, *Lakota Belief and Ritual*, 264-268.

They are commanded not to lie. And whatever they give they are
commanded not to take back. Each day they are commanded to
think good thoughts.[94]

In a diary entry in 1899, Digmann indicated that the Omaha society
could eventually be transformed into Catholic society: "This pagan
[Omaha] society may turn out a basis for a Christian brotherhood (St.
Joseph and St. Mary's societies)."[95] Here Digmann showed that he
wanted to retain this society's structure and adapt it to create a Catholic
society.

In the 1910's and 1920's, the Catholic missionaries in different parts
of America had mixed views of the native dances, but several accepted
them. In an article he wrote for the *Sentinel*, John Lucchesi, S.J., a missionary to the Alaskan Eskimos, described a feast he attended in 1917:

> The feast always includes Indian dances, amidst singing and the
> beating of huge whale, or walrus, skin drums. These dances are
> very nice and modest. . . . The dance of the women would put to
> shame the dances of many white, and even Christian, women,
> [since the Eskimo dances] are so modest, so pleasing and so
> graceful.[96]

Also recounting his experience in the *Sentinel*, Ferdinand Ortiz, O.F.M.,
a Franciscan missionary in New Mexico attended a Mescalaro maiden's
dance in 1920 and did not object to it:

> An elderly Mescalero insisted that God had taught this strange
> ceremonial to men. At any rate, it is a mysterious religious
> dance, a remnant of paganism, though it be and is stripped of an-
> cient objectionable features.[97]

Both these missionaries indicated that the dances in themselves were innocent, or could be made innocent if the Native Americans purged them
of the aspects contrary to the Catholic faith.

Henry Grotegeers, a German Jesuit and Mission Superior at Holy
Rosary from 1916 to 1920, however, believed that many of the Lakota
dances led to licentious behavior among the young and to broken marriages among the older people. In 1921, he recommended limiting the
dances to once a month and forbidding the camping out at the dances.[98]
Even though Grotegeers referred to what he called the "dance evil,"[99] this
does not mean that he thought that all the Lakota dances in themselves

94. *Ibid.*, 267.
95. HRM 7-14-8, Digmann, diary, Nov. 21, 1889, p.19.
96. John L. Lucchesi, S.J., "Holy Cross Mission," *Indian Sentinel* 1 (Oct. 1917):23-25.
97. Ferdinand Ortiz, O.F.M., "The Maiden's Dance," *Indian Sentinel* 2 (July 1920):124.
98. BCIM 1-126-3, Grotegeers to Ketcham, Nov. 17, 1921, p.2-3.
99. BCIM 1-132-5, Grotegeers to Hughes, Oct. 26, 1922.

were evil. Rather he was more concerned with the behavior that he believed occurred at the dances. He also pointed to what he thought was the excessive number and length of the Lakota dances, and expressed his desire to limit them, not abolish them totally.

On the reservations during the summer, the dances lasted several days, and often a whole family traveled to the dance grounds and camped out there. Sometimes they traveled from one dance to another. The Jesuits believed that the frequency of absence from the house and farm for this long adversely affected the Lakotas' economic conditions.[100] Additionally, attending the dances was expensive, and when they returned from the dances, sometimes their crops were spoiled.

In a *Sentinel* article in January, 1923, Louis Goll, S.J., suggested that discouraging the dances by ridiculing them was appropriate:

> The solution of the problem concerning the [Lakota] dances would probably be reached if the white people of the surrounding towns would frown upon these ancient practices as foolish and no longer worthy of notice. As a matter of fact, they laugh at the absurd antics of the dancers. Where persuasion fails to have any effect, ridicule often triumphs.[101]

In the next issue of the *Sentinel* (April 1923), however, an editorial conveyed the BCIM's policy toward Native American dances:

> Recent Associated Press dispatches from New Mexico and Washington have contained the story of the protest of the Indians against a supposed order of the Commissioner of Indian Affairs, Charles H. Burke, suppressing all Indian dances. The Indian Office has simply urged the Indians themselves to limit the number of dances. . . . Certainly the Catholic missionaries have been tolerant of all innocent amusements, including dances, of the Indians. . . . At a meeting of Sioux Indians held on the Cheyenne River Reservation in July of last year, the Indians, in response to the advice of the Catholic missionaries that dances should be limited to four times a year, voluntarily voted the number be reduced to three.[102]

Reacting to media attacks on the Commissioner of Indian Affairs for his alleged dance policy and also hoping to avoid criticism, the BCIM decided to inform its patrons and missionaries that it supported the toleration of "innocent" dances. At this time, the missionaries at Holy Rosary and St. Francis began to adopt a more tolerant position on the Lakota dances.

---

100. BCIM 1-217-2, Fr. Goll, Dec 15, 1933, notes, 10 pages, p.4.

101. Louis Goll, S.J., "Catholic and Protestant Missionaries Confer at Pierre," *Indian Sentinel* 3 (Jan. 1923):13.

102. "Indian Dances," *Indian Sentinel* 3 (April 1923):58-59.

Also in the 1920's, Father Philip Gordon, a Chippewa priest who occasionally came to the Sioux Congresses, was active in preserving Native American traditions and encouraging his Minnesota congregation to perform the traditional dances. In 1926 the federal government attempted to restrict Chippewa tribal dances, claiming that they inhibited the Chippewa's progress. Arguing that the Chippewa dances were as harmless as those of white people, Gordon protested against the government policy:

> The different tribal dances constitute about all there is left to the present day Indians to connect them with their savage ancestors who roamed the prairies and woods of America before this continent was discovered. The dances are a tradition with them, and are consequently dear to the heart of every Indian. Some of the dances are ceremonial in nature, others are indulged in merely for recreation and entertainment, just as white folks do. The federal government officials are in for a difficult job if any serious attempt is made to deprive the Indians of this traditional custom.[103]

Yet even though he supported the Native dances, Gordon, like the Jesuits in the Dakotas, voiced his disapproval of the types of dances that involved drinking, late nights, and licentiousness.[104]

By the 1920's the Jesuits at Holy Rosary and St. Francis allowed Catholics both to view the dances and participate in them. The Jesuits also attended the dances at this time. Beginning in 1926, the Jesuits ran a summer camp for Catholic boys on St. Francis Mission called Camp De Smet, and each year the Jesuits took the boys to see the traditional Lakota dances.[105] In the 1930's, the Lakotas also performed their traditional dances during the Fourth of July celebrations which the Jesuits attended. For example, in 1934 Leo Cunningham, S.J., said that on their Fourth of July celebration, the Lakotas of Holy Rosary Mission held "various Indian dances" on the mission grounds.[106] The Jesuits even sponsored an event in 1936 at which the Lakota boys performed the Omaha dance in traditional Sioux garb at the St. Francis Mission School.[107] Though the Jesuits did not take part in the dances except as spectators, their willingness to allow the dances to take place on the mission grounds indicated that they accepted them. The Jesuits in attendance often took photographs of the

---

103. Paula Delfeld, *The Indian Priest Father Philip B. Gordon: 1885-1948* (Chicago: Franciscan Herald Press, 1977), 104. Quote from *St. Paul Daily News*, August 22, 1926.

104. *Ibid.*, 104.

105. Thomas Bowdern, S.J., "Boy's Summer Camp Among Sioux," *Indian Sentinel* 6 (Summer 1926):115-116. Thomas Bowdern, S.J., "A Jesuit Summer Camp for Boys," *Jesuit Bulletin* 5 (March 1926):13.

106. Leo Cunningham, S.J., "Fourth of July with the Sioux," *Indian Sentinel* 14 (Summer 1934):53.

107. "Pageant Grand Success," *The Sioux Chieftain* 3 (June 1936):3, St. Francis collection, Missouri Province Archives of the Society of Jesus in St. Louis.

dances which they published in the *Sentinel*. Furthermore, several of the Catholic Lakota elders who were at Holy Rosary and St. Francis in the 1930's said that the Jesuits at this time objected to neither the Lakota dances nor the Lakota Catholics' participation in them.[108] Further evidence to support this was an article in 1936 in the *Sina Sapa Wocekiye Taeyanpaha, The Catholic Sioux Herald* which set down guidelines for the St. Joseph's society: "A member of the St. Joseph Society may go to Indian dances, but must govern his conduct properly."[109] Again, the emphasis was on the conduct at the dances, and not on the dances themselves.

In the 1930's, even those elder Jesuits who may have had some reservations about the Lakota dances, still did not regard them as sinful. For example, Sialm said of Black Elk (c.1935):

> He was well-educated in the faith, because he remembered many things which the fathers told him. He then gave up dancing for some years, but in the last years he fell back into the old Indian dances without losing the faith.[110]

Since he said that Black Elk danced "without losing the faith," he indicated that the dances did not conflict with Catholic practice.

Lawrence Helmueller, S.J., a Jesuit scholastic at St. Francis Mission from 1938 to 1939 who returned there as a priest in 1944, said that the Jesuits at that time did not believe that the Lakota dances were objectionable in any way. But like Groteegers, Helmueller commented that the problem with the dances was that they often lasted weeks. He said that commonly Lakota families traveled from one dance to another for a large part of the summer and this diminished their ability to support their families.[111]

From 1939 to 1941, when he taught at the Holy Rosary Mission School, John Scott, an American Jesuit, often went to the Lakota dances. He enjoyed the dances and said that the Jesuits did not object to them. He commented that the Jesuits did not mind at all if Catholics took part in these dances, and agreed with Helmueller the Jesuits did not believe they threatened the Catholic religion in any way.[112] In 1941 Scott attended one of the Sun Dances and wrote about it in the *Jesuit Bulletin*. In this article he

---

108. Jessie Crow, interview, Oglala, S.D., May and Sept. 1992. Viola Packard, interview, St. Francis, Sept. 1992. Myrtle Crow Eagle, interview, St. Francis, Sept. 1992. Bernard Flood, interview, Okreek, Rosebud Reservation, S.D., Sept. 1992. Phyllis Clifford, interview, Kyle, S.D., May 1992. Maggie Brown (Randall was her maiden name) interview, Wanblee, S.D., May 1992. Leo Chasing-In-Timber, interview, Two Strike District, Rosebud Reservation, Oct. 1992.

109. Raymond DeMallie, *The Sixth Grandfather*, 16. "Rules for St. Joseph's Society." *Sina Sapa Wocekiye Taeyanpaha: The Catholic Sioux Herald.* (Marty, S.D.: St. Paul's Catholic Indian Mission) 5(18) (Nov. 1, 1936):7.

110. HRM 7-17-6, Placidus Sialm, S.J., *Camp Churches*, 51.

111. Lawrence Helmueller, S.J., interview, Creighton University, Omaha, Oct. 1992.

112. John Scott, S.J., interview, Creighton University, Omaha, Oct. 1992.

was not critical of the Sun Dance at all, but rather enjoyed the celebration. This particular Sun Dance did not involve piercing, so it was a variation of the original. In his conclusion to his article, Scott praised the dance:

> Once more the Sioux could lift his head and walk erect, for he
> was a brother of Christ. Again he could dance and sing, but no
> longer would he have to scarify his body and subject himself to
> the long fast of the Sun Dance. This time it was a dance of joy
> for *Wakan Tanka* was his Father.[113]

Scott indicated that the Jesuits allowed Lakota Catholics to take part in the Sun Dance since the Lakotas removed the aspects that the Jesuits found objectionable and transformed this dance so that it was consistent with Catholic morals. Though the Lakota Catholics' participation in traditional Lakota ceremonies led some to think that they were superficial Catholics, this was not the case, and those who made this error confused syncretism with missionary adaptation. Native participation in these ceremonies was actually an indication of the Church's tolerant attitude at this time towards those aspects of indigenous culture that were not antagonistic to the Catholic faith.

Another part of Lakota culture that the Jesuits permitted was the Lakota games, and the Lakotas played many of their traditional games at Catholic celebrations.[114] The Jesuits considered these games innocent amusements that were part of the traditional Lakota celebration. The Lakotas played them sometimes after Mass when they gathered together for picnics. In 1946, Peter Price, S.J., of Holy Rosary Mission, described one of these picnics:

> First there were the foot races. Everyone who was strong enough
> took part in the contests according to custom. All the married
> men raced, then the married women, and last the boys and
> girls. . . . The most strenuous and the most popular of the con-
> tests that day was the Indian ball game. This is somewhat like
> lacrosse.[115]

The Lakota games were one more aspect of their culture that the Jesuits did not try to change since they understood that these games were connected neither to religious practices to which the Jesuits objected nor to practices which they believed were detrimental to the Lakotas' well-being.

At their feasts and celebrations which the Jesuits attended, the Lakotas also retained their culinary traditions and continued to eat dog-meat.

113. John Scott, S.J., "Sun Dance in Dakota," *Jesuit Missions* 15 (June 1941):167.

114. BCIM 14/1-26-3, *Sina Sapa Wocekiye Taeyanpaha*, "The Congress of Catholic Indians at St. Francis Mission S.D. July 1, 2, 3, and 5," (Oct. 15, 1905) supplement.

115. Peter Price, S.J., "Grey Hills People," *Indian Sentinel* 26 (June 1946):85-86.

The Jesuits took part in these feasts and also became accustomed to them. In 1892 when he visited a Lakota friend, Digmann asked his host,

> "Where did you get the young pigs from?" He smiled and said: "It is not pork." It was a young dog. Hungry as I was I never had tasted any meat like this but it tasted good and I kept it with me.[116]

At least through the 1920's, the Jesuits ate dog when the Lakotas offered it to them, and the Lakotas continued this custom through the 1930's.[117]

Wasna was another traditional Lakota food that they served to the Jesuits. The Lakotas made it of cherries and meat, and served at feasts such as Christmas.[118] Throughout their time in the Dakotas, the Jesuits enjoyed and recommended the use of Lakota foods. For example, in 1935 Sialm wrote that he noticed a tree that had much of its bark cut off of it. When he asked a Lakota man about this, the man replied,

> "We have no coffee so we cut the bark to make something to drink. It tastes good." I encouraged the Indians in their inventions, as did the missionaries of old who induced the Indians to use home products and medicines.[119]

Often the Jesuits were impressed with the Lakotas' ingenuity and ability to make use of all at their disposal to make their lives better. Certainly the use of indigenous food was not a controversial aspect of missionary adaptation, since it was clearly indifferent to the Catholic faith. Nevertheless, the survival of the Lakota culinary habits was just one more indication that the Jesuits did not hold total Americanization as an ideal and did not attempt to eliminate those Lakota customs that were inoffensive to Christian ethics.

The Sacred Pipe

Another example of an aspect of the Lakota culture that the Jesuits accepted was the smoking of the sacred pipe. The pipe, sometimes called the calumet, was the most sacred piece of religious paraphernalia of most Natives of North America including the Lakotas. Native Americans used the pipe at sacred celebrations as a means of contact and communion with

---

116. HRM 7-14-8, Digmann, diary, Oct. 29, 1892.

117. Leo Cunningham, S.J., "Fourth of July with the Sioux," *Indian Sentinel* 14 (Summer 1934):53. Charles Weisenhorn, S.J., "A Missionary Trip in South Dakota," *Woodstock Letters* 49 (1920):161. Stephen McNamara, S.J., "Black Elk and Brings White," *Indian Sentinel* 21 (Nov. 1941):140.

118. Joseph Zimmerman, S.J., 1930 circular letter in *High Eagle and His Sioux* John Scott, S.J. ed. (St. Louis, 1963), p.14.

119. BCIM 1-229-15, Fr. Sialm to Fr. Hughes, Holy Rosary Mission, Pine Ridge, Feb. 2, 1935.

the Great Spirit. In almost all their ceremonies, they prayed with the pipe, and smoked the pipe with others as a sign of good will. According to Lakota tradition, the Great Spirit gave the pipe to the Lakotas for the purpose of communicating with him. The Lakotas believed that the White Buffalo Calf Woman (sometimes called the Buffalo Cow Woman) brought the sacred pipe to the Lakotas when she appeared magically out of a cloud of mist to two men. One man, however, had improper sexual intentions towards her and approached her. He was summarily turned into a pile of bones with snakes crawling among them.[120] The White Buffalo Calf Woman then told the other man to gather the people. After he did she instructed them on the use of the pipe and gave it to them. She told them a common version of Lakota tradition which explained that the pipe was a symbol of everything in the world: the red stone bowl was a symbol of the earth, the pipe-stem represented the plants; the buffalo carved on the bowl represented the animals; the eagle feather attached to the pipe represented the birds. She told them that the smoking of the pipe linked the smoker to all the things in the universe including ones' relatives and *Wakantanka*. When people smoked the pipe together, this ceremony bound them together in friendship, and thus one of the pipe's uses was to make peace between people.[121]

De Smet often smoked the pipe with the Sioux, and the Jesuits at Holy Rosary and St. Francis were quite familiar with De Smet's letters. Quoting one of De Smet's letters in his notes, Sialm wrote:

> They immediately brought the calumet after having offered it to the Master of Life imploring his blessing, the savages in their engaging simplicity, presented it to his visible representative, entreating us to make known to him their esteem and love which they bear to him.[122]

Even though they realized that the sacred pipe was a central piece of religious paraphernalia, the Jesuits at Holy Rosary and St. Francis did not prohibit its use. The Benedictine missionaries to the Sioux also accepted the use of the sacred pipe. In the early years of the Standing Rock mission, Father Jerome Hunt allowed the Sioux to come to the altar to light their pipes from the candles during Mass.[123] One of the Standing Rock Sioux, Weasel Bear, described the atmosphere of the first masses at Ft. Yates:

---

120. Joseph Epes Brown, *The Sacred Pipe*, 3-5.

121. Powers, *Oglala Religion*, 82. Walker, *Lakota Belief and Ritual*, 90.

122. HRM 7-17-9, Placidus Sialm, S.J., "Ethnological Notes," Quote from Chittenden, 2:634.

123. Sister M. Claudia Duratschek, O.S.B., *Under the Shadow of His Wings* (Aberdeen: North Plains Press, 1971), 86.

I recall clearly how we old-time Indians acted when we first attended mass. It was our custom, while assembled in council, to sit on the ground in a circle and pass the pipe. To us, at that time, attendance at Mass was but another council where we came to hear a message for our benefit. So we came into the church and sat down on the floor, while one of the party filled a large, red-stone pipe, lit it, and sent it around the circle.[124]

The Jesuits at Pine Ridge also tolerated the use of the pipe and even participated in this custom. At Pine Ridge, in an attempt to pacify the Ghost Dancers before Wounded Knee, Digmann met with them a month before the massacre, and he described the meeting in his diary: "I called the meeting in the large loghouse of Old Chief High Bear, the pipe of peace went round and the situation was talked over."[125] In this situation, Digmann must have smoked the pipe with them since to refuse would have been a great insult, and would have ended the negotiations. Writing in 1913, Henry Westropp, S.J., from Holy Rosary described his visit with Blue Cloud, a Yankton Sioux acquaintance, who knew De Smet when he was young:

[Blue Cloud] welcomed us with true hospitality, and filling his calumet with chan-sha-sha (Indian Tobacco made from the red willow) he courteously begged Little Owl (my Indian name) to smoke the "pipe of peace" with him. Amid the soft smoke curling about us he told us many tales of his good friend Father De Smet, told them as though they happened but yesterday.[126]

Fr. Helmueller, S.J., of St. Francis and Fr. John Scott of Holy Rosary, also said that the Jesuits in the 1940's did not consider smoking the pipe sinful and did not forbid its use.[127]

An indication that the hierarchy did not condemn the use of the sacred pipe, which was sometimes refered to as the calumet, was the fact that the Marquette Society published a magazine called *The Calumet*. Moreover, other Catholic periodicals like *The Indian Sentinel* and *Jesuit Bulletin* often published photographs of Lakota men smoking the pipe. In the December, 1939 issue of the *Jesuit Bulletin*, the magazine featured a photograph of Chief Standing Bear holding the pipe and instructing Lakota children in Catholic doctrine.[128] Even at the Catholic Sioux Congresses some Lakotas smoked the pipe. A photograph showed the Director of the BCIM, Fr. J.B. Tennelly, lighting the pipe of one of the Lakotas at

---

124. *Ibid.*, 87.

125. HRM 7-14-8, Digmann, diary, Nov. 20, 1890.

126. BCIM 14/1-4-2, Henry Westropp, S.J., "A Relic of Father DeSmet," *The Calumet* (Dec. 1913).

127. Lawrence Helmueller, S.J., interview, Creighton University, Omaha, Oct. 1992.

128. *Jesuit Bulletin*, (Dec. 1939).

the 1936 Catholic Sioux Congress at St. Francis.[129] Though the man with the pipe was probably not using it in the context of a religious rite, Tennelly, by his actions, encouraged the Lakota tradition of smoking the sacred pipe.

The sacred pipe, however, was such an important religious artifact even out of the context of a formal ceremony that to some Lakotas, it was never just a pipe. Though the Lakotas smoked the pipe for enjoyment as well as in the context of rituals, smoking the pipe for many Lakotas was not simply a secular event. One of the sacred functions of the pipe was to bring people together in a trusting relationship when they smoked it. Even after becoming Catholics, some of the Lakotas continued to believe that the pipe was sacred. For example, in Black Elk's forward (c.1947) to Joseph Epes Brown's book, *The Sacred Pipe,* Black Elk affirmed his faith in Christ but also stated that he believed that the White Buffalo Calf (Cow) Woman brought the sacred pipe to the Lakotas.[130] By the 1940's, however, most Lakota Catholics were not particularly interested in the pipe as a religious artifact. Nevertheless, for some Lakota Catholics, the pipe was still a sacred and significant object. The Jesuits also knew the pipe's traditional significance, but still permitted its use. Since most of the Catholic Lakotas did not use the pipe in the context of the traditional pipe ceremonies, the Jesuits did not fear that they were practicing any rituals contrary to the Catholic faith.

Lakota Names

The Jesuits valued many aspects of the Lakota culture, especially the tight-knit, extended family structure that pervaded the Lakota community. A conversation between Henry Westropp, S.J., and Brings White illustrated the familial relationship that existed between the Jesuits and Lakotas. Brings White was a Lakota woman who married Black Elk after his first wife died, and was Westropp's close friend. After taking a long trip by horse and buggy, Westropp arrived at her tent late at night. Stephen McNamara, S.J., of Holy Rosary, described their meeting: Westropp called to her saying "*Tunwin*" which means "Aunt," and she replied

> "Yes, my nephew." Again, Father cheerfully spoke out; "*Tunwin, wanagi ki palek cek ama u pelo,*" meaning, "Aunt, the ghosts have pushed me here." This expression in the Sioux language conveys the picture of a tired and hungry Indian who after a long journey has been guided by a spirit, maybe his Guardian Angel, to a place where he could get a bite to eat.[131]

---

129. BCIM 9/1/1-45-1, photograph, St. Francis, 1936 Catholic Sioux Congress.

130. Joseph Epes Brown, *The Sacred Pipe,* xix-xx.   Black Elk wrote the forward to this book c. 1947.

131. Stephen McNamara, S.J., "Black Elk and Brings White," *Indian Sentinel* 21 (Nov,

The Jesuits used familial terms like "aunt" to refer to their Lakota friends, and this indicated that they adapted themselves to the extended family structure of the Lakota community.

Another sign that the Lakotas considered the Jesuits a part of their family was their practice of giving Lakota names to the Jesuits. Usually the Lakota practice of giving names to white people was an informal custom that indicated that they accepted that person into the community. On occasion, however, the Lakotas gave the Jesuits names at a formal name-giving ceremony. Just which Jesuits received their names either formally or informally is difficult to determine. Nevertheless, the Lakotas gave names to most of the Jesuits at Holy Rosary and St. Francis. The Lakotas named John Jutz "Iron Gaze;" they named Henry Westropp "Little Owl;" Joseph Lindebner "Little Father;" Henry Billings "Good Horse;" Florentine Digmann *Putin Sapa* meaning "Black Beard;" Eugene Buechel *Wanbli Sapa* "Black Eagle;" Otto Moorman *Wanbli Ska* "White Eagle;" Brother Schilling *Si La* "Little Foot" (he had huge feet); Henry Groteegers *Putin Shasha* "Red Beard;" Joseph Zimmerman *Wambli Wankatuya* "High Eagle;" Albert Riester *Canku Tanka* "Big Road;" and Leo Cunningham *Wambli Makeskan Un* "Eagle of the Lonely Country." The Lakotas also gave William Ketcham a name: *Wambli Wakita*, "Watching Eagle." In turn, the Jesuits gave the Lakotas Christian names as first names. The Lakotas used the names that they gave the Jesuits in everyday conversation and many Jesuits became quite attached to their Lakota names. Several of the Jesuits like Zimmerman, Cunningham, Moorman and Buechel often signed their letters with their Lakota name.[132] Another indication that the Lakotas held the Jesuits in high regard was their use of the term "eagle" in several of the Jesuits' Lakota names. For the Lakotas, the eagle was a sacred animal, and a name with "eagle" in it was an honor.[133]

Sometimes the Lakotas gave the Jesuits names at formal name-giving ceremonies at which they adopted the Jesuits into the Sioux Nation. The local Catholic Lakota communities sponsored these ceremonies, however, and not the band as a whole. At the Catholic Sioux Congress at

---

1941):139-140.

132. Otto Moorman, S.J., "White Eagle, the Blackrobe," *Indian Sentinel* 4 (July, 1924):134. SFM 7-1-8, Eugene Buechel, S.J., correspondence, 1937-1940. HRM 7-17-1, John Scott, S.J., *High Eagle and His Sioux* (1963).

133. "A Missionary Among the Sioux," *Social Justice Review* 37 (Nov. 1944):245. Leo Cunningham, S.J. letter, Holy Rosary Mission, Sept, 12, 1929, Holy Rosary Mission folder, Missouri Province Archives of the Society of Jesus in St. Louis. *Red Cloud's Dream* p.27. Albert Muntsch, S.J., "White Eagle," *Indian Sentinel* 34 (Jan 1954):15-16. Joseph Zimmerman, S.J., "How the Sioux Indians Keep Christmas," *Indian Sentinel* 12 (Fall 1932):164. John Scott, S.J., *High Eagle and His Sioux* (St. Louis, 1963). Bernard Flood, interview, Okreek, Rosebud Reservation, S.D. Oct. 1992. John Scott, S.J., interview, Creighton University, Omaha, Oct. 1992. Fr. C.P. Jordan, interview, St. Francis, S.D. May, 1992.

Holy Rosary Mission in 1946, John Reardon, a Catholic seminarian, went through this name-giving ceremony:

> The Indians immediately showed a marked liking for Mr. Reardon, and during the session they adopted him into the Sioux tribe. . . . Placid faced Sioux, who smoked endlessly, grunted approval periodically as the orator went on and on. . . . The following is a liberal translation of Chief Stabber's speech: "John Reardon has come to us from New York. . . . Tonight he has sung for us the song of the Blessed Virgin Mary. It is the same song that the angel sang when the Blessed Virgin was told she was to be the Mother of God. His voice is rich and strong. It is good. John Reardon is now studying for the priesthood. He is traveling on the long road to that goal. As he travels this road, we see him singing all the way. When he becomes a priest with the powers of the priesthood, we pray that he will use his voice much to speak about God. . . . With your approval I adopt John Reardon into our tribe and name him *Hotanin Mani* (Voice Walking)." The grunts of approval were spontaneous, and John Reardon was officially adopted into the Sioux nation. Every Indian present came forward and shook his hand. They wished him God's blessing in the future and promised to pray for him. It was a thrilling episode of Catholic action and living faith in the midst of four full days of vital Catholic activity.[134]

In these ceremonies, the Lakotas gave names to those people whom they wanted to honor, and the people who received these names entered into a special relationship with the Lakotas. By giving a person a Lakota name in these ceremonies, the Lakotas adopted him or her into the Sioux nation. Though most of the Jesuits received names, few most likely went through the name-giving ceremony. At this ceremony, usually a sponsor of the one to be named explained that through the ceremony the person became more closely bonded to the Lakota people. The sponsor also described the significance of the name. Then the Lakotas prayed over the person, and finally sang an honoring song.[135]

Similarly, Catholics on other reservations had no qualms about participating in the name-giving ceremonies and other traditional ceremonies. In Michigan in 1938, two nuns of the School Sisters of Notre Dame went through the Ottawa naming ceremony, which Sister Mary Devota, S.S.S.D., described in the *Sentinel*:

> Painted and dressed in their old Indian costumes, [the Ottawas] performed, first, the traditional pipe-smoking ritual and then, to the accompaniment of tom-toms and Indian chants, the Ottawa dances. These included versions of the medicine-pipe dance, the

---

134. BCIM 14/1-4-4, Edward Laskowski, S.J., "Indian Congress," *Calumet* (Winter 1946):2.
135. William Stoltzman, S.J., *The Pipe and Christ* (Chamberlain: Tepee Press, 1986), 30-32.

challenge dance, the humorous one-legged dance, the scalp dance and the sun dance. The high point was the conferring of honorary names upon Sisters Mary Zachary and Honesta of Holy Childhood Indian School.[136]

The participation of the nuns in this event indicated that they did not object to the dances, which were most likely variations of the originals (particularly in the case of the scalp dance). Like the Jesuits in the Dakotas, these nuns believed that the name-giving ceremony was not opposed to the Catholic faith.

Hunka Lowampi

The Lakota custom of giving a name to a person was a sign of friendship, and the Lakota name-giving ceremony was a more formal way of showing respect for a person. But the Lakotas had another ceremony in which a Lakota person adopted someone else into his or her family. The Lakotas called this adoption ceremony the *hunka lowampi*, meaning "the singing over the relatives."[137] In this ceremony, a Lakota person decided to adopt another person because he or she had great respect for that person. In the *hunka* ceremony, usually one Sioux, male or female, adopted another by this ritual and they became relatives. If a man and a woman who were close in age wished to undergo the *hunka* ceremony, they became brother and sister to each other even though they were not actually siblings. If a woman adopted a girl who was considerably younger than her, the girl referred to the woman as "mother." If the woman was only a few years older than the girl, the younger referred to her as "aunt." To undergo the ceremony, the only thing necessary was desire on the part of both parties, and some Lakotas participated in the *hunka* ceremony many times, acquiring several relatives. In some cases, the Lakotas also adopted white people or Native Americans of other nations into Lakota families.[138] The *hunka* ceremony was especially significant to the Lakotas because it reinforced the already tight-knit nature of the Lakota families. Traditionally, the Lakotas treated each other as part of a large extended family, and the *hunka* ceremony was a way for the Lakotas to acknowledge in a special and formal way a person's bond with another.

A Lakota elder, George Sword said (c.1910) that the *hunka* ceremony varied considerably:

---

136. Sister Mary Devota, S.S.S.D., "Ottawa Naming Ceremonial," *Indian Sentinel* 18 (Sept. 1938), 101.

137. Powers, *Oglala Religion*, 100.

138. James Walker, *Lakota Belief and Ritual* (Lincoln: University of Nebraska, 1980), 193-240.

If one was poor, the ceremony did not amount to much. If one was unpopular, the ceremony did not amount to much. If one had much, the ceremony was largely attended and lasted many days.[139]

Sword added that anyone may perform the ceremony but usually the medicine men did this. The ceremony itself was complex and during the ceremony, the participants waved horse-tails, smoked the pipe, shook rattles, played the drum, painted themselves with red paint, and feasted on dog. Often the adopted person provided the feast for all who attended. After undergoing this ceremony, those people who became related were obligated to help and counsel each other whenever aid was necessary.[140]

Before the Jesuits founded St. Francis, several missionaries went through the *hunka* ceremony: the Santee chief Aquipaguetin adopted Hennepin, Two Bears adoped De Smet, and Chief Spotted Tail's family adopted Craft. Many of the later adoptions, the Lakotas performed at the Congresses. The Lakotas formally adopted several Jesuits into their families, and the Jesuits were happy to participate in this custom. From the Jesuits' descriptions, some adoption ceremonies seemed more elaborate than others. Nonetheless, several Jesuits underwent adoption ceremonies that were quite long, and they were quite proud of the fact that the Lakotas adopted them.

A *Sentinel* article mentioned that at the 1916 Sioux Congress, the Chippewa Priest, "Father Gordon was formally adopted into the Sioux receiving two names."[141] In 1926, the Lakotas adopted Fr. Riester, S.J., Superior of Holy Rosary Mission, and gave him the name "Big Road." Describing his adoption, Riester explained how it gave him more responsibility and status in the Sioux community:

> The Indians call me *Canku Tanka*, Big Road. It was four years ago that I was rather formally adopted by the Sioux. After much consultation among some of the old chiefs, the ceremony of adoption took place in the *maza tepee*, or meeting house. It lasted all afternoon. *Ptehincala Ska*, White Calf, was the spokesman. He said that once upon a time there was a great chief named *Canku Tanka*. He was the Big Road for the Indians. By following his words of wisdom they had happiness and prosperity. The great chief died and the people were *lila chanteshicha*, sad at heart. The honor of being the Big Road for the Indians was conferred upon me. I must lead them on the right road and they will follow and have peace and prosperity here and happiness hereafter. The

---

139. George Sword, "The Hunka" in *Lakota Belief and Ritual*, James Walker, ed. (Lincoln: University of Nebraska Press, 1980), 198-199.

140. Walker, *Lakota Belief and Ritual*, 200-219.

141. "The Sioux Congress," *Indian Sentinel* 1 (Oct 1916):30.

Indians presented me with bead work and I shook hands with them and passed around cigarettes.[142]

In the cases of Riester and Gordon, however, determining whether they underwent the name-giving ceremony, the *Hunka*, or some combination of the two is difficult. Whether the Lakotas adopted them into a particular family or into the Sioux nation as a whole is unclear. Either way, Riester and Gordon participated in Lakota adoption ceremonies. William Stoltzman, S.J., who studied the Sioux religion, noted that in the name-giving ceremony, the Lakotas often "follow the format of a brief *hunkayapi* [or *hunka*] ceremony,"[143] thus indicating that the two ceremonies were closely related. Both the name-giving ceremony and the *hunka* ceremony were similar in that both involved the Lakotas' adoption of people. The fact that Riester's adoption lasted "all afternoon," indicated that his was a rather formal adoption.

The Lakotas adopted several Jesuits, and this was a formal way of saying that they accepted the Jesuits as a part of the Lakota extended family.[144] The Lakotas adopted Father Westropp who lived at Holy Rosary Mission until 1915.[145] Also when Father Otto Moorman, S.J., was at Holy Rosary Mission between 1920 and 1928, first the Lakotas named him *Wanbli Ska*, "White Eagle," and later they formally adopted him. Albert Muntsch, one of the Jesuits at Holy Rosary, described Moorman's adoption ceremony as a "rare honor" and said that "it was a real adoption, not the sort of mock adoption that many white men have received, merely having a war bonnet put on their heads to the sound of the tom-toms."[146] Furthermore, Joseph Zimmerman, S.J., of Holy Rosary, went through the *hunka* ceremony at a Congress in the 1930's.[147] Although some American Jesuits did not learn Lakota, Riester, Zimmerman, and Moorman all spoke Lakota fluently,[148] and thus became quite close to the elders. The Lako-

---

142. Fr. Albert Riester, S.J., "Sioux Trails all Lead to Big Road," *Indian Sentinel* 11 (Winter 1930-31):7.

143. William Stoltzman, S.J., *The Pipe and Christ*, 31.

144. *Ibid.,* 21. In this section, Stoltzman discussed the *hunka* ceremony in general, and did not refer to the Jesuits.

145. "Otto Moorman," *News-letter: Missouri Province*, Society of Jesus Missouri Province News-letter, 18 (March 1954):70. In Moorman's obituary when the author mentioned that Moorman was adopted, he also mentioned that Westropp was previously adopted.

146. Albert Muntsch, S.J., "White Eagle," *Indian Sentinel* (Jan. 1954):15-16. "Otto Moorman," *News-letter: Missouri Province*, Society of Jesus Missouri Province News-letter, 18 (March 1954):70.

147. Olivia and Hobert Pourier, interview, Sharps Corner, Pine Ridge Reservation, June and October, 1992. Lawrence Whiting, interview, October 1992. Whiting recalled that Zimmerman was adopted but did not witness the ceremony.

148. Albert Muntsch, S.J., "White Eagle," *Indian Sentinel* 34 (Jan 1954):15-16. Rosie Redhair, interview, Pine Ridge, S.D. Oct. 1992.

tas' decision to adopt Riester, Moorman, and Zimmerman may have been related to their willingness to learn the Lakota language.

In 1938 a Holy Rosary Mission newsletter reported that a Lakota woman adopted Brother Henry Billings, S.J.: a Lakota woman had a son who was close to Billings, and after her son died "in Indian fashion the mother of the boy adopted Brother Billings and gave him the name Good Horse."[149]   In this case, Billings clearly participated in the *hunka* ceremony since this woman adopted him directly into her family. Following a longstanding Sioux tradition, this woman adopted Billings in place of her son. Thus, the circumstances of Billings' adoption were actually quite similar to those of Hennepin's adoption. After Aquipaguetin lost his son in a battle, he adopted Hennepin in place of his lost son.

The Lakotas may have formally adopted other Jesuits, but the accounts of such matters are incomplete. Other Native American nations, however, even adopted Catholic bishops into their nations, which indicated that the Catholic hierarchy did not object to this custom. For example in Baltimore in 1927, a group of Blackfeet, including several chiefs, adopted Archbishop Michael Curley into the Blackfeet Nation and gave him the name "Three Persons."[150]

Though the adoption ceremony and name-giving ceremony came from the traditional Lakota religion, the Jesuits were willing to participate in these ceremonies, or versions of them, and report their participation in the mission journals. They obviously did not think these ceremonies were opposed to Catholic practice. Quite the contrary, the Jesuits whom the Lakotas adopted were proud of this distinction since it meant the Lakotas accepted them as part of their extended family.

Theories of Missionary Adaptation

In addition to their acceptance of the adoption ceremonies, the Jesuits accepted many other Lakota customs and, by the 1930's, explicitly stated their policy of preserving Lakota customs. Mary Gannon, one of the Catholic Social Workers at Pine Ridge, worked closely with the Franciscan sisters and Jesuits at Holy Rosary and believed that the reason that the Catholic Church was successful among the Sioux was that Catholics accepted many Lakota customs. In 1932 she wrote BCIM Director Hughes saying that "nothing is dearer to the Indian today than their Indian customs. I believe that is why the Catholics have more of a hold on the Indians because they tolerate their Indian ways."[151]

---

149. *Tom Tom* 4 (June 1938):3, Holy Rosary Collection 4-11, Missouri Province Archives of the Society of Jesus in St. Louis.

150. "Archbishop Curley Adopted into Blackfoot Tribe," *Indian Sentinel* 8 (Winter 1927-28):2. This article refers to the Blackfoot or Blackfeet Nation not the Blackfeet Sioux.

An example of the Jesuits' encouraging the Lakotas to continue their traditions was illustrated in an article that Father Sialm wrote to *The Indian Sentinel* in 1937. In this article, Sialm described his participation in a baptismal feast which retained some aspects of the traditional Lakota name giving ceremony:

> Old Mary Kills Two announced the other day that she was going to give a feast to celebrate the Baptism of her little grandchild, the first born of one of her youngest daughters, Lydia. Sioux grandmothers have always been their grandchildren's second mother, the old Indians say. . . . Mary had the feast announced beforehand, just as the Indians used to do in the old days. The Sioux always held a naming ceremony a few days after a child's birth. A messenger was sent around the camp to announce the celebration. Friends and kinsman would gather around the tepee to congratulate the proud parents, who would in turn feast them and give away presents. Catholic Indians like Mary Kills Two like to keep up the old custom in a Christian way. . . . When the basement hall was rather well filled, the ceremonies began. First the prayers, the songs, and the speeches. Thus it was in the olden times. Indians expect instruction from their leaders and elders whenever there is a gathering. The missionary is expected of course to speak first. . . . Next we all say some prayers in Sioux. Then the catechist speaks. After him both the men and women are called upon to say something too. Indian gatherings of this kind are real schools of instruction for young and old. It was thus that they passed on their tribal lore, their beliefs, their experience, renowned deeds of their heroes, and now, their Catholic practices and the memory of good old people. . . . [He described the feast following the speeches] This feast is also a sample of how old customs have been transformed and transfigured into Christian customs, with still a strong flavor of their Indian character. . . . Christianity has helped the Sioux to preserve many of their fine old customs and by its touch has made them finer. It has deepened and strengthened their natural virtues.[152]

Mary Kills Two preserved the structure of the traditional ceremony: the announcement, the prayers, the songs, the speeches, and the name giving ceremony in which the child was "adopted" into the band. The Lakotas changed the content of the prayers and songs, but retained the traditional form. By combining the two traditions, Mary Kills Two and many other Lakota Catholics on their own initiative adapted their traditions to make them consistent with Catholic traditions. Just as Black Elk appreciated

---

151. BCIM 1-209-7, Mary Gannon to Fr. Hughes, Pine Ridge, Oct. 25, 1932.

152. Fr. Placidus Sialm, S.J., "Mary Kills Two's Party," *Indian Sentinel* 17 (May 1937):67-68.

the distinction between the medicines themselves and the *yuwipi*, the Lakota Catholics distinguished between the aspects of their culture that were permissible and impermissible for Catholics to preserve. In Sialm's opinion, the ceremony was perfectly acceptable since in this case Catholic teaching preserved and yet perfected the Lakota customs, rather than eliminating them. Explicitly adopting a natural law approach, Sialm acknowledged that some aspects of Lakota culture were good and supported the idea of building on these good characteristics.

Mary Kills Two preserved the structure of the traditional ceremony: the announcement, the prayers, the songs, the speeches, and the name giving ceremony in which the child was "adopted" into the band. The Lakotas changed the content of the prayers and songs, but retained the traditional form. By combining the two traditions, Mary Kills Two and many other Lakota Catholics on their own initiative adapted their traditions to make them consistent with Catholic traditions. Just as Black Elk appreciated the distinction between the medicines themselves and the *yuwipi*, the Lakota Catholics distinguished between the aspects of their culture that were permissible and impermissible for Catholics to preserve. In Sialm's opinion, the ceremony was perfectly acceptable since in this case Catholic teaching preserved and yet perfected the Lakota customs, rather than eliminating them. Explicitly adopting a natural law approach, Sialm acknowledged that some aspects of Lakota culture were good and supported the idea of building on these good characteristics.

Joseph Zimmerman, S.J., shared Sialm's appreciation of Lakota culture. With the exception of a few years, Zimmerman was part of either the St. Francis or Holy Rosary mission from 1922 until he died in 1954.[153] From 1924 to 1930 he was the Superior of St. Francis Mission, and he had the reputation of being well-loved by the Lakota people. In turn he said that the Lakotas "for the most part are very devout Catholics who go to the Sacraments each time the missionary goes there."[154] Along with Buechel, Zimmerman had the desire to preserve Lakota culture and he aided in the organization of the Lakota museum at St. Francis. Zimmerman also made the clearest statement of the Jesuits' pastoral theology:

> The work of the missionary is spiritual. But in order to labor
> with maximum efficiency, the missionary must know the customs
> of the people with whom he works. He must be acquainted with
> their background, their environment, and heritage. The Church
> has always emphasized that the missionary should adapt himself
> to the ways of thinking of his converts, should take what is good
> and noble in their way of life and preserve it not destroy it.[155]

---

153. John M. Scott, S.J., *High Eagle and His Sioux* (St. Louis, 1963), 5-12.
154. *Ibid.*, 12.
155. *Ibid.*, 5-6. No date for this quote was recorded, but was probably written in the 1930's or 1940's. Nevertheless, Joseph Zimmerman's nephew, Eugene Zimmerman, S.J., who also

In a 1939 article in *The Indian Sentinel*, William Moore S.J., who was a scholastic at St. Francis Mission at the time, also showed that the Jesuits at Holy Rosary and St. Francis encouraged the retention of the Lakota customs. In this article, he described how the Lakotas gathered for celebrations. They camped out together, "with tents pitched a few feet apart and the whole band living as one large family."[156] He said that the missionaries were happy to celebrate the Mass in the physical setting which fit in with the Lakota customs. In this article, he also explained the Jesuits' attitude concerning missionary adaptation:

> The missionaries of St. Francis Mission on the Rosebud reservation, South Dakota, try to adapt their work to the Indian spirit. They are concerned about instilling the life of grace into the souls of their people, not about imposing alien customs upon a race which clings to its traditional ways.[157]

Moore clearly stated that the Jesuits sought to preserve many aspects of the Sioux culture. Distinguishing between customs and religion, Moore said that the Jesuits did not want to impose "alien customs," but rather wanted to change their religious orientation. He also gave an example of how the Jesuits preserved Sioux customs in their liturgy. At a Fourth of July celebration in 1938 on Rosebud Reservation, Moore described a Mass that the Jesuits held in a rather informal setting, even though the Director of the BCIM, J.B. Tennelly attended the Mass:

> In a small tent, just wide enough for a portable altar, and just high enough to stand erect in, Father Tennelly said Mass for some sixty Catholic Sioux who knelt on the grass outside. Forty of the Indians received Holy Communion, after confessing to Father Buechel in their own language. The absence of kneeling benches, communion rail, and arched aisles leading to handsome altars did not affect the devotion of the brown-skinned Sioux. From their Lakota prayerbooks they sang hymns and prayed as devoutly as they would in a Gothic cathedral. They love simplicity; elegance disturbs them. Twenty feet from the tent in which the Mass was said, coffee pots were boiling over stone fireplaces, and the aroma of breakfast bacon spread over the camp. In the distance, horses champed coarse grass. . . . A semi-circle of tents shone bright in the morning light. The scene was fundamentally like those in which De Smet himself took part a hundred years ago. When Mass was over, and after coffee pots and bacon pans had been emptied, Father Tennelly mingled among the people. They had

---

spent time at Holy Rosary and John Scott, S.J., both said that the ideas expressed in this quote were characteristic of his approach throughout his time in the Dakotas.

156. William Moore, S.J., "With the Sioux in Camp," *Indian Sentinel* 19 (Oct. 1939):118.

157. *Ibid.*, 118.

him speak to them in the bower, an out-of-doors meeting place, made up of rough board seats forming a circle of 200 feet in circumference and covered over by branches of trees. . . . The assembly closed in characteristic Sioux fashion. Around the circle the people passed, men women, and children, each shaking hands with Father Tennelly, and Father Buechel, and thanking them for their visit.[158]

Moore's description mentioned that the "scene was fundamentally like those in which De Smet himself took part a hundred years ago," and showed that even after a hundred years of Jesuit influence, Lakota customs were still present. Moore, Zimmerman, and Sialm all advocated the same idea of preserving indigenous customs that Pius XII put forward in *Summi Pontificatus* (1939):

All that in such usages and customs is not inseparably bound up with religious errors will always be subject to kindly consideration and, when it is found possible, will be sponsored and developed.[159]

---

158. *Ibid.*, 118-119.

159. Pius XII, *Summi Pontificatus. The Papal Encyclicals*, Claudia Carlin, ed. p. 11, paragraph 46.

CHAPTER SEVEN

Conclusion

TRADITIONALLY THE LAKOTAS WERE A DEEPLY RELIGIOUS PEOPLE AND THE converts to the Catholic faith retained their devotion to religion. The Second World War, however, was a period of great transition for the Lakotas. By leaving the reservation to fight in the war or to work in factories supporting the war effort, the Lakotas exposed themselves to a secular environment that often discouraged zealous devotion to Christianity. During the war, the Lakotas had to discontinue the Congresses. But even after they began to hold them again in 1946,[1] the Congresses never regained the popularity they once had. After the war, the Lakotas' interest in the Church and the institution of the Lakota catechists dwindled.[2] Transportation and roads improved and the Jesuits were more mobile. They were able to respond more quickly to sick calls, and thus they took on responsibilities that the catechists usually accomplished. After the war, towns also sprang up on the reservations and people lived closer together. In the 1950's, rather than circuit riding, the Jesuits took up residence in the small towns. But they noted that interest in the Catholic way of life diminished at that time. Richard Jones, a priest at St. Francis in the 1940's, attributed this reduced interest in the Catholic Church to the secularizing influence of white society.[3] As so many before him, he claimed that the Lakotas' contact with whites during this period adversely affected their religious devotion. The Jesuits realized that the secularism of American society was the real threat to the Catholic Church. They never wanted the Lakotas to adopt all the habits and customs of white America, but rather were primarily concerned that the Lakotas become good Catholics.

The Jesuits did not force the Catholic faith on the Lakotas. They offered them new ideas, many of which the Lakotas accepted. The Lakotas

---

1. Edward Laskowski, S.J., "Victory Indian Congress," *Indian Sentinel* 26 (Oct. 1946):121.

2. Paul Manhart, interview, Wanblee, South Dakota, May 1992.

3. Fr. Richard Jones, interview, St. Francis, S.D. Oct. 1992.

changed themselves by accepting these ideas, just as they had been changing throughout their history as a result of contact with other nations. Lakota culture was never static and had been changing even before they had
contact with the whites. European culture actually had a profound impact
on the Lakotas even in the seventeenth century because of the introduction
of horses that the Spanish brought. These horses enabled the Sioux to
hunt buffalo much more efficiently. They also induced those Sioux who
lived in the woodlands to move further west since the horses allowed
them to adapt more easily to the plains economy. The introduction of
horses significantly altered the Sioux culture, and showed that the Lakotas
adopted foreign elements into their culture long before the Jesuits arrived.

Many traditional Lakota legends were also not native to the Sioux, but
rather they adopted them from other Native American nations. Even before
the arrival of the Europeans in the New World, the Native American cultures changed as a result of borrowing from each other. In pre-contact days,
native cultures also changed through conquest of each other. When the Native Americans encountered a legend that expressed some truth, sometimes
they adopted it as their own, not because others forced it upon them, but
because they found it appealing.

Though the introduction of Christianity into the Lakota culture resulted in profound change, it was not the cause of the religious change.
The cause was the Lakotas' acceptance of Christianity. Throughout history in many different circumstances, governments attempted to pressure
many different religious groups to change their religion. But despite pressure and persecution, many retained their faith even in places where they
were only small minorities. In some circumstances, the persecution of a
particular religion led to a resurgence in interest and zeal in that religion.
The Sioux could have rejected or ignored the missionaries, and some certainly did. Most of the Sioux, however, did not ignore the Jesuits because
they were curious about their ideas of God. Ever since De Smet visited
them, they asked for Catholic priests to stay among them and teach them.
By signing the annual petition for the St. Francis and Holy Rosary mission schools, the Lakotas on Pine Ridge and Rosebud showed that they
wanted their children to have a Catholic education. Even though the government attempted to discourage the Lakotas from attending the mission
schools, they still went.

The Jesuits accepted the idea that some truth was in the Lakota religion and customs. Though they believed that the Lakotas had only an
incomplete knowledge of God, they still recognized that the Lakota religion had some virtue. Rather than condemning all the Lakota rituals, they
participated in those rituals and customs that were not contrary to Catholic
teaching, and encouraged the alteration of certain religious rituals to make
them unobjectionable. Even with a custom like the give-away that the
Jesuits opposed on economic grounds, they still believed that Catholics
could participate in this custom and still remain Catholic. During their

mission to the Lakotas, Jesuits smoked the sacred pipe, participated in adoption ceremonies, received Lakota names, ate at Lakota feasts, encouraged Lakota art, attended Lakota dances, encouraged the use of the Lakota language, and preserved Lakota legends. The Jesuits also made significant efforts to integrate many Lakota customs into the Catholic lifestyle. At the Congresses, they created an environment in which they showed appreciation for Lakota art and Lakota heroes. They also allowed the Lakota Catholics to participate in the traditional dances, smoke the pipe, practice some of the traditional funeral ceremonies, and integrate many other Lakota customs into the Catholic life on the reservations.

The Lakotas were not simply followers of the Jesuits, and the Jesuits did not simply lead them like the blind. During the Congresses, at their weekly St. Joseph's and St. Mary's society meetings, and whenever they thought necessary, the Lakotas exhorted the people on the reservations to follow the faith. Drawing on their formidable oratorical skills, the Lakotas made long speeches in their native language. Even though they respected the authority of the priests and bishops, they also openly disputed with them if they believed they were mistaken.

The Jesuit mission to the Lakotas was successful in converting many of the Lakotas because the Jesuits built on what they believed were the good aspects of the Lakota religion and directed these positive characteristics toward Catholic practice. The Jesuits, to some extent, presented Catholicism in continuity with the Lakota religion, and they used the similarities between the Lakota and Catholic traditions to lead the Lakotas to the Church. Since the Jesuits believed that the Lakotas were monotheists, this allowed them to use *Wakantanka* as a translation for God, and thus indicated to the Lakotas that by adopting the Catholic faith they continued to pray to the same God to whom they always had prayed. Moreover, the Jesuits realized that the Lakotas were a religious people who stressed prayer, and so the Jesuits channelled this tendency to Catholic prayers and hymns. By encouraging the Lakota traditions of oration, they directed the Lakotas' oration to the catechesis of the Lakotas.

The Jesuits' mission method also stressed ritual: the Jesuits encouraged the *Corpus Christi* processions, the Rogation days, the Congresses, the Decoration days, and the plays. Since ritual was a central part of the Lakota religion and the Catholic tradition, this similarity helped to draw the Lakotas to the Church. Building on the Sioux sense of tribal unity, the Jesuits transformed the traditional tribal councils and Sun Dances into the Catholic Sioux Congresses. The Lakotas also had a strong sense of family unity, and the Jesuits adapted to this social structure by becoming part of their families through visiting with them, bringing them food, living in their houses, receiving Lakota names, and undergoing adoption. The Jesuits did not simply use Lakota traditions to win converts, but rather they expressed a great satisfaction about certain Lakota traditions and about their close familial ties with the Lakotas. Since many of the Jesuits were foreigners who had left their families in Europe, they valued the Lakotas' hospitality, their tradition of visiting with their neighbors, and their sense of family. The Jesuits also realized that the closeness of the Lakota community, their charity, and their religious zeal were more Christian than that of many Europeans.

The Jesuits' pastoral theology was a dialogue between them and the Lakotas because the Lakotas on their own initiative integrated their customs into the Catholic celebrations, and also because the Jesuits built on the virtues that they recognized in the Lakota culture. By preserving what they considered to be the good aspects of the Lakota culture, the Jesuits followed the dictates of the Church on this matter. In 1944 Pope Pius XII addressed the Directors of the Pontifical Mission Works and advocated the preservation of indigenous culture whenever possible:

> The specific character, the traditions the customs of each nation must be preserved intact, so long as they are not in contradiction with the divine law. The missionary is an apostle of Jesus Christ. His task is not to propagate European civilization in foreign soil. Rather it is his function so to train and guide other peoples, some of whom glory in their ancient and refined civilization, as to prepare and dispose them for the willing and hearty acceptance of the principles of Christian life and behavior.[4]

Even from its beginning, the Catholic Church took native feasts and transformed them into Christian celebrations. At Holy Rosary and St. Francis Missions, the Jesuits continued this tradition in the Congresses, baptisms, and several other ceremonies which incorporated elements of traditional Lakota dances, rituals, and councils. The Jesuits spoke their language, lived with them, participated in their ceremonies, and became part of Lakota families. The Jesuits adapted to Lakota culture and became a part of it. Consequently, the Lakotas trusted them and many accepted the Catholic faith.

---

4. Pope Pius XII, "Address to the Directors of Pontifical Mission Works (1944)" in *The Christian Faith*, 317.

Epilogue[1]

THE SECOND VATICAN COUNCIL CONTINUED THE LIBERALIZING TREND IN pastoral and mission theology that had been developing throughout the twentieth century. The Council's *Pastoral Constitution, Gaudium et Spes* (1965), strongly backed the idea of missionary adaptation and spoke about the perfection of the good tendencies already found in the indigenous cultures:

> Missionary activity is nothing else, and nothing less, than the manifestation of God's plan, its epiphany and realization in the world and in history. . . . [Missionary activity] purges of evil associations those elements of truth and grace which are found among peoples, and which are, as it were, a secret presence of God; and it restores them to Christ their source who overthrows the rule of the devil and limits the manifold malice of evil. So whatever goodness is found in the minds and hearts of men, or in the particular customs and cultures of peoples, far from being lost is purified, raised to a higher level and reaches its perfection, for the glory of God. . . . [Missionaries] should be familiar with [the indigenous people's] national and religious traditions and uncover with gladness and respect those seeds of the Word which lie hidden among them.[2]

This passage acknowledges that in indigenous religions are "seeds of the Word," truths from God, that may grow into the full acceptance of the Christian faith. Another of the Council's documents, *Lumen Gentium*, expanded on this idea:

> Those who, through no fault of their own, do not know the Gospel of Christ or his Church, but who nevertheless seek God with a

---

1. This epilogue is not intended to be a complete study of the Jesuits' mission method in the Dakotas after 1945. Rather it is intended to explain briefly a few major developments in mission method since 1945.

2. Austin Flannery, ed. *Vatican Council II: The Conciliar and Post Conciliar Documents* (Collegeville: Liturgical Press, 1975), paragraph 9 and 11, p.823-825.

sincere heart, and, moved by grace, try in their actions to do his
will as they know it through the dictates of their conscience –
those too may achieve eternal salvation. Nor shall divine provi-
dence deny the assistance necessary for salvation to those who,
without any fault of theirs, have not yet arrived at an explicit
knowledge of God, and who, not without grace, strive to lead a
good life. Whatever good or truth is found amongst them is considered by the Church to be a preparation for the Gospel . . .[3]

Through these documents, the Council was teaching that God has been
working through history, preparing different cultures to receive the Christian faith, and pushing the development of cultures through missionary
activity toward the point where they would be harmonized with the Gospel.

The Council's teaching on the liturgy in *Sacrosanctum Consilium,
The Constitution on the Sacred Liturgy* (1963) also illustrated its openness
to other cultures. In addition to allowing the clergy to celebrate Mass in
the vernacular, the Council decided to allow the inclusion of indigenous
customs in the liturgy, subject to the discretion of the local bishop:

Even in the liturgy, the Church does not wish to impose a rigid
uniformity in matters which do not involve the faith or the good
of the whole community. Rather does she respect and foster the
qualities and talents of the various races and nations. Anything
not bound up with superstition and error she studies with sympa-
thy, and if possible, preserves intact. She sometimes admits such
things into the liturgy itself, provided they harmonize with its true
and authentic spirit.[4]

Though the Church encouraged Catholic priests prior to Vatican II, to
preserve native customs, this constitution allowed them to incorporate indigenous customs directly into the liturgy, and thus make the liturgy conform more closely to the traditions and aesthetics of different cultures.

The Council also produced *Nostrae Aetate, The Declaration on the
Relation of the Church to non-Christian Religions* (1965), which accepted
the teaching that non-Christian religions have some degree of truth. After
writing of the search for God and truth in Hinduism and Buddhism, the
document clearly stated that some virtue dwelt in these religions:

The Catholic Church rejects nothing of what is true and holy in
these religions. She has a high regard for the manner of life and
conduct, the precepts and doctrines which, although differing in
many ways from her own teaching, nevertheless often reflect a
ray of that truth which enlightens all men.[5]

---

3.   Flannery, paragraph 16, p.367-368.
4.   Flannery, paragraph 37, p.13.
5.   Flannery, paragraph 2., p. 739.

The organization of this document also indicated that the Church accepted the notion that some religions were closer to the truth than others. Implicit in the document was the idea that the more similar a religion was to Christianity, the more advanced that religion was. The relative amounts of praise that the document gave to the different religions indicated the distance that a particular religion stood from the Catholic faith. While this document acknowledged the search for God and the practice of love in Hinduism, it indicated that those religions like Islam and Judaism that were monotheistic and shared a religious heritage with Christianity were closer to the truth than was Hinduism:

> Throughout history even to the present day, there is found among different peoples a certain awareness of a hidden power, which lies behind the course of nature and the events of human life. At times there is present even a recognition of a supreme being, or still more of a Father.[6]

In this document, the recognition that non-Christian religions reflected some truth necessarily indicated that some religions reflected more than others. The Council regarded those religions that were monotheistic as having a greater knowledge of God through natural law than did the polytheistic religions. Moreover, acknowledging the close kinship among the Protestants, Orthodox, and Catholics, the Vatican encouraged cooperation and dialogue among these groups. For Catholic scholars, Vatican II created an increased sense of openness towards foreign cultures and religions, and led to a growth in study of the similarities between Christianity and other religions.

The Jesuits on Pine Ridge and Rosebud welcomed the Council's teaching and many studied more deeply the traditional Lakota religion. At this time, they also began to adopt a tolerant attitude toward medicine men. In 1972, William Stoltzman, S.J., who worked at Holy Rosary and St. Francis, organized a series of meetings between a group of six Lakota medicine men (some of whom were Catholics), Lakota friends, and eight Jesuits for the purpose of discussing the relationship between the Catholic faith and the Lakota religion.[7] Stoltzman indicated that the purpose of the meetings was to create mutual understanding between the parties involved.[8] The meetings lasted hours and included the traditional speeches and prayers given in English and Lakota. These meetings, which occurred usually every month, lasted for six years, and were a part of the increased discussion that took place between the Catholic church and many other religions and denominations all over the world.[9]

---

6. Flannery, paragraph 2, p.738-739.
7. William Stoltzman, S.J., *The Pipe and Christ* (Chamberlain: Tipi, 1991), 17.
8. *Ibid.,* 17-18.
9. *Ibid.,* 13-20.

Paul Steinmetz was another Jesuit at Holy Rosary Mission who explored the relationship between the Lakota religion and the Catholic Church in the 1960's and 70's. Describing the Lakota religion as a preparation for the Gospel (a phrase which comes out of *Lumen Gentium*), Steinmetz indicated that the Lakota religion contained ideas that directed the Lakotas toward accepting Christianity. Comparing the conversion of the Jews and Lakotas, Steinmetz noted that when Jews converted to Christianity they reinterpreted their traditions in light of Christianity. The Lakota Christians, Steinmetz argued, could also look into their traditions to see a foreshadowing of Christ:

> If the Christian Indian today is going to understand correctly his own religious tradition he must find in Christianity the fulfillment of that tradition: he must Christianize his own tradition. . . . This will change his tradition but will not destroy it; rather enrich it and make it more perfect. In God's Providence, the Indian religious tradition was a foreshadowing of Christ, preparing the Indian to accept Christ.[10]

On the Lakota reservations today the Jesuits are continuing their efforts to encourage inculturation, the process of using native symbols to promote the understanding of Christianity. Working closely with the Lakota laity on the issue of inculturation, they are studying Lakota religion and culture. The Jesuits believe that missionary adaptation and inculturation should involve the missionaries, deacons, bishops, and the Lakota laity all working together in dialogue to preserve the integrity of both the indigenous cultural symbols and the Church's tradition. This approach is consistent with Pope John Paul II's teaching in the encyclical *Redemptoris Missio* (1990):

> Inculturation must involve the whole people of God, and not just a few experts, since the people reflect the authentic *"sensus fidei"* which must never be lost sight of. Inculturation needs to be guided and encouraged but not forced, lest it give rise to negative reactions among Christians. It must be an expression of the community's life, one which must mature within the community itself, and not be exclusively the result of erudite research.[11]

Since Vatican II, the Jesuits have been quite active at the Holy Rosary and St. Francis missions, and the Jesuits still run the Red Cloud School on Holy Rosary. They have also been promoting native leadership by encouraging Sioux men to become permanent deacons, a position which the Vatican restored in 1967 and which is open to married men. In

---

10. Paul B. Steinmetz, S.J., "The Relationship between Plains Indian Religion and Christianity," *Plains Anthropologist* 15 (1970):83-86.

11. *On the Permanent Validity of the Church's Missionary Mandate: Redemptoris Missio*, (United States Catholic Conference: Washington, D.C.,1990), paragraph 54, p. 94.

1975 the Catholic Church ordained the first permanent deacons from the Sioux nation. The Jesuits also work closely with the Sioux deacons on issues concerning inculturation.

In regard to the Lakota reservations today, some people believe that a conflict exists between the "traditionalists" and the "progressives." But dividing the complex diversity on the Lakota reservations into two parts is an over-simplification. Many different people live on the reservations including Catholics, Episcopalians, members of the Peyote Religion (now called the Native American Church), some who espouse the "traditional" Lakota religion, and many others. Since some Lakota Christians participate in both the Catholic and Lakota ceremonies, labeling them as "progressive" or "traditional" is problematic. Even those Native Americans who claim to live a "traditional" lifestyle or practice the "traditional" religion actually have taken some aspects or forms of the traditional Lakota culture and combined them with aspects of American culture. For example, the Lakotas perform the Sun Dance during the summer on the Pine Ridge and Rosebud reservations. Yet this is not the same Sun Dance that the Lakotas performed of old. In the old days the Lakotas did not allow women to dance the Sun Dance, but now because of the influence of American feminist sentiments, often women can dance. Moreover, formerly the Sun Dancers stared at the sun for long periods of time, fasted, deprived themselves of water for days, cut off pieces of their flesh, and danced to exhaustion. Realizing the physical damage that staring at the sun has on the eyes, modern Sun Dancers do not do this. Also since modern Americans are extremely reluctant to endure any prolonged inconvenience or suffering, the modern Sun Dancers do not physically challenge themselves nearly as much as they did in the past. In the old times, the Lakota nation as a whole would sponsor a Sun Dance and it would be an expression of national unity; today several private Sun Dances take place on Pine Ridge and Rosebud.

The Sun Dance is not now as it was in the old days, but rather is an example of the blending of modern Western values and Native American practices. Just as they have always done, the Lakotas adapted to changing conditions and incorporated new practices into their religion. Some of the structure, some of the forms of the traditional Native American practices remain but the content is different. Traditionally, the Sun Dance was principally concerned with the success of the buffalo hunt or of a war party. But because of modern conditions and concerns the significance of the Sun Dance is not the same. Moreover, today almost all of the Native Americans on these two reservations are Lakotas of mixed ancestry, and the idea of them returning to their "traditional" religion becomes more complex since their ancestors came from Europe as well as America. In South Dakota, both the "traditionalists" and the Jesuits combined aspects of the Lakota culture and with other beliefs and rituals.

During the late 1970's and 1980's, Native Americans including the Sioux renewed their commitment and interest in the Catholic Church. One of the reasons for this resurgence of zeal was the Tekakwitha Conference. Though this began in 1939 as a Conference of those Catholic clergy who served Native Americans, by the late 1970's it became an annual national Conference for the Catholic Native American laity and clergy. The local organizations that grew out of the Tekakwitha Conference also were active during the entire year working to promote spiritual growth among the Catholic communities on the reservations. Furthermore, Sioux deacons helped in the organization of these Conferences, and inspired other Sioux Catholics by their commitment to the Church.[12]

At the Tekakwitha Conferences and among many other Catholics, the practice of incorporating Native American customs and symbols into Catholic services still provokes debate.[13] The Second Vatican Council's teaching to allow some indigenous traditions to be included in the liturgy actually has opened up a new field of debate and inquiry to the clergy and laity. Though the bishops at Vatican II decided to allow some native customs in the liturgy, the Church still faces the task of distinguishing between missionary adaptation and syncretism. The way that the Church has decided to approach this task is to study the indigenous cultures and religions, and establish a dialogue among the bishops, nuns, priests, deacons, and laity. This would allow all to be involved the process of inculturation, and would maintain the integrity of the native symbols and Catholic doctrine.

---

12. Christopher Vecsey, "Sun Dances, Corn Pollen, and the Cross," *Commonweal* (June 5, 1987):345-351.

13. Catherine Walsh, "Native American Catholics at a Crossroads," *America* (Oct. 31, 1992):328-331.

Appendix[1]

Holy Rosary Jesuit Mission Superiors

1888-1892 1895-1896	John Jutz (1832-1924)
1892-1895	Florentine Digmann (1846-1931)
1896-1903	Aloysius Bosch (1852-1903)
1903-1908	Mathias Schmitt (1862-1936)
1908-1916	Eugene Buechel (1874-1954)
1916-1920	Henry Grotegeers (1871-1957)
1920-1926	Louis Goll (1877-1946)
1926-1932	Albert Riester (1874-1951)
1932-1934	Aloysius Keel (1876-1936)
1934-1936	Daniel McNamara (1895-1986)
1936-1941	Martin Schiltz (1891-1979)
1941-1947	Francis Collins (1903-1972)

Superintendents of Red Cloud School at Holy Rosary Mission

1888-1895	Emil Perrig (1846-1909)
1895-1896	John Jutz (1838-1924)
1896-1903	Aloysius Bosch (1852-1903)
1903-1908	Mathias Schmitt (1862-1936)
1908-1916	Eugene Buechel (1874-1954)
1916-1920	Henry Grotegeers (1871-1957)
1920-1926	Louis Goll (1877-1946)

---

1. All of this appendix was copied from the Marquette University archives guides to the "Holy Rosary/Red Cloud Indian School Records" and "St. Francis Mission Records."

1926-1931	Albert Riester (1874-1951)
1931-1932	Joseph Melchiors (1895-1961)
1932-1933	Joseph Zimmerman (1885-1954)
1933-1934	Aloysius Keel (1876-1936)
1934-1936	Daniel McNamara (1895-1986)
1936-1941	Martin Schiltz (1891-1979)
1941-1942	William Fitzgerald (1904-1987)
1942-1944	Anthony Adams (1908-

St. Francis Jesuit Mission Superiors

1886-1893	Emil Perrig (1846-1909)
1893-1896	John Jutz (1838-1924)
1896-1916	Florentine Digmann (1846-1931)
1916-1923	Eugene Buechel (1874-1954)
1923-1924	Florentine Digmann (1846-1931)
1924-1930	Joseph Zimmerman (1885-1954)
1930-1936	Martin Schiltz (1891-1979)
1936-1946	Matthew Connell (1894-1957)

Superintendents of St. Francis Mission School

1886-1893	Emil Perrig (1846-1909)
1893-1896	John Jutz (1838-1924)
1896-1916	Emil Perrig (1846-1909)
1916-1923	Eugene Buechel (1874-1954)
1923-1924	Florentine Digmann (1846-1931)
1924-1930	Joseph Zimmerman (1885-1954)
1930-1936	Martin Schiltz (1891-1979)
1936-1943	Matthew Connell (1894-1957)
1943-1946	George Klaus (1903-1954)

Bibliography

Archives

Archives of the Diocese of Rapid City, Rapid City, South Dakota.

Archives of the Missouri Province Society of Jesus, St. Louis, Missouri.

Marquette University Archives, Milwaukee, Wisconsin. Containing the Bureau of Catholic Indian Missions Collection, the Holy Rosary Mission collection, and the St. Francis Mission collection.

National Archives. Washington, D.C. and Kansas City, Missouri.

Books

Afraid-of-Hawk, Emil. *Watakpeya Tanka, St. Francis Xavier.* New York: Catholic Book Publishing Co., 1925.

Bantin, Philip and Thiel, Mark. *Guide to Catholic Indian Mission School Records.* Milwaukee: Marquette, 1984.

Brown, Joseph Epes. *The Sacred Pipe.* Norman: University of Oklahoma, 1953.

Buechel, Eugene and Jesuit Fathers of St. Francis Mission. St. Francis, S.D. *Lakota Wocekiye na Olowan Wowapi: Sioux Indian Prayer and Hymn Book.* St. Louis: Central Bureau of the Catholic Central Verein of America, 1927.

Buechel, Eugene. *Wowapi Wakan, Wicowoyake Yuptecelapi: Bible History In the Language of the Teton Sioux Indians.* Paul Manhart, ed. New York: Benziger Brothers, 1924.

_____. *A Dictionary of the Teton Dakota Sioux Language.* Pine Ridge: Red Cloud Indian School, 1970.

_____. *A Grammar of Lakota.* St. Francis: Saint Francis Mission, 1939.

Burns, Robert Ignatius. *The Jesuits and the Indian Wars of the Northwest.* Moscow: University of Idaho Press, 1966.

Carlin, Claudia, ed. *The Papal Encyclicals.* Wilmington: McGrath, 1981.

Carson, Mary Eisenman. *Blackrobe for the Yankton Sioux: Fr. Sylvester Eisenman, O.S.B.* Chamberlain: Tipi, 1989.

163

Chittenden, Hiram Martin. *Life, Letters and Travels of Pierre-Jean De Smet.* New York: Francis P. Harper, 1905.

David, Cyprian. *The History of Black Catholics in the United States.* New York: Crossroad, 1990.

Delfeld. *The Indian Priest Father Philip B. Gordon: 1885-1948.* Chicago: Franciscan Herald Press, 1977.

DeLoria, Vine. *Custer Died for Your Sins.* New York: Avon, 1969.

DeMallie, Raymond J. *The Sixth Grandfather: Black Elk's Teachings Given to John G. Neihardt.* Lincoln: University of Nebraska, 1984.

DeMallie, R.J. and Parks, D.R. *Sioux Indian Religion.* Norman: University of Oklahoma, 1987.

Pierre Jean De Smet. *New Indian Sketches.* New York: D. & J. Sadler, 1863.

_____. *Letters and Sketches with a Narrative of a Year's Residence among the Indian Tribes of the Rocky Mountains.* Philadelphia: M. Fintian, 1843.

_____. *Oregon Missions and Travels over the Rocky Mountains in 1845-46.* New York: E. Dunigan, 1847.

Duratschek, Sister M. Claudia. *The Beginnings of Catholicism in South Dakota.* Washington D.C.: Catholic University Press, 1943.

_____. *Crusading Along Sioux Trails.* St. Meinrad, Indiana: The Grail Press, 1947.

_____. *Builders of God's Kingdom.* Yankton: Sacred Heart Convent, 1985.

_____. *Under the Shadow of His Wings.* Aberdeen: North Plains Press, 1971.

Ellis, John Tracy. *The Life and Times of James Cardinal Gibbons.* Westminster: Christian Classics, 1987.

Flannery, Austin. *Vatican Council II.* Collegeville: Liturgical Press, 1975.

Ganss, George. *The Constitutions of the Society of Jesus.* St. Louis: The Institute of Jesuit Sources, 1970.

Garraghan, Gilbert. *The Jesuits of the Middle United States.* New York: America Press, 1938.

Goll, Louis. *Jesuit Missions among the Sioux.* St. Francis: St. Francis Mission, 1940.

Grant, John. *Moon of Wintertime.* Toronto: University of Toronto Press, 1984.

Hennepin, Louis. *A New Discovery of a Vast Country in America.* Chicago: A.C. McClurg, 1903.

_____. *A Description of Louisiana.* University of Minnesota Press, 1938.

Hunt, Jerome. *Catechism, Prayers, and Instructions in the Sioux Indian Language.* Cincinnati: Jos. Berning Printing Co. c. 1900.

_____. *Katolik Wocekiye Wowapi: Prayers, Instructions, and Hymns in the Sioux Indian Language.* Fort Totten: Catholic Indian Mission, 1899.

Ignatius of Loyola. *The Spiritual Exercises of St. Ignatius.* Translated by Anthony Mottola. New York: Image, 1964.

Jahner, Elaine A. *Lakota Myth.* Lincoln: University of Nebraska, 1983.

Karolevitz, Robert F. *Bishop Martin Marty: The Black Robe Lean Chief.* Yankton, 1980.

Kardong, Terrance. *Catholic Life at Fort Berthold: 1889-1989.* Richardton: Assumption Abbey Press, 1989.

LaBarre, Weston. *The Ghost Dance.* New York: Delta, 1970.

_____. *The Peyote Cult.* Hamden: Shoe String Press, 1959.

Lijek, Sister Mary. "Relations between the Office of Indian affairs and the Bureau of Catholic Indian Missions, 1885-1900." Master's Thesis. Washington, D.C.: Catholic University, 1965.

Miller, David Humphreys. *Ghost Dance.* Lincoln: University of Nebraska Press, 1959.

Mooney, James. *The Ghost-Dance Religion and Wounded Knee.* New York: Dover, 1973.

Moore, James T. *Indian and Jesuit: A Seventeenth Century Encounter.* Chicago: Loyola University Press, 1982.

Neihardt, John. *Black Elk Speaks.* New York: Washington Square Press, 1959.

Neuner, J. and DuPuis, J. *The Christian Faith in the Doctrinal Documents of the Catholic Church.* New York: Alba, 1982.

Nolan, Hugh. *Pastoral Letters of the United States Catholic Bishops.* Washington: National Conference of Catholic Bishops, 1884.

Olsen, James C. *Red Cloud and the Sioux Problem.* Lincoln: University of Nebraska, 1965.

Pfaller, Louis. *The Catholic Church in Western North Dakota 1738-1960.* Mandan: Crescent Printing, 1960.

Powers, William K. *Oglala Religion.* Lincoln: University of Nebraska, 1975.

Prucha, Paul. *The Churches and the Indian Schools.* Lincoln: University of Nebraska, 1979.

Radin, Paul. *The Trickster.* New York: Schocken, 1956.

Rahill, Peter J. "The Catholic Indian Missions and Grant's Peace Policy, 1870-1884." Dissertation. Washington, D.C.: Catholic University of America, 1953.

Ravoux, A. *The Labors of Mgr. A. Ravoux among the Sioux or Dakota Indians.* St. Paul: Pioneer Press, 1897.

_____. *Reminiscences, Memoirs, and Lectures of Monsignor A. Ravoux, V.G.* St. Paul: Brown, Treacy, and Co., 1890.

Rogers, Dilwyn. *Lakota names and Traditional Uses of Native Plants by Sicangu (Brule) People in the Rosebud Area, South Dakota: A Study Based on Father Eugene Buechel's Collection of Plants of Rosebud around 1920.* St. Francis: The Rosebud Educational Society, 1980.

Scott, John. *High Eagle and His Sioux.* St. Louis, 1963.

Seminara, Manhart, Simurdiak, Steinmetz, and Cassidy. *Canku Wakan.* Pine Ridge: Holy Rosary Mission, 1981.

Standing Bear, Luther. *My People the Sioux.* Lincoln: University of Nebraska, 1975.

Steinmetz, Paul B. *Pipe, Bible, and Peyote among the Oglala Lakota.* Knoxville: University of Tennessee, 1990.

Steltenkamp, Michael F. *Black Elk: Holy Man of the Oglala.* Norman: University of Oklahoma Press, 1993.

Stoltzman, William. *The Pipe and Christ.* Chamberlain: Tipi Press, 1991.

Tedlock, D. and Tedlock, B. *Teachings from the American Earth.* New York: Liveright, 1975.

Thwaites, Reuben. ed. *Jesuit Relations and Allied Documents, Travels and Explorations of the Jesuit Missionaries in New France, 1610-1791.* 73 vols. New York: Pagent Book Company, 1959.

Walker, James R. *Lakota Belief and Ritual.* Lincoln: University of Nebraska, 1980.

_____. *Lakota Society.* Lincoln: University of Nebraska, 1982.

Unpublished Manuscripts

Foley, Thomas. "Hovering Eagle: The Lives, the Legends, the Letters, and the Journals of Francis M. Craft." Marquette University Archives.

Sialm, Placidus. "Camp Churches." Marquette University Archives.

Steltenkamp, Michael. "No More Screech Owl." Marquette University Archives.

Zaplotnik, John. "Bishop John N. Stariha." Archives of the Diocese of Rapid City.

Unpublished Articles

Moore, William. "The Importance Placed on Ranching, Agricultural, and Shop Training at the St. Francis Mission School, Rosebud Reservation." Marquette University Archives. (April 1938):1-12.

Thiel, Mark. "The Omaha Dance in Oglala and Sicangu Sioux History, 1883-1923." Marquette University Archives. (1983): 1-29.

Articles in Periodicals

Afraid-of-Hawk, Emil. "Sam Little Bull." *Indian Sentinel* 23 (April 1943):63-64.

Berheide, Edward. "Crow Hill Indian Congress." *Indian Sentinel* 19 (Sept. 1939):100, 108.

Bischofberger, George. "Holy Rosary Turns Golden." *Jesuit Missions* (June 1938):155.

Bosch, Aloysius. "Indians in Council." *Sacred Heart Messenger* (1893):876-886.

Bowdern, Thomas. "A Jesuit Summer Camp for Boys." *Jesuit Bulletin* 5 (March 1926):3-4, 13.

_____. "Boy's Summer Camp Among Sioux." *Indian Sentinel* 6 (Summer 1926):115-116.

_____. "Diamond Jubilee of Father Digmann." *Jesuit Bulletin* 4 (Dec. 1925):7, 13.

Brey, Floyd. "Fills-the-Pipe Entertains." *Calumet* (July 1934).

_____. "The Sioux Indian Boy." *Jesuit Missions* (Sept. 1932):175, 190.

Buechel, Eugene. "Hired at the Eleventh Hour." *Indian Sentinel* 21 (May 1941):70, 80.

_____. "Frank Arrowside." *Indian Sentinel* 16 (Oct. 1936):122.

_____. "Joe White Hat." *Indian Sentinel* 17 (May 1937):79.

Bull Head, Francis. "Sioux Catholic Congress at Holy Rosary Mission." *Indian Sentinel* 11 (Fall 1931):173-174.

Cody, Alexander. "Chief Big Head." *Indian Sentinel* 2 (July 1920):140-143.

Coffey, Francis. "Frolic and Festival." *Indian Sentinel* 22 (June 1942):91-92.

_____. "Rev. Placidus Sialm." *Indian Sentinel* 20 (May 1940):71-72, 80.

_____. "Sioux Craftsmen." *Jesuit Missions* (Nov. 1940):276.

Cooper, John. "Present-Day Anthropology: Its Spirit and Trend." *Primitive Man* 1 (Jan. 1928):4.

Craft, Francis. "Indian Belief in Purgatory and Prayers of the Dead." *Poor Souls Advocate* 2 (2 June 1890):194-196.

Cunningham, Leo. "A Catholic Meeting House." *Indian Sentinel* 9 (Spring 1929):57.

_____. "Fourth of July with the Sioux." *Indian Sentinel* 14 (Summer 1934):53.

_____. "Interesting Notes from South Dakota." *Jesuit Bulletin* 6 (Dec. 1927):4.

_____. "The Great Spirit." *Indian Sentinel* 8 (Spring 1928):60.

Devota, Sister Mary. "Ottawa Naming Ceremonial." *Indian Sentinel* 18 (Sept. 1938):101.

Digmann, Florentine. "Catholic Indian Schools: St. Francis." *Indian Sentinel* (1907):21-28.

_____. "I Want to see the Great Spirit." *Indian Sentinel* 4 (Jan. 1924):26.

_____. "The Old Guard," *Indian Sentinel* 6 (Winter 1926): 44.

_____. "St. Francis Mission." *Indian Sentinel* 1 (April 1919):9-13.

_____. "Thunderbird Keeps His Word." *Indian Sentinel* 8 (Spring 1928):67.

Donnelly, W.P. "The White Indian—A Century After." *Jesuit Bulletin* 17 (Jan. 1938):1-2.

Fallon, James. "Indian Sodality." *Indian Sentinel* 19 (May 1939):77.

Frech, Vincent. "The Creation of Man as told by the Sioux." *Indian Sentinel* 4 (April 1924):91.

Goll, Louis. "Holy Rosary School." *Indian Sentinel* 1 (April 1919):24-26.

_____. "The Peyote Cult." *The Catholic Herald* 9 (1 Aug. 1940):1-2.

Gordon, Philip. "The Potawatomies of Kansas." *Calumet* (Christmas 1916).

Grotegeers, Henry. "Catholic Indians: Joe Horn Cloud." *Indian Sentinel* 2 (July 1921): 332-334.

Gschwend, Joseph. "Catholic Sioux Indians in Council." *America* (20 June 1931):253-254.

Henry, T. "Holy Rosary Mission." *Indian Sentinel* 1 (April 1919):15-17.

Holler, Clyde. "Black Elk's Relationship to Christianity." *The American Indian Quarterly* 8 (Winter 1984):37-47.

Huffer, William. "Catholic Sioux Congress of South Dakota." *Indian Sentinel* 3 (Oct. 1923):147-148.

Hunt, Jerome. "The Catholic Sioux Congress." *Indian Sentinel* (1910):13-14.

Ketcham, William. "Father Ketcham Explains Work of Indian Catechists." *Calumet* (April 1917).

Laskowski, Edward. "Indian Congress." *Calumet* (Winter 1946).

_____. "Victory Indian Congress." *Indian Sentinel* 26 (Oct. 1946):121-122.

Luther, Joseph. "High Lights from a Hundred Per Cent American Convention." *Jesuit Bulletin* 3 (Dec. 1924):13.

Madlon, Daniel. "Fifty Years Progress." *Indian Sentinel* 16 (Sept. 1936):107, 111.

Mattingly, Francis. "Red Scaffold Congress." *Indian Sentinel* 29 (Oct. 1949):122-126.

McNamara, Stephan. "Big Boy is a Girl." *Indian Sentinel* 20 (Dec. 1940):159.

"Black Elk and Brings White." *Indian Sentinel* 21 (Nov. 1941):139-140.

Meyer, Alfred. "The Gathering of the Sioux Clans." *Indian Sentinel* 21 (Sept. 1941):99-100, 110.

Moore, William. "Black Eagle on Sioux Syntax." *Jesuit Missions* (Nov. 1939):262-263, 279.

_____. "A New Indian Mission." *Indian Sentinel* 17 (Nov. 1937):134.

_____. "Preparing for Tomorrow." *Indian Sentinel* 19 (Feb. 1939):19-20, 28.

_____. "With the Sioux in Camp." *Indian Sentinel* 19 (Oct. 1939):118-119.

Moorman, Otto. "Passing of the Log Chapel." *Indian Sentinel* 8 (Fall 1928):161.

Muntsch, Albert. "White Eagle." *Indian Sentinel* 34 (Jan. 1954):15-16.

Ortiz, Ferdinand. "The Maiden's Dance." *Indian Sentinel* 2 (July 1920):124-128.

Prendergast, George. "Orators of the Plains." *Jesuit Bulletin* 11 (Feb. 1932):35,46.

Price, Peter. "Grey Hills People." *Indian Sentinel* 26 (June 1946):85-86.

Regnet, Henry. "The Buffalo Mission." *Jesuit Bulletin* 38 (Oct. 1959):8-9, 16.

Riester, Albert. "Progress at Pine Ridge." *Indian Sentinel* 8 (Summer 1928):105.

_____. "Sioux Trails All Lead to Big Road." *Indian Sentinel* 11 (Winter 1930-31):7-8.

Scott, John. "Getting the Right Start." *Indian Sentinel* 20 (June 1940):91-92.

_____. "Sioux Boys Learn Carpentry." *Indian Sentinel* 19 (Dec. 1939):155-156.

_____. "Sun Dance in Dakota." *Jesuit Missions* 15 (June 1941):146-147, 167.

_____. "Where Summer Trails End." *Indian Sentinel* 20 (Sept. 1940):108-109.

Sialm, Placidus. "A Retreat to Catechists." *Indian Sentinel* 3 (April 1923):78.

_____. "A Trip of 200 Miles Costs Father Sialm only Ten Cents." *Calumet* (Jan. 1921).

_____. "Dakota News." *Indian Sentinel* 18 (April 1938):64.

"Dedication of Kyle Chapel." *Indian Sentinel* 17 (Jan. 1937):5-6.

_____. "In Memory of Those who have Labored among the Sioux." *Indian Sentinel* (April 1919):37-39.

_____. "Ivan Star-Comes-Out." *Indian Sentinel* 19 (March 1939):44.

_____. "Holy Rosary Mission." *Jesuit Bulletin* 1 (Dec. 1922):12.

_____. "Left-Hand Heron: Sioux Story Teller." *Indian Sentinel* 11 (Spring 1931):54.

_____. "Mary Kills Two's Party." *Indian Sentinel* 17 (May 1937):67-68.

_____. "Potato Creek People." *Indian Sentinel* 19 (Nov. 1939):139-142.

_____. "A Retreat to Catechists." *Indian Sentinel* 3 (April 1923):78.

_____. "Sioux Catechists' Retreat." *Indian Sentinel* 6 (Fall 1926):171-172.

_____. "Sioux Laymen's Retreat." *Indian Sentinel* (Winter 1927-28):11-12.

_____. "White Crow: Sioux Catechist." *Indian Sentinel* 13 (Summer 1933):140.

Steinmetz, Paul. "The Sacred Pipe in American Indian Religion." *American Indian Culture and Research Journal* 8 (1984):27-80.

_____. "The Relationship between Plains Indian Religion and Christianity: A Priest's Viewpoint." *Plains Anthropologist* 15 (1970):83-86.

Strassmaier, Bernard. "Sioux Congress of North Dakota." *Indian Sentinel* 8 (Fall 1928):161.

Tennelly, J.B. "Catherine Tekakwitha." *Indian Sentinel* 22 (Sept 1942):99-100.

_____. "The Indian Missions." *Indian Sentinel* 18 (May 1938):67-69.

_____. "Place of the Cottonwood Trees." *Indian Sentinel* 19 (June 1939):83-84, 95.

_____. "The Romance of Anadarko." *Indian Sentinel* 18 (Jan. 1938):3-4, 13.

Van der Velden, A. "A Cheyenne Legend." *Indian Sentinel* 2 (July 1920):147-148.

Vecsey, Christopher. "Sun Dances, Corn Pollen, and the Cross." *Commonweal* (5 June 1987):345-351.

Vrebosch, Aloysius. "The Crow Indians." *Indian Sentinel* (1909):25-39.

Walworth, Ellen. "Our Little Sister Kateri Tekakwitha, the Lily of the Mohawks." *Indian Sentinel* (1908):5-14.

Weisenhorn, Charles. "Sioux Congress on Pine Ridge Reservation." *Indian Sentinel* 2 (Oct. 1920):169-173.

Westropp, Henry. "A Relic of Father De Smet." *Calumet* (Dec. 1913).

_____. "Little Owl's Account of the Congress." *Indian Sentinel* (1911):9-13.

Woods, John. "27th Annual Sioux Congress." *Indian Sentinel* 4 (Oct. 1924):147-151.

Zabolio, Albert. "The Sioux and Catholic Action." *Jesuit Missions* 17 (Sept. 1943):210-211.

Zimmerman, Joseph. "Catechist Nick Black Elk." *Indian Sentinel* 30 (Oct. 1950):101-102.

_____. "Flying Owl." *Indian Sentinel* 23 (Oct. 1943):127.

_____. "Great Sioux Chief Passes Away." *Indian Sentinel* 7 (Fall 1927):180-181.

_____. "How the Sioux Indians Keep Christmas." *Indian Sentinel* 12 (Fall 1932):163-164.

_____. "In the Bad Lands." *Jesuit Missions* 7 (May 1933):101.

_____. "Kateri Tekakwitha Still Lives." *Indian Sentinel* 15 (Fall 1935):87.

_____. "Mile and a Half Down the Road." *Indian Sentinel* 22 (May 1942):71-72.

_____. "The Owancaya Omniciye." *Indian Sentinel* 27 (June 1947):95-96.

_____. "The Sioux Taste War." *Indian Sentinel* 23 (Jan. 1943):12-13.

_____. "The True Faith versus Paganism." *Calumet* (May 1944):16-17.

_____. "Thy Kingdom Come." *Indian Sentinel* 18 (Nov. 1938):137-138.

"Abbot Martin Visits Sitting Bull." *Annals of the Catholic Indian Missions* 2 (Jan. 1878):7-10.

"All Aboard for a Visit to the Missions." *Calumet* (Oct. 1940):6-7.

"Andrew Sockalexis." *Indian Sentinel* (1913):48.

"Archbishop Curley Adopted into Blackfoot Tribe." *Indian Sentinel* 8 (Winter 1927-28):2

"Catholic Indians: Peter Big Turkey." *Indian Sentinel* 2 (Jan. 1921):237-239.

"Catholic Indians and the War." *Indian Sentinel* 1 (July 1918):15-33.

"Catholic Sioux Congress." *Calumet* (Oct. 1919).

"*Corpus Christi* Procession at Holy Rosary Mission." *Jesuit Bulletin* 3 (March 1924):14.

"*Corpus Christi* at Holy Rosary Mission." *Jesuit Bulletin* 5 (Sept. 1926):6-7.

"Financial Statement." *Annals of the Catholic Indian Missions* 1 (Jan. 1877):26-28.

"First Priest of His People." *Indian Sentinel* (1904-1905):32.

"Golden Jubilees." *Indian Sentinel* 2 (Oct. 1922):564-565.

"The Great Catholic Sioux Congress of 1910." *Indian Sentinel* (1911):3-8.

"Great Mission Encyclical." *Jesuit Bulletin* 6 (Sept 1927):7.

"Heritage of the F-Lazy-S.' *Jesuit Bulletin* 15 (March 1936):4-5, 8.

"The Holy Father and the Missions." *Jesuit Bulletin* 7 (June 1928):12.

"Holy Rosary Mission School." *Indian Sentinel* (1908):27-32.

"Indian Dances." *Indian Sentinel* 3 (April 1923):58-59.

"Indian Legend: the Creation of the World." *Indian Sentinel* 2 (July 1921):339.

"Indian Legend: The Stolen Fire." *Indian Sentinel* 2 (Oct. 1921):385-386.

"Indians Meet in Convention." *Calumet* (Oct. 1920).

"Indians Trained as Catechists." *Calumet* (July 1916).

"James Thorpe." *Indian Sentinel* (1913):48.

"The Jesuit Indian Missions of South Dakota." *Jesuit Bulletin* 1 (Sept. 1922):4-8.

"Kateri: A Bright Light in a Vast Darkness." *Jesuit Missions* 17 (Nov. 1943):266-267.

"Legend of the Chipmunk." *Indian Sentinel* 2 (Oct. 1920):179.

"Monsignor Stephan." *Indian Sentinel* (1902-1903):2-5.

"A Little Indian Life." *Indian Sentinel* (1902-1903):14-23.

"A Missionary among the Sioux." *Social Justice Review* 37 (Nov. 1944):245-246.

"Pagent Grand Success." *The Sioux Chieftain* 3 (June 1936):3.

"Peter Big Turkey," *Indian Sentinel* 2 (Jan. 1921): 237-239.

"The Sioux Congress." *Indian Sentinel* 1 (Oct. 1916):27-30.

"William Ketcham." *Calumet* (April 1917) supplement.

"Work of a Native Priest." *Calumet* (Nov. 1915).

"Work of the Bureau." *Annals of the Catholic Indian Missions of America* 2 (Jan. 1878):30-31.

Index